Law, Technology and Disruption

Law, Technology and Disruption investigates how technological innovation affects legal systems together with regulatory frameworks. This volume brings together leading scholars to examine the evolving relationship between law and technological disruption, as digital advancements challenge long standing legal principles.

The book examines key areas such as algorithmic decision-making and digital agricultural intellectual property to assess how disruptive technologies are testing legal norms. The book examines Chinese online platform copyright governance along with algorithmic bias risks and regulatee design for legal compliance while studying publicly accessible datasets regulation and online review regulation and how emerging technologies impact fundamental rights and market dynamics.

Through analysis of contemporary debates on legal adaptation and enforcement in the digital age, this book provides valuable insights for academics, policymakers and professionals who work at the intersection of law and technology. This book provides both accessible and rigorous analysis of the challenges and opportunities presented by rapid technological change, and the need for legal systems to adapt to an era of continuous innovation.

This book was originally published as a special issue of *Law, Technology and Disruption*.

Tianxiang He, Associate Professor, School of Law, City University of Hong Kong.

Law, Technology and Disruption

Towards a Comprehensive Regulatory Framework

Edited by
Tianxiang He

Routledge
Taylor & Francis Group
LONDON AND NEW YORK

First published 2026
by Routledge
4 Park Square, Milton Park, Abingdon, Oxon OX14 4RN

and by Routledge
605 Third Avenue, New York, NY 10158

Routledge is an imprint of the Taylor & Francis Group, an informa business

British Library Cataloguing in Publication Data
A catalogue record for this book is available from the British Library

ISBN13: 978-1-041-09013-7 (hbk)
ISBN13: 978-1-041-09014-4 (pbk)
ISBN13: 978-1-003-64802-4 (ebk)

DOI: 10.4324/9781003648024

Typeset in Minion Pro
by Newgen Publishing UK

Publisher's Note
The publisher accepts responsibility for any inconsistencies that may have arisen during the conversion of this book from journal articles to book chapters, namely the inclusion of journal terminology.

Contents

Citation Information

The chapters in this book were originally published in *Law, Innovation and Technology*, volume 14, issue 1 (2022). When citing this material, please use the original page numbering for each article, as follows:

Introduction
Tianxiang He
Law, Innovation and Technology, volume 14, issue 1 (2022), pp. 1–4

Chapter 1
Law, authority, and respect: three waves of technological disruption
Roger Brownsword
Law, Innovation and Technology, volume 14, issue 1 (2022), pp. 5–40

Chapter 2
Rule-following robots? Transitional legal disruption through regulatee design and engineering
Hin-Yan Liu
Law, Innovation and Technology, volume 14, issue 1 (2022), pp. 41–70

Chapter 3
Online content platforms, copyright decision-making algorithms and fundamental rights protection in China
Tianxiang He
Law, Innovation and Technology, volume 14, issue 1 (2022), pp. 71–94

Chapter 4
Algorithmic bias and the New Chicago School
Jyh-An Lee
Law, Innovation and Technology, volume 14, issue 1 (2022), pp. 95–112

Chapter 5

Intellectual property in digital agriculture
Anselm Kamperman Sanders
Law, Innovation and Technology, volume 14, issue 1 (2022), pp. 113–127

Chapter 6

Good advice is expensive – bad advice even more: the regulation of online reviews
Mateja Đurović & Tim Kniepkamp
Law, Innovation and Technology, volume 14, issue 1 (2022), pp. 128–156

Chapter 7

The eligibility requirements for legal protection of publicly accessible datasets
Guobin Cui
Law, Innovation and Technology, volume 14, issue 1 (2022), pp. 157–203

Notes on Contributors

Roger Brownsword holds professorial positions in law at King's College London, UK, and Bournemouth University, UK; and, together with Han Somsen, he was (and continues to be) the founding general editor of *Law, Innovation and Technology*.

Guobin Cui is Professor of Law as well as the Director of the Center for Intellectual Property at Tsinghua University Law School, China.

Mateja Đurović is Professor in Contract and Commercial Law, in the Dickson Poon School of Law at King's College London, UK, and Judge of the European Court of Human Rights. He is Co-Director of the School of Law's Centre for Technology, Ethics, Law and Society (TELOS) and Academic Director of the Executive Programme on Consumer Law.

Tianxiang He is Associate Professor at School of Law, City University of Hong Kong, Hong Kong.

Anselm Kamperman Sanders is Professor of Intellectual Property Law at Maastricht University, the Netherlands, and he is Deputy Judge in the Court of Appeal, The Hague.

Tim Kniepkamp studied Law at Humbold University of Berlin, Germany, and at King's College London, UK.

Jyh-An Lee is Professor and Executive Director of the Centre for Financial Regulation and Economic Development (CFRED) at The Chinese University of Hong Kong Faculty of Law, Hong Kong.

Hin-Yan Liu is Associate Professor and Coordinator, Artificial Intelligence and Legal Disruption Research Group, Faculty of Law, University of Copenhagen, Denmark.

Introduction

Tianxiang He

The disruptive power of new technologies in relation to our legal systems is evident. We have witnessed the rise of platforms, blockchain, artificial intelligence, big data, virtual and augmented reality, and the advancement of biotechnology and their power to better our lives. Yet the close but unpleasant encounters of these technologies with our regulatory system have demonstrated that the latter needs an update to cope with all the technological challenges. With regard to the study of law and technology today, it is often observed that the traditional focus is on matching facts with legal rules and delivering an answer. However, a verdict from the courts might not be a real solution to the technological challenges, and without a thorough examination of the relevant national policy, the laws designed in a pre-digital era may not render a satisfactory result that fits the current agenda. For scholars, it has created the need for a regulatory framework to the study of law and technology that can accommodate consideration of the stability of our legal system, as well as the efficiency of other legal and non-legal instruments such as technology and community norms.

Although much of the literature in the field of law, regulation and technology reflects North American and European thinking, the challenges and opportunities presented by new technologies have both local and global dimensions. There need to be conversations about the disruptive effects of emerging technologies amongst legal and regulatory scholars in the East, just as much as in the West, in the South just as much as in the North. Accordingly, in an attempt to extend the conversation, in March 2021, Hong Kong Commercial and Maritime Law Centre of the School of Law, City University of Hong Kong hosted a conference entitled 'Law, Technology and Disruption'. This conference—which was held virtually and which was viable only because of the rapid development of online meeting platforms—was designed to address the question of how technological advancements might disrupt different fields of law and how scholars from these fields might respond to these challenges. With support from the journal of *Law, Innovation and Technology*, we are able to select and publish seven articles that were presented in the said conference to form this special issue.

The collection starts with an extended version of one of the two keynotes given at the conference.[1] This article, by Roger Brownsword, outlines three waves of technological disruption to the authority of law and to the claim that we should respect the law (just because it is the law and even though we might have reservations about it). Brownsword goes into the root of law and governance and depicts how technological advancements disrupt our belief in and respect for the law. He argues that if and when perfect order can be achieved by governance by machines (or simply if machines can 'do governance' better than humans), then human societies will need to make major decisions about their future governance models. For, quite simply, governance by machines follows a different logic than that of governance by humans and rules. These decisions will have a profound impact on our societies as the two models are similar in function but fundamentally different in their mode of performance.

Hin-Yan Liu with his paper further develops Brownsword's idea by digging deep into the concept of 'disruption' with regard to law, regulation, and governance. He uses the convergence of artificial intelligence and extended realities as an example to illustrate the power inequities between the regulator and the regulatee. He distinguishes two different types of legal disruption that are driven by new technologies: the overt form that we scholars are often focusing on and a transitional legal disruption where 'new technologies create new worlds by invoking and connecting new capabilities.' He argues that the latter is more dangerous as it changes 'the surrounding benchmarks of expectations and normative values around a new equilibrium' and 'the new paradigms that follow may have lasting consequences that become costly and difficult to change'. He shares the same worries as Brownsword about a Law 3.0 world in which the focus is on designing the regulates,[2] as the concept will be changed from manipulation to regulatee design and engineering that erases agency and autonomy in the process and prunes variance. He thereby argues the importance of regulatory responsibility of preserving the commons in the aftermath of legal disruption.

Following the same logic, my contribution focuses on the challenges brought by the concentration of power in content platforms to the copyright jurisprudence and other content regulation laws. This author uses China as a case study and finds that the evolvement of content platforms and digital

[1] Professor Julie Cohen from Georgetown University opened the conference with a keynote speech entitled 'Designing Information-Era Countermovements'. Professor Cohen's speech (and the Q and A), which summarized the main themes of her book, *Between Truth and Power: The Legal Constructions of Informational Capitalism* (Oxford University Press, 2019), and offered some insightful reflections on the governance challenges that are now presented by platforms, standards, and the networked economy, is available to be viewed at https://drive.google.com/drive/folders/1psQNxPcdQEU5O3IL1FDuM6VGrnlkASI0?usp=sharing.

[2] Roger Brownsword, *Law 3.0: Rules, Regulation, and Technology* (Routledge, 2020).

creative tools has not only curtailed direct online piracy to a large extent but has also facilitated partial copying activities and related businesses. It has incidentally generated 'information cocoons' and provided the Chinese government with a strong tool to regulate online content. This author identifies three related challenges that require theoretical responses: the 'micro-copyright' enforcement, the introduction of algorithmic decision-making filtering mechanism in detecting copyright piracy and illegal contents, and the possible invasion of freedom of speech and privacy by algorithmic censorship applications. The paper also uses Brownsword's concept of Law 1.0-3.0 and argues that the solution lies in a regulatory framework that consists of legal and non-legal solutions such as technology and norms.

The next contribution focuses on the issue of algorithmic bias and the proper regulatory approach. Jyh-An Lee approaches the said issue that happens in the collection or processing of data from the New Chicago School framework developed by Lawrence Lessig.[3] Lee uses the four modalities highlighted by Lessig, which are social norms, market, architecture, and the law that regulate human behaviour, to discuss the proper regulation of algorithms. He argues that law could address the algorithmic bias problem by regulating the other three modalities and should be extra cautious about imposing a legal requirement of transparency on AI algorithms.

The fifth paper underlines the breadth and depth of platform power, investigating the impact of digitisation of the agricultural market in assessing the market definitions in the context of potential harm to competition in this sector. Anselm Kamperman Sanders in his paper identifies the challenges brought by the digitisation of the agricultural market, such as market concentration and issues of trust, and how the intellectual property regime intensifies them. He argues that various regulatory options, including the law against unfair competition and other non-legal options such as codes of conduct, can help to alleviate the problem.

The sixth paper also implicates platforms. Co-authored by Mateja Đurović and Tim Kniepkamp, this contribution explores the legal challenges raised by online reviews (particularly concerning their reliability and their authenticity). The authors observe the risks relating to consumer protection that are brought about by the shift in reference point: from credible resources to unreliable and often manipulated online reviews. The authors notice the failure of EU legislative moves in addressing this problem and propose a co-regulatory approach that includes laws such as a new EU directive and norms such as the ISO Norms and similar standards as side-by-side solutions to increase accountability of online platforms.

The final article in the special issue argues that there is an urgent need to provide legal protection of publicly accessible datasets and to set the possible

[3]Lawrence Lessig, 'The New Chicago School' (1998) 27 *Journal of Legal Studies* 661.

eligibility requirements for them in China. The protection of big data has long troubled Chinese legal scholars, and they have suggested a broad legislative framework for datasets protection. Guobin Cui finds this kind of proposal misleading as various kinds of information contained in the dataset are already covered by different laws such as property law and intellectual property laws. He argues that only publicly accessible datasets that contain no original contents, selections, or compilations requires sui generis protection and proposes a narrow property right regime to protect them. He then further elaborates the eligibility requirements for the protection of publicly accessible datasets: the dataset is made public, it contains a substantial number of data entries, and it reflects a substantial collection cost of the collector.

All seven articles compiled reflect the bafflement of the law and our regulatory system in the face of certain new technologies and the various approaches to address the problems and their potential risks. Taken together, they represent the change of mindset of the legal profession from believing that law can be a perfect system that can solve all the problems to admitting that law is just part of the regulatory framework and, to solve technological challenges our societies require help from regulatory instruments other than law.

The School of Law at City University of Hong Kong has been actively promoting and is spearheading law and technology in its teaching and research. Besides the acclaimed series of regular and short-term law and technology courses for both graduate and undergraduate level of students, we hope and have the confidence to make the 'Law, Technology and Disruption' conference a famous brand and a regular event that serves as a platform for lawyers, especially Asian lawyers interested in law and technology topics.

Acting as the guest editor of this special issue, I would like to express my gratitude to all the authors for their contribution to this important topic, and to the journal of *Law, Innovation and Technology* for providing the invaluable platform for us.

OPEN ACCESS

Law, authority, and respect: three waves of technological disruption

Roger Brownsword

ABSTRACT

This article identifies and discusses three waves of technological disruption to the authority of law and, concomitantly, to the demand for respect for the law.

The first wave disrupts the claim made by national legal systems to recognise their authority and the demand that their decrees and decisions should be respected. This disruption, which is particularly associated with cybertechnologies and actions in cyberspace, is likely to occur whenever technologies develop significant new regulatory spaces in which humans (or their extensions) transact and interact (such as the metaverse).

The second wave disrupts the debate about the demand that the law should be respected, simply because it is the law and any reservations notwithstanding. Traditionally, this demand is justified by reference to a picture of law as a *rule*-based *order* or as an aspiration for *just* order. However, this is disrupted by the prospect of technologies that promise to 'do governance' better than humans with rules, this generating a picture of law as governance by smart technologies and, in opposition, a picture of law as self-governance by *humans*. Instead of a debate between two modes of governance by rules, we now have a debate between various modes of human governance by rules and governance by technologies.

The third wave disrupts the conceptual scheme that underlies our thinking about the authority of, and respect for, the law. In particular, the picture of law as governance by smart technologies throws into doubt the relevance of questions about the authority of law (when law is no longer governance by humans and governance by rules) and about respect for the law (when the reservations that we have about governance by fellow humans are no longer applicable).

1. Introduction

In our technologically sophisticated societies, we act, interact, and transact in environments that are located at various points on a spectrum running from offline (analogue) to online (digital). Typically, the more that we move away from offline environments, the more that technologies bear the weight of governance; and, concomitantly, the greater the range and intensity of questions about the authority of law's governance and why we should respect it. To be blunt: why should we respect the governance of law simply because it is the law? It is a question that persists whether our societies are low-tech or high-tech.

Given today's setting for this question, the purpose of this article is to open up a research agenda relating to three technologically-provoked waves of 'disruption'[1] to traditional ideas about both the authority of law (the authority of the rules and institutions of Westphalian legal systems) and respect for the law. Although, in the present article, I will not explicitly address a further related form of disruption, namely disruption to various forms of *discontent* with law's governance, it is implicit in my discussion that such disruption is also taking place.[2]

Having already experienced the first of these waves of disruption, we are currently experiencing the second; and, the third is on the horizon. While the first wave has brought with it a significant disruption, an amplification of discontent with the law, it is not a game-changer. However, the second wave is a game-changer, rewriting the terms of the traditional debate. In that debate, law is presented as better than various kinds of arbitrary and disordered alternatives; but, if technologies are able to 'do governance' better than law, the challenge to law comes from a different direction—instead of law looking down on worse alternatives, it now has to look up at arguably better options. This presages a third wave of disruption when governance

---

[1]There are many ways in which Law might be 'disrupted'. It might be that the application of traditional legal doctrines, concepts, templates, classifications, and the like, to novel phenomena or circumstances associated with a new technology is problematic. Or, it might be that the disruption impacts on legal practice, on what we do and how we do it. Or, as in the current paper, the disruption might impact on our conceptual thinking, our values, or our attitudes, and so on. For discussion, see, e.g., Roger Brownsword, 'Law and Technology: Two Modes of Disruption, Three Legal Mind-Sets, and the Big Picture of Regulatory Responsibilities' (2018) 14 *Indian Journal of Law and Technology* 1, 'Law Disrupted, Law Re-imagined, Law Re-invented' (2019) 1 *Technology and Regulation* 10, and 'Political Disruption, Technological Disruption, and the Future of EU Private Law' in Mateja Durovic and Takis Tridimas (eds), *New Directions in EU Private Law* (Hart, 2021) 7.

[2]This related line of disruption, not so much to law itself but to discontent with law's governance, is something that I am currently working on in 'Law's Imperfect Governance: Discontent, Disruption, and Reconstruction' (forthcoming). Briefly, even without recent technological disruption, there are many reasons to be discontent with law's governance. First, there might be a deep-rooted discontent with the credentials of those who are undertaking governance. This is not a matter of competence in the sense of capability but of mandate. By what right, on what basis, do *these* particular humans subject other humans to their regime of governance? Secondly, there is a broad sweep of discontent where governance is judged to be 'bad' or ugly' relative to an ideal of 'good governance'. For example, the complaint might be that governance makes no attempt to serve the interests of the governed, or that it is inconsistent in its administration, or that its lacks flexibility, and so on. Thirdly, even if governance is guided by the relevant desiderata, it might provoke discontent, either because of the way in which it interprets a particular desideratum or translates it into practice, or because of its handling of tensions between conflicting desiderata. Once we add new technologies back into the mix, we might find that some of our discontent is exacerbated but, in other respects, as we put our faith in governance by technologies, some might find that their discontent with governance is relieved.

is predominantly by machines and technological management rather than by humans with rules; in this changed context, the question is whether it remains meaningful to employ concepts that were designed for a human rule-based enterprise and, indeed, whether the questions that we have about authority and respect are any longer relevant. If not, this third wave is more than a game-changer, it is a game-ender.[3]

Potentially, the first kind of disruption can occur whenever technologies create new but controversial options for humans; and, it is particularly when new and alternative regulatory spaces are created (such as the spaces now being promised by the development of the Metaverse[4]) that this kind of disruption is provoked. Indeed, it has been particularly with the development of the online social spaces of the Internet that we have experienced the first wave of challenges as doubt is cast on which system of legal rules has authority and whether legal rules are to be respected *at all* by agents who act in cyberspace. In cyberspace, land-based and territorially-defined legal systems no longer are controlling; cyber-borders do not map onto land borders; it is not obvious that land-based orders maintain their monopoly on authority and jurisdiction.[5] While this development foreshadows a radical challenge to legal authority and to respect for the law, even in its more aggressive cyber-libertarian forms, it does not depart from the traditional paradigm of governance by humans and governance by rules.

---

[3]Compare William Lucy, 'The Death of Law: Another Obituary' (2022) 81 *Cambridge Law Journal* DOI: https://doi.org/10.1017/S0008197321001021. Concluding his essay on the 'death of law', Lucy observes (footnotes omitted):

> Will the death of law be a cause for regret? The existence of technologies that ensure regulatees comply with the law, often regardless of their agency, is surely a good thing. Golf carts or shopping trolleys that cannot be stolen, cars that cannot exceed the speed limit and contracts that cannot be breached, look like positive developments, a protection of or increase in human well-being. How can more of this kind of regulation, which deprives those so inclined of the opportunity to do bad things, be objectionable? Jurists have nevertheless objected to it on a number of grounds. The most common is that technological management seems prone to transgress the principles that inform the rule of law. Slightly less common are the objections that technological management undermines human dignity, on the one hand, and freedom, on the other, since it either treats human beings as objects or illegitimately limits their sphere of action. I do not doubt the weight of some versions of these objections, but wish instead to highlight another worry additional to or possibly latent within them. It is this: if technological management is generalised as a means of regulation, then the space for human agency will contract and, as a result, agency may wither and die.

[4]https://en.wikipedia.org/wiki/Metaverse.

[5]Anticipating such radical change, see David R. Johnson and David Post, 'Law and Borders—The Rise of Law in Cyberspace' (1996) 48 *Stanford Law Review* 1367. Opening their paper, Johnson and Post state (at 1367):

> Global computer-based communications cut across territorial borders, creating a new realm of human activity and undermining the feasibility—and legitimacy—of laws based on geographic boundaries. While these electronic communications play havoc with geographic boundaries, a new boundary, made up of the screens and passwords that separate the virtual world from the 'real world' of atoms, emerges. This new boundary defines a distinct Cyberspace that needs and can create its own law and legal institutions. Territorially based law-makers and law-enforcers find this new environment deeply threatening.

However, the first disruptive wave is followed by a second, this time raising the prospect of governance by machines and technological management that present more fundamental questions about modes of governance and, with that, about how we now view the idea of the authority of law, its institutions and officials, and respect for the rules of law.

Lest this prospect seems a bit fanciful, we should note how governance by technologies has insinuated itself into many professional sports. Once upon a time, horse races were started by an official who dropped a flag; and, at the finishing line, an official called the winner of the race. Nowadays, we have mechanical starting stalls and, at the finishing line, we have cameras. More significantly, in soccer, rugby, cricket, and tennis, off-pitch officials and technologies play a role in supporting and correcting on-field decisions. In some sports, the authority of human officials (umpires) is open to limited challenge—interestingly, with the appeal being from solely human on-field decisions to off-field technological review rather than (as Article 22 of the EU General Data Protection Regulation contemplates) this being an appeal from the technology to a human[6]; and, in other sports, off-field humans assisted by technology make the decisions. In professional soccer, where on-field respect for officials had reached an all-time low, the players now submit to the technology. Whether or not the players respect the technology and whether or not spectators prefer their sport (like their music) 'unplugged' or technologically-assisted is another matter.

In these sports, it seems like a time of technological transition and, for our purposes, the question is this: what are the implications for legal authority and respect for legal rules and officials if a similar transition takes place in the law? To the extent that legal authority and respect for the law hinge on law being better than the alternative, what are the implications of a technological alternative?

While this second wave of disruption is currently in the spotlight, it presages a third wave. In his influential book, *After Virtue*, Alasdair MacIntyre argued that, even though the language of morality might persist, its concepts lose their meaning when the context in which they have been developed itself changes.[7] So, updating this argument, we might say that the concept of moral virtue loses its meaning where, in technologically managed contexts, agents are free to act only in the way that the technology permits. Where technological management forces or disables a particular action, this might not reflect

[6]Regulation (EU) 2016/679. To claim the protection of Article 22, the data subject must show (1) that there has been a decision based solely on automated processing (2) which has produced adverse legal effects or (3) which has significantly affected him or her. This is a provision that poses more questions than it answers. For discussion of several nice points of interpretation, see Roger Brownsword and Alon Harel, 'Law, Liberty and Technology—Criminal Justice in the Context of Smart Machines' (2019) 15 *International Journal of Law in Context* 107.

[7]Alasdair MacIntyre, *After Virtue* (Duckworth, 1981).

badly on the agent, but there is no virtue in so acting.[8] Accordingly, the third wave of disruption impacts on a raft of concepts that are meaningful when the context is governance by humans and by rules but not so once the context is governance by technology—and, moreover, not so even though we might persist in trying to transplant the language of one context to the other.

While the article is specifically about technological disruption to the authority of law and to its demand for respect, it supports the view that the disruption of law is rarely a single occurrence at a particular point in time.[9] Rather, we have different technologies contributing in different ways and at different times to the ongoing disruption of law and, in this case, disrupting its foundational ideas, claims and demands (as well as, implicitly, the reservations and discontent that we have with its governance).[10]

Starting with Section 2, in which we sketch the first disruptive wave with its amplification of disrespect for the law, the article has six principal sections.

In Section 3, the traditional debate about the authority of, and respect for, the law is outlined. That debate, I will suggest, bottoms out on whether we have prudential or moral reasons to treat law as 'preclusionary'[11] in the way that the claims to authority and for respect have it—that is to say, in the way that it is claimed that we should recognise the authority of legal rules simply because they are 'the law'; and that we should respect legal requirements and prohibitions simply because they are provided for by 'the law'. Crucially, such respect is demanded even though we might have reservations about the prospectus for law or about its performance, or discontent with its particular decrees and decisions.

Section 4 engages with the traditional justifications, prudential and moral, for such demands. Here, I will suggest that the plausibility of the traditional justifications is context dependent. In some contexts, the prudential case

[8]See, e.g., Roger Brownsword, 'Lost in Translation: Legality, Regulatory Margins, and Technological Management' (2011) 26 *Berkeley Technology Law Journal* 1321; Ian Kerr, 'Digital Locks and the Automation of Virtue' in Michael Geist (ed), *From 'Radical Extremism' to 'Balanced Copyright': Canadian Copyright and the Digital Agenda* (Irwin Law, 2010) 247; and Shannon Vallor, *Technology and the Virtues* (Oxford University Press, 2016).

[9]Compare Hin-Yan Liu, Matthijs Maas, John Danaher, Luisa Scarcella, Michaela Lexer, and Leonard Van Rompaey, 'Artificial Intelligence and Legal Disruption: A New Model for Analysis' (2020) 12 *Law, Innovation and Technology* 205; and, taking this forward, see Hin-Yan Liu, 'Rule-following Robots? Transitional Legal Disruption through Regulatee Design and Engineering' (2022) 14 *Law, Innovation and Technology* (this special issue).

[10]See (n 2).

[11]By 'preclusionary', I mean that the imprimatur of 'Law' (in relation to an institution, official, rule, decisions, requirement, and so on) is decisive; there is nothing further to be said; Law precludes debate. Law, per se, has authority, and commands unquestioning respect and compliance. Compare the analysis of 'authority' in Joseph Raz, *The Authority of Law* (Oxford University Press, 1979). Raz devotes only one chapter, Ch 13, to 'respect' for the law. His position is (i) that, because (so he contends) there is no general obligation to obey the law, this cannot be the basis for an attitude of practical respect for the law, but (ii) it is nevertheless permissible (optional) for a person to adopt an attitude of respect for the law (in a way analogous to friendship) which then gives reasons for obeying the law (other things being equal).

looks plausible; in others, the moral case looks plausible; but, in too many contexts today, neither case looks plausible. In contexts of plurality and scepticism, I will identify two pressure points for the plausibility of either of the traditional views. One pressure point is revealed when individuals question the sense of particular legal requirements; and the other arises when a hard look is taken at the supposed source of legal authority.

In Section 5, we get to the second wave of challenges and questions, as the prospect of governance by technical measures and technology disrupts the traditional debate. On one analysis, the debate still rests on a choice between prudential and moral justifications, but the relevant considerations are now quite different. Instead of comparing law with a worse alternative, we now have to compare it with a seemingly better-performing alternative. However, on another analysis, this does not capture the nature and significance of the disruption. Prefiguring the third wave of disruption, the thought is that what is disrupted is not so much the terms of the debate but the context in which the traditional debate is located—a context in which it is meaningful to ask whether law has 'authority' and whether we should 'respect' it, and which supports human communities to exercise their prudential and moral judgments.

In Section 6, I characterise the choice that our communities now face as one between, on the one hand, human-centric governance, not perfect but always an expression of human striving and, on the other, a technological form of governance that is human protective in a paternalistic way but not truly human-centric. Stated shortly, this is a choice between some version of governance by humans (self-governance) and benign governance for humans (but not by humans). On this analysis, we need to be very careful about paving the way for governance by machines, no matter how well such governance seems to serve our collective interests and how well it seems to articulate the community's morality.

Section 7 introduces the third wave of disruption. Here, I start by sketching a short agenda of questions that are prompted by this wave of disruption; and, this is followed by some reflections on how we might consider relaxing the demand for respect or even reimagining it. In particular, we might ask: how far do the conceptual ideas and the questions that accompany governance where humans are still the authors of regulatory measures remain meaningful once that context changes to governance by technologies? Is it helpful or appropriate to try to transplant the language of authority, respect, trust, justice, and so on that is characteristic of human governance to governance by machines? And, should we try to rework the ideas that stand behind this language or start again with a conceptual scheme that fits a world of governance by technology?

Finally, in some short concluding remarks, I underline the significance of these disruptions. It would be no exaggeration to say that, in what are still the early years of our technological societies, humans face some fundamental choices about how they relate to technology.[12]

2. The first wave of disruption

Where agents act in cyberspace in ways that have some connection with more than one legal system, there is an obvious question about which rules of which legal system will be treated as applicable. However, this is not a radically disruptive question; this is a question that conflicts lawyers are used to asking in offline cross-border disputes.[13] The radical challenge is provoked by the question: why should we recognise the rules of any legal system as having authority, why not treat our own codes of conduct as authoritative?

Perhaps the most evocative articulation of this radical challenge is to be found in John Perry Barlow's declaration of independence which, memorably, opens in the following terms:

> Governments of the Industrial World, you weary giants of flesh and steel, I come from Cyberspace, the new home of Mind. On behalf of the future, I ask you of the past to leave us alone. You are not welcome among us. You have no sovereignty where we gather.
>
> We have no elected government, nor are we likely to have one, so I address you with no greater authority than that with which liberty itself always speaks. I declare the global social space we are building to be naturally independent of the tyrannies you seek to impose on us. You have no moral right to rule us nor do you possess any methods of enforcement we have true reason to fear.
>
> Governments derive their just powers from the consent of the governed. You have neither solicited nor received ours. We did not invite you. You do not know us, nor do you know our world. Cyberspace does not lie within your borders. Do not think that you can build it, as though it were a public construction project. You cannot. It is an act of nature and it grows itself through our collective actions.[14]

Picking up this thread, Chris Reed and Andrew Murray[15] argue that, whatever the plausibility of claims to authority in offline analogue legal systems, these do not translate across to the online environments of cyberspace. In the latter, where individuals are presented with a plurality of authority and legitimacy claims, the self-validating claims of national legal systems will

---

[12] Compare Victoria Sobocki, 'Avoiding the Gilded Cage of Tech, Striking the Balance Between too Little and too Much Technology: Artificial Intelligence and Legal Disruption' paper presented at conference on 'Law, Technology, and Disruption' held at City University Hong Kong, March 19–21, 2021.

[13] Compare Uta Kohl, *Jurisdiction and the Internet: Regulatory Competence over Online Activity* (Cambridge University Press, 2007).

[14] https://www.eff.org/cyberspace-independence (last accessed September 16, 2021).

[15] Chris Reed and Andrew Murray, *Rethinking the Jurisprudence of Cyberspace* (Edward Elgar, 2018).

not suffice. Summing up their analysis in four key points, Reed and Murray say:

> The first [point] is that law has two main sources of authority: that deriving from the lawmaker's constitution, which in the case of state law is clear authority only for persons physically present in the state's territory; and the authority which comes from acceptance of a rule by a community. The second is that jurisprudence in cyberspace is exclusively concerned with the second source of authority, and needs to identify it at the level of individual rules rather than considering the authority of the entire body of the lawmaker's output. Third, laws compete for authority in cyberspace, and they compete with social and other norms as well as other laws, so that the authority of a law and also the demands it is able to make depend on how well it does in that competition. Finally, although lawmakers may be able to do little to enhance their authority claims, they can certainly weaken them by failing to establish the legitimacy of those claims and by impairing the rule of law through making authority claims which go beyond the boundary of the lawmaker's community.[16]

This critique of authority is closely related to Reed and Murray's analysis of legitimacy and the Rule of Law.[17] Taking acceptance by the individual as focal, their 'message' is that 'the legitimacy, efficacy and normative acceptance of law norms in the online environment are predicated upon their acceptance by the community and by the individual in that community.'[18] In other words, claims to authority are not vindicated by constitutional declaration or by the practice of officials who are authorised by such declaration, but depend on recognition and acceptance by the community and its individual members.

Once those who act in cyberspace question the authority of national legal systems, respect for the law is thrown into jeopardy; and, whatever commitment there is to the Rule of Law, it does not align with the rule of national legal systems. Now, it might be argued that respect per se has been done no favours by cyberspace. For example, a decade ago, in their book, *The Offensive Internet*, Saul Levmore and Martha Nussbaum highlighted concerns about the way in which online anonymity seemed to encourage a level of incivility and offence that one would not expect to encounter offline where those acting in such a manner could be identified.[19] Since then, it has become all too easy to point to the culture of online disrespect for others—indeed, the Internet has brought us a whole lexicon of disrespectful acts, such as 'flaming', 'trolling', and 'doxxing'—as well widespread disrespect for IP laws such as copyright and trade marks (witness, for example, illegal peer-to-peer file sharing and the thousands of web sites that trade

[16]Ibid., at 234–35.
[17]For legitimacy, see ibid. Ch 7, and for the Rule of Law, see ibid Ch 8.
[18]Ibid. p 228.
[19]Saul Levmore and Martha C. Nussbaum(eds), *The Offensive Internet* (Harvard University Press, 2010).

in counterfeit designer goods). However, it is specifically a lack of respect for the law that is at issue.

What is at issue, is the disrespectful attitude that Joel Reidenberg detected amongst the 'Internet separatists',[20] who seemed to think that the Rule of Law (and national rules of law) simply do not apply to their on-line activities. This seems to be the case, for example, when millions of youngsters engage in unlawful file-sharing, when thousands of users of Twitter conspire to disclose the identity of persons in defiance of protective court orders,[21] and when trolling and online racial abuse is rampant. Hence, as Reidenberg says:

> The defenses for hate, lies, drugs, sex, gambling, and stolen music are in essence that technology justifies the denial of personal jurisdiction, the rejection of an assertion of applicable law by a sovereign state, and the denial of the enforcement of decisions .... In the face of these claims, legal systems engage in a rather conventional struggle to adapt existing regulatory standards to new technologies and the Internet. Yet, the underlying fight is a profound struggle against the very right of sovereign states to establish rules for online activity.[22]

Not only that: what is also at issue is Yahoo's famous refusal to accede to the order of the French court in the LICRA case.[23] What is at issue is Mark Zuckerberg's well-publicised reluctance to appear before parliamentary committees concerned about Facebook, fake news, disinformation, and data privacy issues.[24] In other words, what is at issue, too, is the attitude and culture of big tech.[25]

So, whether we focus on the attitude of cyberlibertarians who deny that the writ of legal authority extends to cyberspace, or the disrespect of the Internet separatists, or the attitude of the big tech CEOs, we have a direct challenge to traditional demands made for the authority of and respect for the law. In all these instances, the question is: why should we recognise the authority of your rules simply because they are presented as 'the Law'; why should we respect the requirements and prohibitions of your rules simply because they are presented as 'the Law'?

---

[20]Joel R. Reidenberg, 'Technology and Internet Jurisdiction' (2005) 153 *University of Pennsylvania Law Review* 1951.

[21]See, e.g., Frances Gibb, Anushka Asthana, and Alexi Mostrous, 'Paper Faces Legal Threat over Picture of Footballer' *The Times*, May 23, 2011, p1 (the Ryan Giggs case).

[22]Reidenberg (n 20), at 1953–1954.

[23]The story has been told many times but, for one of the best renditions, see Jack Goldsmith and Tim Wu, *Who Controls the Internet?* (Oxford University Press, 2006) Ch 1.

[24]See. e.g., Lauren Feiner, 'Mark Zuckerberg turns down UK Parliament Request to Answer Questions about Fake News and Data Privacy on Facebook', CNBC November 7, 2018: available at https://www.cnbc.com/2018/11/07/mark-zuckerberg-declines-uk-parliament-invite-to-discuss-privacy.html (last accessed March 6, 2021). For further discussion, see Howard Davis, 'Obtaining Information from an Over-Mighty Subject: The Parliamentary Experience' in Maurizio Borghi and Roger Brownsword (eds), *Informational Rights and Informational Wrongs: Questions of Law, Regulation and Governance* (Routledge forthcoming).

[25]Compare the critique in Shoshana Zuboff, *The Age of Surveillance Capitalism* (Profile Books, 2019).

Disruptive though these questions provoked by cyberspace are, they are still posed within the traditional paradigm of governance by humans and governance by rules. In this article my question is: if we move away from governance by humans and by rules to governance by technologies, how does this impact on our traditional questions about authority and respect for the law? If we do move to a more technological mode of governance, we come to a second wave of challenges to traditional thinking about law, authority, and respect. Here, the main challenge to the authority of law and respect for the law is not so much a failure by citizens to comply with the legal rules, or a problem about knowing which set of rules is authoritative, or even to press for self-governance, but the replacement of governance by rules by governance by technology.

3. The second wave I: the traditional debate

The backcloth to traditional jurisprudential debates about either the authority of, or respect for, the law is the opposition between legal positivist and legal idealist conceptions of law. While the former relies on prudential reasons (law being favourably compared with less well-ordered alternatives, primarily some 'lawless' alternative),[26] the latter relies on moral reasons (law being viewed as an essentially moral enterprise and, if comparisons are being made, being favourably compared with an enterprise that simply has no aspiration systematically to do justice).

Broadly speaking, the shape of the arguments is similar whether we are focusing on legal authority or on the question of respect. In both cases, the key question is why we should defer to the directives, decrees and decisions of others simply because they come with the imprimatur of 'the Law'. Even if we disagree with the sense of the position taken by lawmakers, or if compliance raises questions of conscience, the demand to recognise the authority of the law and to respect its rules is unqualified. In this part of the article, we will outline the salient features of the two positions, the prudential and the moral, that purport to justify such a demand.

3.1 The legal positivist/prudentialists' view

The paradigmatic setting for the legal positivist/prudentialist view is that of a community that treats law and morals as independent spheres, each being a discrete department of practical reason, each being a distinct practical

[26]Often, the moral alternative is also compared unfavourably with the order promised by the legal positivist version of legal order. However, the reasons given for the supposed practical superiority of a legal positivist conceptualisation of law do not stand up to close examination: see Deryck Beyleveld and Roger Brownsword, 'The Practical Difference Between Natural-Law Theory and Legal Positivism' (1985) 5 *Oxford Journal of Legal Studies* 1.

discourse. Like planets that occupy the same Universe but orbit independently of one another, law and morals are always separate and distinct although there will be cases where they come quite close to one another. If law is to be respected in such a community, this is not to be understood to be an appeal to good morals (although, no doubt, the moral high ground will be taken by those who demand respect if the opportunity presents itself).

This is not to say that law is not valued in this community of legal positivist prudentialists; and, indeed, by and large, members of such a community might happily comply with legal rules. Nevertheless, to use HLA Hart's terminology[27], the internal aspect of those who comply for prudential reasons is not the same as the internal aspect of those who comply for moral reasons. The question is: what is it about law so conceived, the positive requirements of which will quite possibly conflict with an individual's sense of their (at any rate, short-term) self-interest, that reasonably commands not just a modicum of respect but unquestioning compliance?

In the 1970s, E.P. Thompson shocked some fellow left-leaning intellectuals when he declared that the Rule of Law, the rule of rules, was an unqualified good.[28] What Thompson meant was that the rule of rules was a better option than the alternative, where that alternative was the arbitrary rule of the powerful. At least, with the rule of rules, the powerful would be constrained by their own rules; and, given a reasonable warning of what the sanctions would be for breach of the rules, the less powerful would have a chance of avoiding unanticipated penalties and punishments. In this way, Thompson echoed not only Lon Fuller—who argued that the procedural constraints of his idea of legality would tend to discourage the exercise of arbitrary power[29]—but also Judith Shklar who had already highlighted the virtues of legalism in preference to the lawlessness of both fascist and Stalinist regimes.[30]

Similarly, we might hear echoes of this line of thinking in Alain Supiot's commentary on the replacement of law with governance, the flattening of relevant considerations for governance, and the decline of respect for law.[31] Once the 'law' ceases to offer any resistance and is used merely as a tool, those who are subjected to its instrumentalism no longer have any reason to pledge their allegiance to it.

So, from a prudential perspective, it is arguable that the rule of rules is unquestioningly to be preferred to the lawless and order-less alternative (the rule-less Wild West); and, it is also arguable that, where people want

---

[27]HLA Hart, *The Concept of Law* (Clarendon Press, 1961).
[28]EP Thompson, *Whigs and Hunters: The Origin of the Black Act* (Pantheon Books, 1975) at 266.
[29]Lon L. Fuller, *The Morality of Law* (Yale University Press, 1969).
[30]Judith N. Shklar, *Legalism* (Harvard University Press, 1964).
[31]Alain Supiot, *Governance By Numbers* (trans by Saskia Brown) (Hart, 2017).

to know where they stand, the legal positivist version of rule by rules is to be preferred to any moral conception that invites contestation around its central idea of a *just* order.[32]

3.2 The legal idealist/moralists' view

The paradigmatic context for the legal idealist/moralist view is an aspirant moral community, its members not only committed both individually and collectively to doing the right thing, but also sharing a view as to the guiding principles for the community. Such principles might be founded on a religious code or credo, as in the Thomist tradition.[33] Equally, though, the picture might be entirely secular.[34] In such a context, the Law, as a direct translation of the Moral Law, would necessarily be regarded as authoritative and it would command respect.

Where the life and times of a community are fairly static, where little changes from one generation to the next, and where there is little communication or interaction with other communities, then the moralists' picture might be both plausible and sustainable.

Crucially, in this picture, the members of a moral community respect the Law not only when, by their lights, the Law's prescriptions guide correctly towards doing the right thing but even when it is either unclear or controversial whether they are guiding in the right direction. The argument is that, because those who are responsible for making the Law are attempting in good faith to maintain the community's moral commitments, this suffices to treat the mere fact that this is the Law as a good reason for respecting the institution, respecting its officials, and respecting its prescriptions. Moreover, members are reminded that the consequences of not respecting the Law might be to undermine and destabilise the moral aspiration of the

---

[32]Such a preference is in line with both 'exclusive legal positivist' thinking (as, commonly associated with Joseph Raz's conceptualisation of law and authority) and Scalian 'originalism'. On the latter, see, Antonin Scalia, 'Originalism: The Lesser Evil' (1989) 57 *U. Cin LR* 849, at 862:

> I take the need for theoretical legitimacy seriously, and even if one assumes (as many nonoriginalists do not even bother to do) that the Constitution was originally meant to expound evolving rather than permanent values ... I see no basis for believing that supervision of the evolution would have been committed to the courts. At an even more general theoretical level, orginalism seems to me more compatible with the nature and purpose of a Constitution in a democratic system. A democratic society does not, by and large, need constitutional guarantees to insure that its laws will reflect 'current values.' Elections take care of that quite well. The purpose of constitutional guarantees ... is precisely to prevent the law from reflecting certain changes in original values that the society adopting the Constitution thinks fundamentally undesirable. Or, more precisely, to require the society to devote to the subject the long and hard consideration required for a constitutional amendment before those particular values can be cast aside.

[33]The leading example in modern jurisprudence is John Finnis, *Natural Law and Natural Rights* (Oxford University Press, 1980).

[34]As argued, for example, in Deryck Beyleveld and Roger Brownsword, *Law as a Moral Judgment* (Sweet and Maxwell, 1986; reprinted by Sheffield Academic Press, 1994).

community. For the legal enterprise to command our respect, to appreciate why Law really matters, it must be conceived of as an integral part of the practice of an aspirant moral community.[35] So viewed, the legal enterprise does not need to align perfectly with the Moral Law but it must represent a good faith and serious attempt to do the right thing.[36] The reason why Law should be respected is not because it is the perfect articulation of the Moral Law but because it is a very human enterprise guided by moral aspirations. Communities that fully commit to Law are making a moral, not a prudential, declaration.

Accordingly, as this sketch would have it, respect for the law is largely a matter of respect for moral aspiration and integrity. Respect for the authority of legal officials is respect for persons who are trying to do the right thing, and respect for their rules and decisions is respect for an enterprise that is predicated on translating moral pluralism into provisional regulatory positions and determinations.

4. The traditional views: plausibility and context

Once we take the traditionally opposed views out of their paradigmatic contexts, the plausibility of their respective justifications for deference to legal authority and respect for the law is reduced. In communities that are secular, where citizens are used to forming their own judgments (prudential and moral, individual and collective), and where 'ethics' is widely thought to be 'just a matter of opinion', these views come under strain. Once citizens start to question the good sense of legal positions, processes, and decisions, or once citizens start to doubt the moral guidance offered by the law, the claims to authority and for respect can look over-demanding or simply implausible.

In what follows we can identify two pressure points at which either view is likely to come apart. In both cases, we are assuming a context in which a hard look is being taken at the demands made by the law. The first pressure point, found in a context of plurality, is revealed where individuals want to make up their own minds about the prudential or moral sense of the law's particular demands; and the second pressure point, found in a context of scepticism, is revealed when citizens ask questions about the source of legal authority.

4.1 In a context of plurality: individuals making their own prudential and moral judgments

In 2022, many societies exhibit high levels of plurality, of competing views about what is in the community's best interest. For example, there have

[35] Here, readers might detect some echoes from Alon Harel, *Why Law Matters* (Oxford University Press, 2014).

[36] This is the thrust of the legal idealist position argued for in Deryck Beyleveld and Roger Brownsword (n 33).

been many different (prudential) judgments about the timing and extent of the legally imposed restrictions on freedom of movement and association at the time of the Covid-19 pandemic. Few would question that their governments have the general authority to respond to public health emergencies and have legal authority to introduce measures of the kind adopted; but, that is not the issue. The question is why one should comply with the particular restrictions that have been imposed simply because they are the law. Indeed, in the United Kingdom, where the government's response was clearly open to question, the former Supreme Court Justice, Jonathan Sumption, was reported as saying that 'people should make their own decisions in the light of their own health and that the law should be a secondary consideration for them.'[37] We might ask: did this evince 'disrespect' for the Law? Would such 'disrespect' be justified or excused if it were based on a good faith and reasonable belief that the 'most draconian of the government's interventions ... [were] imposed under an Act that [did not] appear to authorise them' and with 'limited [or no] parliamentary scrutiny'?[38] If not, would such disrespect be mitigated if those who made their own decisions freely submitted to the penalties where their conduct involved the commission of criminal offences? How high is the bar for respect? How easy is it to evince disrespect?

In such a setting, it is tempting to introduce a proviso that licenses citizens, in exceptional circumstances, to back their own prudential judgments so long as they submit to whatever legal penalties there might be. This seems to be Sumption's position. However, this throws into doubt the background prudential judgment on which the preclusionary demands for respect for the law are made. Once this background judgment is up for debate, it is unclear how broad the proviso should be and where the exceptional case begins and ends. In fact, this is analogous to the familiar vulnerability of the default rules prescribed by rule utilitarians: once (act) utilitarians start reassessing the utilities case-by-case, the benefits of the default rule are compromised.[39]

At the same time, in the world as we know it in the present century, one of the many disruptive effects of emerging technologies is to the conditions that sustain the moralists' picture. When the context for community life changes rapidly, when the application of the guiding principles is moot, it is the task

---

[37] C.J. McKinney, 'Coronavirus laws a "secondary consideration", says Sumption', *Legal Cheek* (September 14, 2020): available at https://www.legalcheek.com/2020/09/coronavirus-laws-a-secondary-consideration-says-sumption/ (last accessed September 16, 2020). Similarly, Sumption has suggested that people should make their own decisions about whether or not to assist family or friends with assisted suicide (although, in this case, the reasons for breaking the law would be a matter of conscience rather than prudence): see Joshua Rozenberg, *Enemies of the People?* (Bristol University Press, 2020) 97–98.

[38] For the context in which the laws were made and for these particular reservations about their legality, see, Jonathan Sumption, *Law in a Time of Crisis* (Profile Books, 2021) Ch 12 and pp 228 and 233.

[39] Compare Raz's example of the traffic signals, (n 11) at 16 and esp 25.

of the law to take a position, a position with which some members might (as the community would see it) reasonably disagree. For example, developments in modern biotechnology have provoked huge challenges for the law—not least in provoking new debates about the interpretation of human dignity[40]—as it is compelled to arbitrate between religious and secular views and between the ethics of prohibition and the ethics of permission.[41] Again, developments in neuroscience and neurotechnologies have raised questions about the fairness of the criminal justice system, especially about penal practice.[42] Nevertheless, in this context, the traditional demand for respect for the law insists that, such disagreement notwithstanding, a positive attitude towards legal prescriptions and legal institutions should be maintained.

Moreover, modern moral communities might be even more pluralistic than this. There might be disagreement not only about the application of guiding principles to particular hard cases but also about which principles should be treated as guiding.[43] Where the reference standards or values for doing the right thing are themselves contested, the law faces a greater challenge because the best attempt at accommodating moral disagreement might mean that very few or even no-one in the community actually supports the (compromise) position that is adopted.[44] Once again, though, to

---

[40]See, e.g., Deryck Beyleveld and Roger Brownsword, *Human Dignity in Bioethics and Biolaw* (Oxford University Press, 2001).

[41]See, e.g., Roger Brownsword, *Rights, Regulation and the Technological Revolution* (Oxford University Press, 2008); 'Human Dignity, Human Rights, and Simply Trying to Do the Right Thing' in Christopher McCrudden (ed), *Understanding Human Dignity* (Proceedings of the British Academy 192) (The British Academy and Oxford University Press, 2013) 345; 'Regulatory Coherence—A European Challenge' in Kai Purnhagen and Peter Rott (eds), *Varieties of European Economic Law and Regulation: Essays in Honour of Hans Micklitz* (Springer, 2014) 235; and 'Developing a Modern Understanding of Human Dignity' in Dieter Grimm, Alexandra Kemmerer, and Christoph Möllers (eds), *Human Dignity in Context* (Nomos and Hart, 2018) 299.

[42]See, e.g., Joshua Greene and Jonathan Cohen, 'For the Law, Neuroscience Changes Nothing and Everything' (2004) 359 *Philosophical Transactions of the Royal Society B: Biological Sciences* 1775; and, for the counter-view, see, Stephen A. Morse, 'Lost in Translation? An Essay on Law and Neuroscience' in Michael Freeman (ed), *Law and Neuroscience* (Oxford University Press, 2011) 529, and 'Law, Responsibility, and the Sciences of the Brain/Mind' in Roger Brownsword, Eloise Scotford, and Karen Yeung (eds), *The Oxford Handbook of Law, Regulation, and Technology* (Oxford University Press, 2017) 153.

[43]In those parts of the world where 'identity politics', fostered by online technologies, has entered the mix, the nature of plurality is likely to be even more complex and problematic. See, e.g., Matthew D'Ancona, *Identity, Ignorance, Innovation* (Bloomsbury, 2021) Chs 1–4. According to D'Ancona, there needs to be 'a new progressivism which respects group identity and … seeks to negotiate the differences that arise from the (endless) collisions of rights that take place in a diverse society' (at 111). Likening such a plural society to a dodgem rink, 'the challenge is to avoid collision … [and] the duty of rink managers is to ensure that nobody sustains injury' (at 112). In this context, we 'must assume that network politics is now the norm and that most of its battles will be fought online' (113). Moreover, we must 'take as read the fact that public trust in most institutions … has plummeted and that one of many formidable tasks facing [new progressivism] is to restore confidence in the organisations, agencies and public bodies that, in the end, will enact it' (113).

[44]Compare Roger Brownsword, 'Regulating the Life Sciences, Pluralism, and the Limits of Deliberative Democracy' (2010) 22 *Singapore Academy of Law Journal* 801.

demand respect for the law is to demand that all members of the community continue to view the law and its prescriptions in a positive light.

As with the prudential view, the default moral argument will be put under stress unless a conscientious objection clause is recognised; and, again the dilemma is the same. Should we decline to recognise an exception and then risk being accused of overclaiming and inviting rejection of the claim as wholly unreasonable? Or, should we create an exception but then risk underclaiming and compromising the preclusionary effect of the imprimatur of Law?[45]

4.2 In a context of scepticism: the question of the source of legal authority

For both legal positivists and legal idealists claims to legal authority (particularly where it is a matter of title that is at issue) are validated by reference back to their source.

According to legal positivists, the answer to a question about the authority (title) of a body or person undertaking a legal function (or claiming to act in a legal capacity) hinges on whether there is an appropriate mandate in a recognised authorising rule. In the case of legislative and judicial bodies, this authorisation might be explicitly declared in the founding constitutional rules; in other cases, the authorisation will be found in rules that have themselves been made by authorised rule-makers. On this account, the chain of title takes us back to the constitution, or the rule of recognition, or the last norm of positive law, or some such apex rule within the particular legal system. This means that, in the final analysis, the system purports to be self-validating. It means that the plausibility of all claims to authority within the system are contingent on acceptance of the apex rule as the ultimate test of authority. Ultimately, the authority of law rests entirely on a convention. Such a contingency is the Achilles Heel of the legal positivist/prudentialist view of legal authority.

There a number of responses to this problem, to the apparently unauthorised nature of the apex authorising rules themselves. One response, famously advanced by Hans Kelsen, treats this as a logical problem because there seems to be no end to the chain of authorisation. Kelsen's proposal is that we should presuppose a hypothetical rule (the 'Basic Norm' in Kelsen's terminology) that stands just outside the legal system and which authorises the apex rule or norm.[46] However, even if we accept the fictitious Basic Norm as a kind of logical full-stop, it does nothing to answer the practical and

---

[45]See, further, the discussion in 7.2.

[46]Hans Kelsen, *The Pure Theory of Law* (2nd ed) (University of California Press, 1967). For critical assessment, see Beyleveld and Brownsword (n 33) Ch 6, 'Methodological Syncretism in Kelsen's Pure Theory of Law' in Stanley L Paulson and Bonnie L Paulson (eds.) *Normativity and Norms: Critical Perspectives on*

normative questions raised by citizens. Another response is to present the apex rule as the agreed reference point for testing authority, the agreement taking the form of a social contract. Those who are parties to the contract are then precluded by their consent from disputing the apex rule as the test. Again, though, while this might be sound in principle, in practice it is also something of a fiction.[47]

For legal idealists, the last norm of positive law is never going to be the ultimate source of legal authority. Law has to be connected to some external moral standard or order and this is where the source of legal authority eventually will be found. While this narrative might be plausible in some contexts, it lacks plausibility where communities have stopped believing in the divine right of Kings, or similar justificatory tales. Particularly in those communities where there is a pragmatic acceptance that the authority of law rests only on a convention, the moral account will be rejected as a legacy of primitive thinking.

While there is a great deal more that could be said about these much-debated jurisprudential puzzles, the bottom line is that the traditional views are in trouble once we take a hard look at them. As Scott Shapiro says of this puzzle (the 'Possibility Puzzle' as he terms it):

> Legal philosophers, therefore, face a terrible dilemma: they are damned if they do ground the law in moral facts and damned if they don't.[48]

In my view, if we are not to give up on the idea of a compelling foundation for law, we should be looking instead at a prospectus that is fully committed to maintaining the 'global commons',[49] understood as the preconditions for humans to exist and to be viable as agents—whether they are forming their own communities with their own distinctive collective values and aspirations, or debating the mode of governance for their community, or developing a sense of their own identity and interests, or having regard to and debating the legitimate interests of fellow humans.[50] Although this is of

---

Kelsenian Themes (Clarendon Press, 1998) 113, and 'Normative Positivism: The Mirage of the Middle-Way' (1989) 9 *Oxford Journal of Legal Studies* 463.

[47]Compare Deryck Beyleveld and Roger Brownsword, *Consent in the Law* (Hart, 2007).

[48]Scott J. Shapiro, *Legality* (The Belknap Press, 2011) at 49.

[49]Let me emphasise that this term is not to be limited to, or equated with, those international spaces that lie beyond the limits of national jurisdiction, open to use by the international community and closed to appropriation by treaty or custom; and, nor is it to be equated with the *jus cogens* or obligations *erga omnes* that happen to be recognised at any one time by international law. Rather, the comparison should be with Karen Yeung's remark that a failure to include adequate safeguards in the governance of new technologies (such as AI), 'may erode our moral, cultural, and political foundations (the "commons") which could fatally undermine our democratic political system and with it our individual freedom, autonomy, and capacity for self-determination which our socio-cultural infrastructure ultimately seeks to nurture and protect [...]' (see Karen Yeung, 'Why Worry about Decision-Making by Machine?' in Karen Yeung and Martin Lodge (eds) *Algorithmic Regulation* (Oxford University Press, 2019) 21 at 42).

[50]See, further, Roger Brownsword, *Law, Technology and Society: Re-imagining the Regulatory Environment* (Routledge, 2019) Ch. 4, *Law 3.0: Rules, Regulation and Technology* (Routledge, 2020) Chs 17 and 20 (the

the first importance, because any picture of law that does not treat this commitment as non-negotiable is certainly not worthy of our respect, for our immediate purposes we do not need to take it any further.[51]

For present purposes, the point is that both sides in the traditional debate might wobble but the shape of the debate has not yet been radically disrupted. It is when we contemplate a switch from governance by rules to governance by rules together with technical measures and governance by machines and 'technological management' that we get to the radically disruptive second wave of challenges and questions.[52]

5. The second wave II: the traditional debate disrupted

The disruption brought about by governance by technology impacts on both sides of the traditional debate. On the one side, the prudential case for law is challenged by technologies that promise to outperform humans and rules in achieving order. It is no longer enough to argue that law, albeit less than perfect, is preferable to a lawless and disordered Wild West. Governance by technology claims that it can put in place a form of order that is closer to perfection.[53] On the other side, technologies promise to outperform

latter for the idea of a triple licence authorising a particular technological application), and *Rethinking Law, Regulation and Technology* (Elgar, 2022) Ch. 6. It should be understood that the conditions that make up the commons are neutral as between humans and as between human projects, whether they are projects for individuals or communities; and, in the same way, the infrastructural conditions are impartial as between particular views of self-interest and particular criteria for moral judgments. Infrastructural conditions that are not neutral and impartial in this way might well be important but, ex hypothesi, they will not be part of the critical infrastructure that supports human social existence. So, the global commons is not the only infrastructure but its conditions are relatively thin, setting the minimum conditions for human social existence. Quite simply all humans have a stake in these minimum conditions; the conditions themselves are neutral between humans but necessary if humans are to flourish; from which it follows that human agents must be positively disposed towards a project that focuses on assuring the conditions for humans to exist and for them to develop their capacity for, and their free exercise of, agency.

51 For application of this scheme of thinking in a context that is not technological, and where the line between cosmopolitan responsibilities and local sovereignty can be more clearly drawn, see Roger Brownsword, 'Migrants, State Responsibilities, and Human Dignity' (2021) 34 *Ratio Juris* 6. One way of understanding the significance of this kind of scheme is that enables us to apprehend the depth of values as well as their breadth and plurality: see Roger Brownsword, 'Informational Wrongs and Our Deepest Interests' in Borghi and Brownsword (n 24).

52 Broadly speaking, by 'technological management' I mean the use of technologies—typically involving the design of products or places, or the automation of processes—with a view to managing certain kinds of risks by excluding (i) the possibility of certain actions which, in the absence of this strategy, might be subject only to rule regulation or (ii) human agents who otherwise might be implicated (whether as rule-breakers or as the innocent victims of rule-breaking) in the regulated activities. See, further, Roger Brownsword, *Law, Technology and Society: Re-imagining the Regulatory Environment* (n 50) 40–42. Compare Ugo Pagallo, *The Laws of Robots* (Springer, 2013) 183–92, differentiating between environmental, product and communication design and distinguishing between the design of 'places, products and organisms' (185).

53 Compare, e.g., Allan C. Hutchinson, *Cryptocurrencies and the Regulatory Challenge* (Routledge 2022) at 81:

> [R]ather than seek to remain within [an old-style] regulatory mind-set or renovate the regulatory tools available, the better option by far is to strike out in new directions with a broader institutional imagination and with a better toolbox of regulatory tools … .As regards

humans in computing the features of, and realising, their aspirant moral order of law. Whether we are thinking just about *order* (as in the legal positivist and prudentialist picture of law), or about order that aspires to be *just* (as in the legal idealist and moral picture of law), the argument for the machines is that they can outperform the human enterprise of law; what we should be deferring to is the judgment of the machines.

According to Karen Yeung and Martin Lodge, what is distinctive about contemporary debates relating to the 'rise of the machines' is:

> the almost limitless domains in which algorithmic systems may be shown to 'outperform' humans on a very wide range of tasks across multiple social domains that have previously been understood as requiring human judgement and intelligence.[54]

To be sure, there will be a debate about whether governance by technology can live up to its promise.[55] If we assume that it can, though, then the traditional debate—which sets one version of human governance against another—is displaced by a quite new debate about authority and respect where the choice is between either governance by humans and rules or governance by technologies.

In a world of rapid technological development and increasing automation, and in the shadow of disruption, we find another picture forming, a picture of law that seeks to preserve self-governance by humans. Relative to Lon Fuller's idea of the legal enterprise as that of subjecting human conduct to the governance of rules,[56] the emphasis in this picture is not so much on rules as on *humans*; and the reasons for respecting law all relate to the virtues of governance by humans rather than governance by machines.[57]

---

cryptocurrency and other Fintech innovations, it would seem best to generate a regulatory way of proceeding that is itself more technological and adaptive—*Regtech*. In a world of super-technology, regulation runs the definite risk of not only missing the opportunities to stay up-to-date, but also of missing the mark unless it becomes more technological and adaptive.

[54]Karen Yeung and Martin Lodge, 'Algorithmic Regulation: An Introduction' in Yeung and Lodge (n 48) 1 at 12.

[55]See, e.g., Alex Griffiths, 'The Practical Challenges of Implementing Algorithmic Regulation for Public Services' in Yeung and Lodge (n 48) 150, especially at 159–169 where the failure of an intelligent monitoring tool employed by the Care Quality Commission and similarly, of an algorithmic approach employed by the Quality Assurance Agency (for higher education) is analysed. For doubts about the claimed superior moral governance by smart machines, see Robert Sparrow, 'Why machines cannot be moral' (2021) *AI & Soc*, available at https://doi.org/10.1007/s00146-020-01132-6; and, Hubert Etienne, 'The Dark Side of the "Moral Machine" and the Fallacy of Computational Ethical Decision-Making for Autonomous Vehicles' (2021) 13 *Law Innovation and Technology* 85.

[56]Lon Fuller (n 29).

[57]See, e.g., Mireille Hildebrandt, *Smart Technologies and the End(s) of Law* (Elgar, 2015). On which, see Roger Brownsword, Disruptive Agents and Our Onlife World: Should We Be Concerned?' (2017) 4 *Critical Analysis of Law* 61. Similarly, emphasising the centrality of *human* agency to the idea of law, see Amnon Reichman and Giovanni Sartor, 'Algorithms and Regulation' in Hans-W Micklitz, Oreste Pollicino, Amnon Reichman, Andrea Simoncini, Giovanni Sartor, and Giovanni De Gregorio (eds), *Constitutional Challenges in the Algorithmic Society* (Cambridge: Cambridge University Press, 2021) 131, at 158:

> Moreover, central to the notion of law in a liberal democracy is its human nature: it is a product of human agency, its values and goals should reflect care for human agency, and its application should ultimately be at the hands of humans exercising agency . . . .[To be sure, as some jurists

This human-centric picture is one of a community that now not only has at its disposal a range of technologies that can be deployed for regulatory purposes but also an appreciation that such tools might be more effective than rules. This is a community that has come to realise that, far from being a regulatory challenge, technologies can be a regulatory opportunity. In other words, this is a community in which 'law 3.0' (as I would term it) is already part of the conversation.[58] However, where the functions of law are automated, we are being asked to respect an enterprise that takes humans out of the loop.

From a prudential perspective, the automation of legal functions, the replacement of human officials with machines, might seem risky relative to one's interests. Teething problems are to be expected and over-reliance on the technology might leave both individuals and communities ill-prepared for situations in which there are technological malfunctions or breakdowns. Without reassurance about the reliability and resilience of the technology, it is unclear whether one should prefer, so to speak, a West coast regulatory approach with its aspiration of total technological management that will guarantee perfect control and compliance or the traditional East coast approach where compliance is far from perfect, where decisions can suffer from human bias and inconsistency, and where detection and enforcement is also far from perfect.[59] In this light, we might recall Samuel Butler's *Erewhon*[60] where the Erewhonians—concerned that their

suggest,] the question of legal validity, scope, and operative meaning of a particular rule as considered for application in a given set of facts cannot be fully separated from the underlying values embedded in the rule (as part of a set of rules and principles, governing a given field of human interaction). If this is indeed the case, discretion is a feature, not a bug. It is not clear that we can fully separate the question of 'what is the operative meaning of the rule with respect to a particular set of facts' from the question 'should we enforce that meaning in the given set of facts'. In that respect, would we rather have bureaucrats fully automated, without seeing the unique circumstances before them – the human being (not only the case number), applying for the exercise of state power (or its withdrawal) in a particular case? Certainly, there is a risk that relaxing the technical commitment to the conventional meaning of rules will result in biases or favouritisms, as may be the case when human judgment is exercised. But the alternative, namely removing all ambiguity from the system, may result in detaching law from its human nature, by removing agency and by supposing that codes can adequately cover all circumstances, and that human language is capable of capturing 'the reality' in a transparent, technical manner. The latter assumption is difficult to support.

[58] See Roger Brownsword, *Law 3.0: Rules, Regulation and Technology* (n 50), and 'Law 3.0: A Conversation for the New Decade?' (2020) *Georgetown Journal of International Affairs*, available at https://gjia.georgetown.edu/2020/07/21/law-3-0-a-conversation-for-the-new-decade/ (last accessed February 2, 2022).

[59] Seminally, see Lawrence Lessig, *Code and Other Laws of Cyberspace* (Basic Books, 1999). Compare, Roger Brownsword, 'Code, Control, and Choice: Why East is East and West is West' (2005) 25 *Legal Studies* 1. See, too, Martin Ebers and Marta Cantero Gamito, 'Algorithmic Governance and Governance of Algorithms: An Introduction' in Martin Ebers and Marta Cantero Gamito (eds), *Algorithmic Governance and Governance of Algorithms* (Springer, 2021) 1 at 3, who observe that 'while it is true that human decision-making is not immune to mistakes and biases, algorithmic decisions can have a much larger effect, as the software not only decides dozens or hundreds of cases, but rather tens of thousands or more.' On this basis, we might judge that it is prudent to stick with human governance as a strategy for limiting the damage that might be caused by the machines.

[60] Samuel Butler, *Erewhon* (Penguin, 1970; first published, 1872).

machines might develop some kind of 'consciousness', or capacity to reproduce, or agency, and fearful that machines might one day enslave humans—decided that the machines must be destroyed. The Erewhonians, so to speak, preferring the devil they knew, opted for the East coast.

Similarly, from a moral perspective, it is unclear whether submitting to governance by smart machines is doing the right thing. If we value human discretion in the application of rules, we might worry that, with automation, this is a flexibility that we will lose.[61] Moreover, to the extent that the morality inscribed in machines tends to be utilitarian, this will be unattractive to those moral constituencies that do not subscribe to such reasoning.[62] As with the prudential rejection of governance by machines, conserving governance by rules, made by humans and administered by humans, might seem to be the morally indicated option.[63]

However, let us suppose that we do radically revise our conceptual thinking so that we come to view law as an expert system, not so much an assembly of philosopher kings as an assemblage of smart machines that can out-calculate, out-compute, and out-perform even the most intelligent and wisest of humans. If this is the relevant picture of law, then would it not be crazy for humans to back their own judgments, both prudential (for order) and moral (for just order), against the machines? Yet, this is exactly what is proposed by the human-centric picture in which the law seems to be celebrated as an expression of (probably) inferior governance simply because it retains its human character. Like a see-saw, the dialectic between those who argue for respect for the law and those who are discontent will move up and down but, as the weight of discontent increases, we might come to think that the form of governance to be respected by humans is after all the law of the machines; given time, even humans will come to realise that relative to governance by humans, it is governance by machines that is better than the alternative.[64]

---

[61] For some pertinent examples, see Robert Veal and Michael Tsimplis, 'The integration of unmanned ships into the lex maritima' [2017] LMCLQ 303.

[62] Again, compare Hubert Etienne (n 55).

[63] Compare Hildebrandt (n 57) where we find this kind of picture of law, with on the one side 'legality' (due process and justice) being valued against mere 'legalism' (mechanical application of the rules) and, on the other, governance by rules being valued against rule by technologies.

[64] Compare the drift of the discussion in Ryan Abbott, *The Reasonable Robot* (Cambridge University Press, 2020); similarly, see Daniel Kahneman, Olivier Sibony, and Cass R. Sunstein, *Noise* (William Collins, 2021) at 337 where, having discussed many examples of the performance of algorithms relative to intuitive human judgments (such as judgments about the appropriate level of punishment for a convicted criminal), the authors conclude that:

> [A]lthough a predictive algorithm in an uncertain world is unlikely to be perfect, it can be far less imperfect than noisy and often-biased human judgment. This superiority holds in terms of both validity (good algorithms almost always predict better) and discrimination (good algorithms can be less biased than human judges). If algorithms make fewer mistakes than human experts do and yet we have an intuitive preference for people, then our intuitive preference should be carefully examined.

Taking stock, whereas in the traditional debate, the principal fault line is between positivist and idealist conceptions of law (where, on both sides of the line, law is characterised as governance by rules), the new fault line (after disruption) is between, on one side of the line, modes of governance that are directed by humans who use rules and, on the other side, governance by technologies where humans no longer direct and rules are no longer the instruments of direction.

6. The second wave III: the new debate

So, to put the question starkly, if our choice is between human-centric governance (with humans making their own decisions) and governance that is designed to ensure that humans come to no harm, then which version of governance should we choose, why so, and what price or risk might there be in making the choice?[65]

First, which version should we choose? Should we choose imperfect self-governance by humans or more perfect governance for humans? If we choose the latter, it makes little sense to worry about authority and respect: the context is no longer one of trusting the judgments of other humans above one's own prudential or moral judgments; it is no longer a matter of deferring to the judgments of other humans. If we choose the former, we still have the traditional question to tackle. To be sure, we might think that we need to cut some more slack to individuals to follow their own prudential judgments or conscience. However, there is still a live question to be asked about why deference to the law should be the default.

Secondly, is there any reason why we should choose one mode of governance rather than another? For moralists, it might seem self-evident that there is no virtue in doing the right thing simply because this is indicated by smart machines or compelled by technological management. For moralists, the inclination might be towards the former version (the East coast). For prudentialists, the inclination might be towards the latter version (the West coast) but some might follow the moralists in thinking that it is important for humans to make their own prudential judgments. What we have here are different conceptions of our humanity and, subject to the critical caveat in the next point, I see no compelling reason to say that one conception is better than the other.

Thirdly, although we might not yet have a clear reason to prefer one conception over the other, human agents should never make choices that compromise the essential conditions for their existence and agency. So, whatever

[65]Of course, this is not to suggest that the choice actually will be presented in such stark terms. The governance designs that are available are likely to be far more nuanced and it will not be a matter of voting for one mode of governance rather than the other. It will not be like a decision to switch off analogue and commit to digital, or vice versa. But, if that were the nature of our choice, how should we decide between the two modes of governance?

we choose we must not adopt a mode of governance that irreversibly compromises the conditions for our human social existence (that is to say, the global commons).

Finally, to return to the nature of the second wave of disruption, we can detect three prongs of disruption. One is the disruption to the prudential case for deference to the Law. The relevant alternative to legal order is not now disorder, but a better technologically controlled regime of governance. The second prong is the disruption to the moral case for deference to the Law. The relevant alternative now is not an inferior order that does not aspire to be just, but a better form of governance by moral machines coupled with technological management. Thirdly, the opposition between the prudential and moral justifications for governance by legal rules is de-centred and disrupted. In place of this traditional opposition, we now have, on one side, advocacy in support of governance by rules (implicating a conception of human-centric governance) and, on the other side, advocacy in support of governance by machines (implicating a conception of human-protective governance).[66] While the traditional jurisprudential question retains its vitality on one side of this new opposition, on the other, it seems to be redundant. If this is correct, then we can already sense the nature and significance of the third disruptive wave.

7. The third wave of disruption: an agenda for debate

As was indicated in my introductory remarks, the second wave of disruption presages a third wave. The disruptive impact that we are highlighting in this

[66] In para 1.1 of its Explanatory Memorandum to the proposed Regulation on AI, Brussels 21.04.2021, COM(2021) 206 final, the European Commission remarks that the purpose of the Regulation is to deliver 'an ecosystem of trust by proposing a legal framework for trustworthy AI. The proposal is based on EU values and fundamental rights and aims to give people and other users the confidence to embrace AI-based solutions, while encouraging businesses to develop them. AI should be a tool for people and be a force for good in society with the ultimate aim of increasing human well-being. Rules for AI available in the Union market or otherwise affecting people in the Union should therefore be human centric, so that people can trust that the technology is used in a way that is safe and compliant with the law, including the respect of fundamental rights.' Does this suggest a human-protective approach, with the emphasis on increasing human well-being as well as the take-up of AI, or does it suggest an approach where humans continue to rely on rules and remain in control?

Of course, in practice, governance might involve elements that are human-protective while also reserving some elements of human-centric oversight and control. Compare, e.g., Saverio Puddu, Ana Isabel Rollán Galindo, and Kay Firth-Butterfield, 'What the EU is doing to foster human-centric AI' (May 3, 2021) (available at https://www.weforum.org/agenda/2021/05/ai-and-ethical-concerns-what-the-eu-is-doing-to-mitigate-the-risk-of-discrimination/)/. Their reading of AI governance in the EU is that the 'strategy … is clear and it places people at the centre of the development of AI, thus designing a human-centric AI.' In particular, the EU's proposed Regulation on AI (COM/2021/206 final) 'is part of a wider effort to develop human-centric AI by eliminating mistakes and biases to ensure it is safe and trustworthy.' It 'includes requirements to minimise the risk of algorithmic discrimination, in particular in relation to the quality of data sets used for the development of AI systems'; and it 'introduces human oversight of certain AI systems to prevent or minimise risks to health, safety or fundamental rights that may emerge when an AI system is used.' For the human oversight provisions in the original draft of the EU Regulation, see Article 14.

third wave is on a raft of concepts that are meaningful when the context is governance by humans and by rules but not so once the context is governance by technology[67]—and, moreover, not so even though we might persist in trying to transplant the language of one context to the other.

In this article, I will start by sketching an agenda of questions that are prompted by the third wave of disruption and then I will speak to the disruption of the idea that we should respect the law—simply because it is the law and our reservations notwithstanding.

7.1 An agenda of questions

The third disruptive wave provokes many questions. In the agenda sketched below, the questions that are put forward are primarily about the disruption to a conceptual scheme of thinking that is associated with governance by rules and by humans.

First, to state the general question: how far do the conceptual ideas and the questions that accompany governance where humans are still the authors of regulatory measures remain meaningful once humans are out the regulatory loop? Similarly, how far do the conceptual ideas and the questions that accompany governance where it is rules that are the instruments of choice remain meaningful once that context changes to governance by technologies?

Secondly, following up on the general question, if and when governance is no longer by rules, how meaningful is it to persist with the idea of 'legality', an idea that is predicated on a commitment to governance by rules?[68] If the mode of governance is no longer rule-based, what will it mean to say that governance is guided by the principles of 'legality'? Possibly, we might be able to derive some generic sense of fair dealing from the rule-based notion of legality; if so, should we persist with it?[69] Or, should we

[67]If a community is fully committed to governance by technology, there will also be disruptions to the back-up layers of governance (in which humans and rules are no longer employed). In other words, the logic of this level of reliance on technologies implies (i) that, in place of primary rules directed at human conduct, we have (primary) technologies doing the governance and (ii) that, in place of the secondary rule structure, we have oversight governance of the operation of the primary technologies by a secondary layer of technologies. How far a particular community will want to back up these technologies (to a third and fourth layer of oversight and checking) will depend initially on its assessment of risk and its prudential judgments. But, this might be the last act of human involvement. From this point on the technologies also undertake risk assessment of their own governance.

[68]See Fuller (n 29).

[69]Seminally, see Lodewijk Asscher, '"Code" as Law. Using Fuller to Assess Code Rules' in E. Dommering and L. Asscher (eds), *Coding Regulation: Essays on the Normative Role of Information Technology* (TMC Asser, 2006) 61, at 86:

> Code can present constraints on human behaviour that can be compared with constraints by traditional laws. We have argued that even though code is not law, in some instances it can be useful to ask the same questions about code regulation as we do about traditional regulation. Code as law must be assessed by looking at the results of regulation in terms of freedom and individual autonomy and compared to the balance struck in traditional law.

abandon this idea lest it should 'legitimate' a quite different mode of governance? Certainly, for communities that are anxious to retain rule-based governance, it would be a hostage to fortune to allow the *language* of legality to be translated without qualification to governance by technologies.[70]

Thirdly, there is the parallel question of whether it is meaningful to persist with the idea of the Rule of Law, understood as the rule of rules, when governance is no longer by rules. Bearing in mind the important thought that it is the Rule of Law that stands between law's governance and a techno-managed future[71], communities need to be very careful (as with legality) about licensing these rule-based ideas—or, at any rate, the language associated with these ideas—to legitimate very different modes of governance.

Fourthly, beyond legality and the Rule of Law, there is a raft of concepts—including authority, respect, trust, justice, due process, and so on that are characteristic of *human* governance—about which we might ask: is it meaningful or smart to transplant these concepts, or this vocabulary, to governance by machines?[72] In each case, the language might persist but the underlying concepts will have undergone a radical change.

Fifthly, if we suppose that the discourse of law's governance is distinctively a discourse of justification, that the power exercised through law is always subject to justification, then should we accept that this discourse is no longer appropriate or required once governance is by machines? In particular, even if it is acknowledged that humans have a right to an explanation where decisions are automated,[73] should we accept that this is merely a (technical) 'explanation' that describes how the system works and, perhaps, gives some assurance that the technology has functioned as per its specification?[74]

For my own attempts to derive some generic guidance from the Fullerian principles, see Roger Brownsword *Law, Technology and Society: Re-imagining the Regulatory Environment* (n 50) 118–32, and *Rethinking Law, Regulation and Technology* (n 50) Ch 4.

[70] In this context, we should heed Mireille Hildebrandt's warning (n 57 at xiii):

> If we do not learn how to uphold and extend the legality that protects individual persons against arbitrary or unfair state interventions, the law will lose its hold on our imagination. It may fold back into a tool to train, discipline or influence people whose behaviours are measured and calculated to be nudged into compliance, or, the law will be replaced by techno-regulation, whether or not that is labelled as law

[71] See, e.g., Mireille Hildebrandt (n 57).

[72] We should note Frank Pasquale's apt remark in 'Inalienable Due Process in an Age of AI: Limiting the Contractual Creep toward Automated Adjudication' in Micklitz et al (n 57) 42, at 43: 'At some point, agencies will adopt automated processes that courts can only recognize as simulacra of justice.'

[73] For discussion of the vexed question of whether data subjects have a right to an explanation under the GDPR, see Sandra Wachter, Brent Mittelstadt, and Luciano Floridi, 'Why a Right to Explanation of Automated Decision-Making Does Not Exist in the General Data Protection Regulation' (2017) 7 *International Data Privacy Law* 76. See, further, Jyh-An Lee, 'Algorithmic Bias and the New Chicago School' (2022) 14 *Law Innovation and Technology* (in this special issue).

[74] See, e.g., Joshua A. Kroll, Joanna Huey, Solon Barocas, Edward W. Felten, Joel R. Reidenberg, David G. Robinson, and Harlan Yu, 'Accountable Algorithms' (2017) 165 *University of Pennsylvania Law Review* 633. Compare, too, OECD/LEGAL/0449, adopted on 22/5/2019, available at https://legalinstruments.oecd.org/en/instruments/OECD-LEGAL-0449 (last accessed June 21, 2019). Here, Article 1.3, headed 'transparency and explainability', states that 'AI Actors should commit to

If so, this is a long way short of the kind of justificatory explanation that we expect from human decision-makers.[75]

Sixthly, do we now face a Copernican revolution in our conceptual thinking, reworking the ideas that stand behind human-centric self-governance and, if so, where do we centre our thinking? For example, Ethan Katsh and Orna Rabinovich-Einy, having rightly observed that 'new forms of resolving and preventing disputes will move us even further away from the idea that the legal system is at the centre of the dispute resolution solar system',[76] then say:

> Adopting technology in the courtroom opens up new opportunities not only for making our existing processes less expensive and cumbersome and more accessible at all hours. It could also change the very nature of court processes, with software playing an increasingly significant role in streamlining, resolving, and preventing claims. Indeed, there is promise for transforming our very understanding of the meaning of *justice*.[77]

This prompts the response, echoing the fourth question above, that our sense of justice is not what needs to be transformed; for sure, unequal justice is not justice,[78] but it is our practice that needs to be transformed not the ideals to which we aspire.

Seventhly, should we now view law as just one kind of patterned order? When we read familiar characterisations of law as governance by rules, should we, instead of putting the emphasis on 'rules', put it on 'governance'? To be sure, an order that emerges from humans who are self-consciously following rules is a distinctive kind of order; and, as traditional jurisprudence

---

transparency and responsible disclosure regarding AI systems.' Hence, such actors 'should provide meaningful information, appropriate to the context, and consistent with the state of the art:

1. to foster a general understanding of AI systems,
2. to make stakeholders aware of their interactions with AI systems, including in the workplace,
3. to enable those affected by an AI system to understand the outcome, and
4. to enable those adversely affected by an AI system to challenge its outcome based on plain and easy-to-understand information on the factors, and the logic that served as the basis for the prediction, recommendation or decision.'

[75]See, Roger Brownsword, 'The Regulation of New Technologies in Professional Service Sectors in the United Kingdom: Key Issues and Comparative Lessons' (published by the Legal Services Board, London, July 4, 2019). Especially para 3.1.3.3 (transparency as justification) and the case of *CCN Systems Ltd v Data Protection Registrar* (Case DA/90 25/4/9, judgment delivered 25 February 1991) on the use of unrelated third-party data. Available at https://www.legalservicesboard.org.uk/wp-content/uploads/2019/07/Professions-RB-Report-VfP-4-Jul-2019.pdf (last accessed January 22, 2022). Compare, too, Michael Veale and Irina Brass, 'Administration by Algorithm?', in Yeung and Lodge (n 47) 121, at 131.

[76]Ethan Katsh and Orna Rabinovich-Einy, *Digital Justice* (Oxford University Press, 2017) 20.

[77]Ibid., at 164–65.

[78]Compare Jerold S. Auerbach, *Unequal Justice* (Oxford University Press 1976) at 12: 'In the United States justice has been distributed according to race, ethnicity, and wealth rather than need. This is not equal justice.' Similarly, see Benjamin H. Barton and Stephanos Bibas, *Justice Rebooted* (Encounter Books, 2017) at p. 4: 'Mothers seeking child support, tenants fighting eviction, and laid-off workers claiming unemployment or disability benefits usually cannot afford lawyers. They routinely endure long delays and great difficulty navigating courts by themselves before they can receive justice.'

emphasises, the internal attitude of those who are following the rules is distinctive.[79] Nevertheless, if the predictability of order is the key characteristic of governance, then (given the unpredictability of human responses to rules) legal order is hardly the paradigm. Rather, the paradigm of governance is technologically secured order.

So much for a sample of questions that flag up the disruption to our conceptual thinking. However, we can add to our list three further questions that are prompted by the narrative that anticipates a third wave of disruption.

One question is this: although we have suspended doubts about the superior performance of machines and technological management, a significant number of humans surely will push-back against this kind of governance.[80] They will contest the claim that machines do governance better than humans. Already, in some sports, there is a push-back against some forms of technological arbitration; for both players and spectators, the technology is an unwelcome interruption.[81] Indeed, some see the technology as exacerbating the inconsistencies in human on-field decisions that were one of the reasons for entrusting the decisions to off-field technologies and human interpreters aided by such tools.[82] Given such resistance, why should we assume that the third wave of disruption will take place? Perhaps, it will always remain on the horizon.

A second question concerns the point at which we should say that governance is no longer an essentially human enterprise. To be sure, humans might not figure in the foreground but how far out of the background loop can they be taken before the enterprise loses its human character? How deep and how broad must be our reliance on machines and technologies? How difficult must it be to identify accountable humans? Should we treat governance as crossing from human to technological when this is recognised de jure or is de facto reliance (when there is no longer a willingness by human reviewers to override the decisions made by machines) sufficient?[83]

Finally, should our working assumption be that, in the bigger picture, most communities will learn to live with (and accept) the rise of, but not

---

[79]Classically, see Hart (n 27).

[80]Compare, e.g., Roger Brownsword, 'From Erewhon to Alpha Go: For the Sake of Human Dignity Should We Destroy the Machines?' (2017) 9 *Law, Innovation and Technology* 117. See, too, various lines of resistance in Brett Frischmann and Evan Selinger, *Re-Engineering Humanity* (Cambridge University Press, 2018); and my remarks in n 59.

[81]Compare, e.g., Matthew Syed, 'VAR is football's passion killer—it's time to bin it' *The Times*, November 6, 2019, 64.

[82]See, e.g., Mark Clattenburg's assessment in the *Daily Mail* (October 20, 2019) available at https://www.dailymail.co.uk/sport/football/article-7594255/Inconsistent-VAR-losing-credibility-PGMOL-need-basics.html (last accessed January 22, 2022); and, recently, 'Arsenal fume over "inconsistent" VAR decisions after Man City loss' ESPN, January 1, 2022 available at https://www.espn.co.uk/football/arsenal-engarsenal/story/4560251/arsenal-fume-over-inconsistent-var-decisions-after-man-city-loss (last accessed January 22, 2022).

[83]See Rebecca Crootof, '"Cyborg Justice" and the Risk of Technological–Legal Lock-In' (2019) 119 *Columbia Law Review Forum* 233.

necessarily the rule of, the robots?[84] Should we assume that human communities will typically adopt a mode of governance that relies on both humans and technologies? Indeed, this might appeal as the optimal mode of governance, a happy conjunction of humans and machines.[85] In this picture, the outliers will be, at one end of the spectrum, the few communities that either reject governance by machines and hold on firmly to governance by humans and rules and, at the other end of the spectrum, the communities that embrace a brave new world of technological governance. For the latter, and possibly also for those communities that rely on hybrid modes of governance, the challenge would seem to be to articulate a theory of 'good governance' that is neutral between particular modalities of governance.[86]

7.2 Respect relaxed

A question that arises some time before we get to the third wave of disruption is whether the demand for respect for the law is simply too demanding. Particularly in a context of prudential and moral plurality, should we not relax the demand?[87] This is not a proposal to go from all to nothing; the demand can be relaxed by degrees.

Relaxing the demand for respect by one notch, it might be accepted that non-compliance or non-acceptance is permissible provided that this is 'for good reasons', that the circumstances are 'exceptional', that non-compliance is a 'last resort', and that those who do not comply submit to their penalty. There is plenty of scope for interpretation here but let us suppose that the good reasons can be either prudential or moral. Even so, this is a very limited relaxation; the expectation is that citizens will be positively disposed towards law's governance, that they will default to compliance, and that the idea of respect is still largely intact.

---

[84] Borrowing, here, from Martin Ford, *Rise of the Robots* (London: Basic Books, 2015) and *Rule of the Robots* (London: Basic Books, 2021). In his more recent book, Ford compares AI with electricity as a generic utility, indeed as 'an electricity of intelligence' (p. 4). The applications of AI's cognitive capability are, thus, virtually limitless 'from medicine to science, industry, transportation, energy, government and every other sphere of human activity' (ibid).

[85] Compare Frank Pasquale, *New Laws of Robotics* (The Belknap Press, 2020), the subtitle of which is 'Defending Human Expertise in the Age of AI'. According to Pasquale, the question is not whether robots can outperform humans, or whether (and when) humans should not use robots, but 'What sociotechnical mix of humans and robotics best promotes social and individual goals and values?' (at 29). What then follows is 'the case that AI supplementing, rather than replacing, human expertise realizes important human values' (ibid). Further, at 32, 'We can uphold a culture of maintenance over disruption, of complementing human beings rather than replacing them. We can attain and afford a world ruled by persons, not machines.' For discussion of machines judging humans, see ibid Ch 5.

[86] Compare, e.g., the Council of Europe's *12 Principles of Good Democratic Governance* (available at https://rm.coe.int/12-principles-brochure-final/1680741931, last accessed January 10, 2022). Although there are some excellent ideas in these principles, their particular focus is local governance and, more importantly, they are predicated on governance by rules and regulations.

[87] See 4.1. above.

Without further relaxation, the law might also be smart in relieving potential tension, for example, by making sympathetic provision for conscientious objectors[88] and for those who contest the prudential judgments made by those who govern (so smart design will favour pilots, provisionality, reviews, and precautions where the evidence is contested).

Taking up the call for relaxation, we might progressively relax the demand, notch by notch, until we get to a point where we find the concept of 'respect' so attenuated that we can no longer think it appropriate to dignify either the law or the attitude of citizens with that term. To identify in this way the minimum conditions for a meaningful claim that the law should be, and is, respected would not be theoretically or practically insignificant. Disrespect, after all, is the other side of the coin.

As a starting point, it might be agreed that respect for the law demands more than going along with its rules only where it suits one's interests. To respect the law is to go along with its requirements even though one might have some reservations about doing so. Respect is a willingness to comply with, to be guided by, and to support the law, such reservations notwithstanding. Indeed, if it is not already apparent, it is the friction between the demand for compliance and our reservations about law that make respect such a significant idea.

For those whose picture of law's governance (and its particular promise) is one of good *order*, it will not matter whether the reservations are prudential or moral: one does not respect the law if one lets one's reservations override the needs of good order. So, when Lord Denning famously rejected the accusation that he did not respect the precedents by saying that this was not so, that he followed the precedents *wherever he agreed with them*, some might have (and, indeed, did) respond to the effect that this was no kind of respect for the law. However, Lord Denning did not depart from the precedents because it suited him; he did so because he judged that justice in the individual case was more important than consistency in decision-making (order).

For those whose picture of law's governance (and its particular promise) is one of *just* order, Lord Denning's approach could be argued to be in line with respect for the law—or, at any rate, his approach was not disrespectful. From this perspective, the reservations that matter are moral reasons; and what might, from another perspective, seem like an act that evinces disrespect for the law, from a moral viewpoint is seen as respectful. Nevertheless,

[88]See, e.g., Davide Paris, 'Reckoning with Growing Pluralism. Potentials and Limits of Conscientious Objection: Conscience Clauses in Abortion Laws in Europe' in Lucia Busatta and Carlo Casonato (eds), *Axiological Pluralism* (Springer, 2021) 89, esp at 101 (on the importance of making space for conscientious objection in 'contemporary democratic and pluralistic societies' and criticising recent decisions at the European Court of Human Rights where challenges to Swedish abortion law, making no allowance for conscientious objection, have been rejected as 'manifestly ill-founded').

even with a moral picture of the law's governance, respect for the law cannot be a licence to act on one's own moral judgments in the face of a moral judgment arrived at through legal processes. The challenge for that kind of picture is to specify the conditions in which one's moral reservations can be acted on without this involving disrespect for the law; or, putting this the other way round, the conditions in which one should respect the law by setting aside one's moral reservations.

In a community that aspires to *just* order, if the Denning response to a charge of disrespect is recognised as acceptable, would it be available to agents other than judges? In particular, would it be available to lawbreakers who maintained that they respected the law by complying with those laws with which they agreed, or by cooperating with the authorities in the event that they broke laws that they judged to be unjust? And, what should we make of the classic Socratic dilemma of whether one should submit to one's punishment even though one might judge that punishment to be unjust? If the community collectively agrees a licence for individuals to act on their own judgments of justice without this amounting to disrespect for the law, the answer to these questions will depend on the terms of this licence. Relative to the community's own lights, an individual who acts on their judgment of justice in circumstances that fall within the terms of the licence should not then be treated as having shown disrespect for the law. Conversely, if their acts fall outwith the protection of the licence, this should be treated as a case of disrespect and the individual will then need to resort to some other standard (such as the licence that some ideal-typical moral community would accord to its members) or find a different line of response altogether (for example, one that argues that the performance of those who govern in the community is so poor that the demand for respect has been forfeited). If the community has not collectively agreed a licence of this kind, then there are likely to be as many different views about whether an act (guided by an individual's sense of justice) evinces disrespect for the law as about the background question of justice itself—which might or might not be a sustainable situation given that the aspiration is to both *order* and justice.[89]

This leaves us with a debate to be continued. If we doubt that the two traditional pictures of respect for the law's governance can sustain the kind of strong demand for respect that we have been considering, then we can articulate the way in which each of those pictures can set the minimum conditions for respect. Each picture treats respect for law's governance as

[89]Similarly, if the aspiration of the Law is simply for order, then there might be a collectively agreed licence to act on one's own judgment that the legal provisions suffer from a deficit in rationality. However, if order is to be maintained, the terms of this licence to act on a judgment that the law is 'irrational' would need to be carefully circumscribed. In this context, compare Jonathan Sumption (n 38) Ch 12 and pp 228 and 233.

requiring compliance with the particular decrees of law even though one has reservations about this. However, as we have seen, these articulations are not identical and, in the end, what we make of respect for the law, and of disrespect, is driven by what we make of the concept of law itself.

That said, while rule-based legal systems that manage plurality more successfully than others might seem to be worthy of greater respect, there is still the headline question of whether they can match the performance of governance by technologies. Moreover, when the machines govern, we might expect plurality to become less problematic. On the East coast, humans might continue to state their own minds, there might be differences of opinion, and plurality will persist; but, on the West coast, such matters will be of less import—for the machines, the opinions of humans, their differences and pluralities will no longer matter.

7.3 Respect reimagined

All our questions about respect for law's governance (or for any other form of human governance) are engaged when we have reservations about acceptance or compliance. On the one side, we might have doubts about the prospectus for law or discontent with its performance; on the other side, we have the call for respect, such reservations notwithstanding. If reservations were taken out of this equation, if we entertained no doubts or discontent, and if respect for the law (or any other mode of governance) signalled 'no reservations' and 'no second thoughts about acceptance or compliance', then the tension that troubles us would be resolved. But, how plausible is this reimagination of respect for the law?

This article is not written on the basis that respect for law's governance entails both an unquestioning attitude and unfailing compliance. Rather, it is based on the assumption that humans who respect the law should have a questioning attitude but should nevertheless comply and be unswervingly loyal their reservations notwithstanding. The reason why equating respect with no reservations lacks plausibility is that it assumes that one group of humans (who submit to the law) will be prepared to put blind faith in a governing group. We do not need to agonise about whether there are some contexts in which this might be plausible; even if there are such contexts, they are special cases. In general, I take the context to be the familiar one of humans having their reservations and there being questions about acceptance and compliance where other humans are responsible for governance. Certainly, if we are assuming an East coast form of law, this seems appropriate. What, though, about the West coast which is emblematic of governance by code and other technologies?

Where governance is by machines, we have wondered whether it is meaningful to continue to ask questions about the authority of law or respect for the law. We sense that we need to have accountable humans in control of the governance to bottom out these questions. However, if a West coast community reaches a point where governance has been left to the machines, and where humans no longer doubt the direction given by the machines or think about compliance or non-compliance in technologically managed environments, then if respect means anything it connotes that humans have given up on having their own ideas about the governance of their communities. On the East coast, and particularly where self-governance is central to our picture of law's governance, this is simply unthinkable; but, on the West coast, perhaps the logic of the evolving form of governance is precisely that of the idea of respect *without reservation*. Dismissing that idea was surely sound in relation to East coast forms of governance; but we should not so easily dismiss this idea of respect where governance is in a West coast form. What, to East coast citizens, might seem like an Alice in Wonderland inversion might be perfectly normal on the West coast.

In an analogous way, we can detect a similar inversion in our conceptualisation of 'trust' (and 'trustworthiness'). On the East coast, to trust a person to do the right thing (or indeed to do anything) is to rely on them without any security or insurance even though one has reservations about doing so and even though one is aware that there is a risk in doing so. To trust another human in such circumstances might or might not be judged to be prudential, but trust belongs in a moral world and it expresses a moral view of a relationship. Trust and trustworthiness come first, reliance on others follows. By contrast, on the West coast, to trust a person or a technology is to rely on them without any security or insurance because one has no reservations about doing so and because one treats such reliance as risk-free (or subject only to acceptable risks). Here, humans calculate prudentially: if fellow humans or machines seem to behave in predictable ways, then (with appropriate hedging of risk) they can be relied on; and, in this sense, they can be trusted. Risk assessment and risk management come first, trust follows. Whereas, on the East coast, to judge that a person is 'trustworthy' is to judge that a person will do the right thing even when they are disposed to (and have the opportunity to) do otherwise, on the West coast it is a proxy for reliability.[90]

[90]Compare the EU's idea of an ecosystem for trust in AI (n 64). It is striking that so much of the EU's background thinking about AI hinges on 'the development of human-centric, sustainable, secure, inclusive and trustworthy AI' (see, e.g., the Commission's press release of April 21, 2021 (on Europe being fit for the digital age) (available at https://ec.europa.eu/commission/presscorner/detail/en/ip_21_1682). Quoting Margrethe Vestager, Executive Vice-President for a Europe fit for the Digital Age, the press release says: 'On Artificial Intelligence, trust is a must, not a nice to have. With these landmark rules, the EU is spearheading the development of new global norms to make sure AI can be trusted' (ibid). Despite this commitment to trustworthy AI, the draft Regulation does not explicitly elaborate this desideratum (although, implicitly, the conspicuous focus on managing risks suggests that AI is trustworthy when it would be reasonable to judge that the risks it presents are acceptable). Moreover, when the focus shifts to trustworthy *humans* (in the provisions on the social scoring of humans), there

In an insightful analysis, Christoph Kletzer hits this nail on the head when he says:

> There are entirely different stakes at play in reliance and trust. Whilst reliance is a mundane and technical issue, trust is a morally laden issue that potentially concerns our very human essence. This makes it crucial to keep these two concepts neatly separated. Failing to do so leads to a host of misunderstandings not only about trust and reliance itself but also about the relationship of technology and law.[91]

So, on this analysis, parties who commit their transaction to a blockchain, do not place their 'trust' in the technology, they merely rely on it; and, although we should not jump too quickly to this conclusion, we might infer that, by relying on the technology rather than their human counterparty, they do not trust the latter (or regard the latter as trustworthy). Moreover, following through with this, we might say that it is not so much the difference between trust and trustworthiness that is critical—although it is no doubt true that we can mistakenly place our trust in one who is not trustworthy and fail to place our trust in one who is trustworthy[92]; rather, what matters is the difference between reliance based on trust (or trustworthiness) and reliance based on the judgment that the level of (managed) risk to which one is exposed is acceptable.

Finally, to return to respect, what this exercise reveals is that there is an intimate relationship between the form of governance that we presuppose and our conceptualisation of respect for the law, for its operators and its operations. On the East coast, respect means different things depending on whether we conceive of law's governance just as *order* or as *just* order; and, what respect for law's governance means on the West coast is radically different to any East coast conception of respect. As Kletzer says of the need to separate reliance (on machines) from trust (in humans), we also need to separate mere reliance on governance by machines from respect for governance by humans.[93]

---

is again no definition or elaboration: see, Michael Veale and Frederik Z. Borgesius, 'Demystifying the Draft EU Artificial Intelligence Act' (2021) 22 *Computer Law Review International* 97, at 100. Should we assume that the criteria for judging a human to be trustworthy are identical to those that are relevant to judging that AI is trustworthy? Or, is this trying to compare, so to speak, apples with oranges?

[91] Christoph Kletzer, 'Law, Disintermediation and the Future of Trust' in Larry A. DiMatteo, André Janssen, Pietro Ortolani, Francisco de Elizalde, Michel Cannarsa, and Mateja Durovic (eds), *The Cambridge Handbook of Lawyering in the Digital Age* (Cambridge University Press, 2021) 312, at 322.

[92] For some interesting reflections on trust, trustworthiness, and transparency, see the British Academy 'Future of the Corporation' briefing on that topic by Onora O'Neill and James Bardrick (January 2017) (available at https://www.thebritishacademy.ac.uk/documents/2563/Future-of-the-corporation-Trust-trustworthiness-transparency.pdf); and, see David Archard's blog on trustworthiness and 'doing ethics' (April 20, 2020) (available at https://www.nuffieldbioethics.org/blog/trustworthiness-and-doing-ethics) and the comments thereon.

[93] In this context, we should also note the difference between the East coast understanding of human 'autonomy' in any of its contested conceptions and the West coast notion of 'autonomous' technologies. Whereas the former connotes a degree of human control, the latter connotes independence

8. Concluding remarks

There is no doubting that the prospect of efficient and effective governance by technology disrupts the traditional debate about the authority of law and respect for the law—a debate where the background choice is restricted to various versions of governance by rules.[94] However, the precise nature and significance of the disruption invites further analysis.

If the choice between governance by rules and governance by machines is to be made on prudential grounds, the choice seems to be between imperfect order and perfect (or near perfect) order; and, if we are to push back against the latter it has to be on the apparently unpromising basis that we believe our self-interest (whether as an individual or as a member of the collective) is better served by imperfect order. If the choice is to be made on moral grounds, and if we are to push back against governance by technology it seems to be on the unpromising basis that we think that we do the right thing by backing our own moral judgments against the more perfectly realised moral order of the machines. In the end, what matters to humans with the capacity for agency is the process, not the product. How irrational, how typically human, technologists might reflect.

However, we might think that there is more to it than this. Governance by machines is not just another version of legal order demanding recognition of its authority and respect for its operation; it is not just another articulation of law to which prudential and moral reason is to be applied. Arguably, governance by machines is radically different to governance by humans; and

from human control. So, any reference to 'trustworthy autonomous systems' should not be taken to signal that such systems are either trustworthy or autonomous in the sense that humans might be trustworthy and autonomous. On 'autonomy' in relation to AI, see the European Group on Ethics in Science and New Technologies, *Statement on Artificial Intelligence, Robotics, and 'Autonomous' Systems* (Brussels, 2018) esp. at 9–10, where we read:

> It is therefore somewhat of a misnomer to apply the term 'autonomy' to mere artefacts, albeit very advanced complex adaptive or even 'intelligent' systems. The terminology of 'autonomous' systems has however widely gained currency in the scientific literature and public debate to refer to the highest degree of automation and the highest degree of independence from human beings in terms of operational and decisional 'autonomy'. But autonomy in its original sense is an important aspect of human dignity that ought not to be relativised.
>
> Since no smart artefact or system - however advanced and sophisticated - can in and by itself be called 'autonomous' in the original ethical sense, they cannot be accorded the moral standing of the human person and inherit human dignity. Human dignity as the foundation of human rights implies that meaningful human intervention and participation must be possible in matters that concern human beings and their environment. Therefore, in contrast to the automation of production, it is not appropriate to manage and decide about humans in the way we manage and decide about objects or data, even if this is technically conceivable. Such an 'autonomous' management of human beings would be unethical, and it would undermine the deeply entrenched European core values. Human beings ought to be able to determine which values are served by technology, what is morally relevant and which final goals and conceptions of the good are worthy to be pursued. This cannot be left to machines, no matter how powerful they are.

[94] Even where the debate moves away from the non-moral/moral dimension of law's governance, and the choice becomes one between traditional Westphalian, transnational, or pluralistic versions of governance, all orders are normative (rule-based).

technological management is radically different to governance by rules. The technological performance simply cannot be compared with the human performance. There might be some functional similarities but the performances are fundamentally different.[95] In that light, we come to see that a key feature of the traditional debate about the authority of, and respect for, the law is that it is predicated on a context in which the enterprise of subjecting human conduct to the governance of rules is an essentially human enterprise that uses rules as its regulatory tools. Once we take humans and rules out of the picture, this is a very different context and, concomitantly, a very different debate. In this context, while we can still ask whether we should defer to the machines, arguably, it no longer makes sense to conceive of law in terms of authority (this being characteristic of human relations) and respect (this being characteristic of situations in which the option of non-compliance is available).

We might also wonder whether the disruption goes even deeper, beyond the terms of the traditional debate, beyond our understanding of law as a human rule-based enterprise, reaching back to the context that supports the human capacity to make our own individual and collective judgments, whether guided by prudential reason or by moral reason. To be sure, if we commit to the authority of law and if we habitually respect it, we have put our prudential and moral trust in the law. In principle, we can recall questions for our own judgment and, as we have seen, that can be problematic. However, if we put our trust in governance by machines, recall might not be so easy. In dystopian scenarios, the machines might have other plans for humans;[96] and, even without dystopias, if governance by machines has disrupted the context in which humans develop their capacities for prudential and moral reason, the retrieval of governance by rules might not be so simple,

Finally, in what I have flagged up as the third disruptive wave, we have reason to wonder whether it is meaningful to question the authority of and respect for the law when the context is no longer one of governance by humans and rules. In the very different context of governance by technology, we might need to modify a broad sweep of our conceptual thinking. If we are reluctant to make such modification, then we need to resist the momentum behind governance by smart machines, lest we find ourselves irreversibly in a place that we humans do not want to be. In an ideal world, this would be the moment to take time out—time out to ask ourselves precisely that question: where do we want to be, what kind of societies do we wish to inhabit, do we want a world of imperfect self-governance or a world

[95]Compare Lyria Bennett Moses, 'Not a Single Singularity' in Simon Deakin and Christopher Markou (eds), *Is Law Computable?* (Hart, 2020) 205.

[96]Nick Bostrom, *Superintelligence* (Oxford University Press, 2014); and, Martin Ford, *Rule of the Robots* (n 83) 253–61.

of benign technological governance? Sadly, our rapidly changing technological societies are not designed for moments of this kind.

Acknowledgements

The ideas in this article formed the basis for a keynote lecture given at the conference on 'Law, Technology, and Disruption' held at City University Hong Kong, March 19–21, 2021 and, subsequently, for the Annual Lecture 2021 at the Allens Hub for Technology, Law and Innovation at UNSW. I am grateful to participants for their comments. An edited version of the keynote was published as 'Law, Authority, and Respect in our Information Societies: Three Waves of Technological Disruption' Bournemouth University CIPPM / Jean Monnet Working Papers No. 03-2021; some of the ideas about respect and the law were included in Roger Brownsword and Han Somsen, 'Law, Innovation and Technology: Fast Forward to 2021' (2021) 13 *Law, Innovation and Technology* 1, and they also feature in Roger Brownsword, *Rethinking Law, Regulation and Technology* (Cheltenham: Elgar, 2022) Chs 12 and 13. The present article is a further, incremental, iteration of this previous work.

Disclosure statement

No potential conflict of interest was reported by the author(s).

Rule-following robots? Transitional legal disruption through regulatee design and engineering

Hin-Yan Liu

ABSTRACT

Artificial Intelligence (AI) and Extended Reality (XR) technologies present regulators with powerful tools to manipulate human behaviour, but more perniciously, human desire and indeed human being. This is because AI applications can interfere with our internal decision-making processes, and XR applications can affect our sensations by creating and mediating our experiences of the external world. When these technologically driven affordances are strained through contemporary cognitive science research to ground the notion that perceptions are processes for prediction error minimisation, such interferences can amount to designing and engineering the regulatee herself. Effectively, regulation no longer needs to be signalled in a normative regulatory environment, nor must it hardcoded into the architecture or technologically managed. Instead, AI and XR make it possible to design and create regulatees that embody the desired regulatory outcome. Paradoxically, however, such regulatory incorporation looks very much like the exercise of the agency of an agent and therefore is not recognised as a problem by contemporary legal principles and processes which seek to push back against obviously external influences or pressures. As a result, it is immensely difficult to articulate the legal or regulatory challenges posed by these developments, and to identify the harms through these doctrinal lenses.

1. Introduction

The idea that legal principles and processes fall short as responses to technologically driven change has been gaining traction to the point of becoming the organising concept for the City University of Hong Kong's inaugural 'Law, Technology, and Disruption' conference.[1] While the term 'disruption' has unfortunately become worn out as a buzzword, its utility as a means of

[1] Convened during 19–21 March 2021 at the City University of Hong Kong.

capturing and articulating the challenging and ever-changing relationship between law, technology, and society, persists.[2]

So what is the concept of legal disruption? Why might it be useful? Where might it be found? What are the ramifications that follow?

In earlier work in this Journal, we proposed a new model of analysis for legal disruption where we were engaged in: defending the necessity for a novel conceptual model; contextualising the model within the preceding debates and surrounding literature; and setting out a detailed model for understanding the legal disruption precipitated by Artificial Intelligence (AI).[3]

In this paper, I hope to deepen our understanding of what 'disruption' might be in relation to law, regulation, and governance, and to draw attention to other facets of technologically driven legal disruption that may prove more challenging than the issues that are being widely discussed at present.[4] In broad brush strokes, this is because of the distance and divergence between expectation and experience, and because technologically driven affordances are unevenly distributed. These two effects intertwine to exacerbate the power inequities between the regulator and the regulatee: as the regulator has ever increasing capabilities to do more and more, the ability for the regulatee to resist or revolt against these restrictions diminishes to a vanishing point.

This is a grand claim in the abstract, but one that I hope to illustrate with the convergence of artificial intelligence and Extended Realities (XR). These two technologies envelope the regulatee in a powerful pincer movement to such an extent as to reduce the regulatee into a mere object for manipulation (in the sense of control) in theoretical terms. This double envelopment is executed by the use of AI on the one wing interfering with the internal decision-making processes of the regulatee,[5] and by the use of XR mediating the experiences of the regulatee in the physical world, and designing and creating the cyberspace and virtual worlds. Through a detour in the

---

[2]Hin-Yan Liu and others, 'Artificial Intelligence and Legal Disruption: A New Model for Analysis' (2020) 12 *Law, Innovation and Technology* 205; Roger Brownsword, 'Law Disrupted, Law Re-Imagined, Law Re-Invented' (2019) 2019 *Technology and Regulation* 10; Hin-Yan Liu, 'The Digital Disruption of Human Rights Foundations' in Mart Susi (ed), *Human Rights, Digital Society and the Law: A Research Companion* (Routledge, 2019); Roger Brownsword, 'Law and Technology: Two Modes of Disruption, Three Legal Mind Sets, and the Big Picture of Regulatory Responsibilities' (2018) 14 *Indian Journal of Law and Technology* 1.

[3]Liu and others (n 2).

[4]For more on a problem-finding orientation, see Hin-Yan Liu and Matthijs M Maas, '"Solving for X?": Towards a Problem-Finding Framework That Grounds Long-Term Governance Strategies for Artificial Intelligence' (2021) 126 *Futures* 102672.

[5]Daniel Susser, 'Invisible Influence: Artificial Intelligence and the Ethics of Adaptive Choice Architectures', *Artificial Intelligence, Ethics and Society* (2019), www.aies-conference.com/wp-content/papers/main/AIES-19_paper_54.pdf; Daniel Susser, Beate Roessler and Helen Nissembaum, 'Online Manipulation: Hidden Influences in a Digital World' (2019) 4 *Georgetown Law Technology Review* 1; Daniel Susser, Beate Roessler and Helen Nissenbaum, 'Technology, Autonomy, and Manipulation' (2019) 8 *Internet Policy Review* 1.

science of perception, I make the case that AI and XR combine to design and engineer the regulatee herself.

The upshot is that AI and XR enable the regulator to 'do regulation' through non-legal, indeed non-normative, means.[6] For our purposes, the important characteristic shared by normative means of regulation is that they are 'leaky'. In other words, they are in the realm of 'should' and 'ought', to varying degrees and with differing consequences for doing otherwise, but at the end of the day *it is possible* to do go against normative injunction and to do something else. What is pernicious about non-normative means of regulation is precisely that *the undesirable is collapsed into the impossible.*[7] The shift to regulatee design and engineering moves the locus of regulation upstream by *directly controlling the internal desire and motivation of the regulatee.*

The point, and problem, here for legal disruption is that we hold on to our legally informed *expectations* as to what power is, how it is exercised, by whom; and how to resist against it, through which procedures, and upon what grounds. Technologically driven *experiences*, however, take us in a radically different direction. Under normative logics of regulation, the regulator essentially configures the incentive structures for the regulatee and attempts to signal these accordingly,[8] but ultimately it is up to the regulatee to decide and to act. Under non-normative logics of regulation,[9] however, the regulatee herself is opened up for control and coercion (albeit by unfamiliar means): not only are choice architectures and thought-processes tampered with, but the very pre-perception sensory inputs can be manipulated through the new affordances and signifiers that are driven by AI and XR. The autonomy of the regulatee has effectively been lost in the translation from normative to non-normative means of regulation and the change in paradigm presents significant obstacles against resistance, roll-back, or revolution.

Thus, there are at least two different types of legal disruption that are driven by new technologies. There is the more overt form of turbulent

---

[6]By normative means of regulation, I draw on the four different regulatory modalities, Lawrence Lessig, 'The Law of the Horse: What Cyber Law Might Teach' (1999) 113 *Harvard Law Review* 501, 507–10.

[7]Roger Brownsword articulates this in crystal clear terms: 'Where a normative strategy is employed, regulators will seek to channel the behaviour of their regulatees by steering them towards one or more (required or desired) actions or away from one or more (prohibited or undesired) actions. In the former case, the steer is positive, in the latter it is negative. Where a non-normative strategy is employed, the steering follows a similar pattern: in order to steer regulatees towards a desired action, other options might be closed off or the regulatee is somehow "locked in" to the required action; and, in order to steer regulatees away from an undesired action, that action is simply closed off (instead of *x* actions being available, it is now *x*–1 actions that are available)'. Roger Brownsword, 'In the Year 2061: From Law to Technological Management' (2015) 7 *Law, Innovation and Technology* 1, 26.

[8]The terms regulator and regulatee are used loosely here, since the bottom-up nature of social norms decentralises this modality of regulation (and similarly with the market modality as well). Lessig, 'Law of the Horse' (n 6) 507.

[9]See Roger Brownsword's progression through three legal mindsets, especially the instrumental and the technocratic. Brownsword, 'Law Disrupted, Law Re-Imagined, Law Re-Invented' (n 2) 14–16.

disruption where the gaps and limits of the law are revealed and subject to analysis and reform, but there appears to be a type of transitional legal disruption where new technologies create new worlds by invoking and connecting new capabilities. The transitional aspect of these latter situations obscures their disruptiveness because, by settling the surrounding social, political, economic and legal context around a new equilibrium, it collapses the distance and divergence between experience and expectation. The effect is to shield transitional disruption from analysis and reform, but the impact of transitional legal disruption is both more fundamental and far-reaching than the more readily apparent turbulent disruption.

2. A roadmap

The opening parts of this paper will examine the idea of disruption, and I will analyse legal disruption as a function of time-frame and rate of change because these appear to be the qualities of change that distinguish disruption from more innocuous forms of change. Delving deeper, I set out the Change-Stability Matrix as a means of teasing out four different types of change. The purpose of this Matrix is to highlight instances where change is likely, or at least liable, to being 'disruptive'.

At this stage, however, the Change-Stability Matrix does not connect to legal disruption: my attempt to do so will situate the 'Change' dimension within sociotechnical change, and pit this against the 'Stability' dimension embodied by orthodox legal responses that seek stability, predictability, and foreseeability. This is essentially a different way of setting out a baseline of expectation and plotting it against the variable of what might be termed 'real world manifestations', bringing the discussion back to legal disruption as a function of time-frame and rate of change but hopefully with a greater appreciation of why legal disruption occurs. Doing so reveals two main forms of legal disruption: turbulent disruption and transitional disruption. The former, being more apparent, receives greater attention but I argue that transitional disruptions are more perilous because these simultaneously change the surrounding benchmarks of expectations and normative values around a new equilibrium. In so doing, the perceptible difference between expectation and experience is artificially suppressed thereby obscuring the prospect of legal disruption while simultaneously stabilising the aftermath.

After setting the scene, I guide us through several iterations of technologically driven legal disruption to make the case that it is *regulatee design and engineering* that constitutes the core concern. To do this, I depart from recent work that sets out AI influences to decision-making, distinguished between persuasion and coercion on the one hand and manipulation on the other on the grounds of hiddenness, towards the notion of regulation as the design of product and places. While this shift from normative to non-normative forms of regulation constitutes a transitional legal disruption in itself, it can still be considered as external influences upon regulatee behaviour and thus distinguishable from the regulatee herself.

To make the claim that regulation is incorporated into the regulatee herself, I guide us through recent work in the behavioural sciences that postulates the process of perception as a prediction error minimisation process. This is necessary because if perception can be understood as a two-way process of calibration between projected expectations and subsequent sensory input, this suggests that influencing sensory input will impact upon what is perceived. If the construction of perception through this adaptive calibration process informs conscious experience and the sense of self, we can see that by influencing sensations we can weave regulation into the fabric of the regulatee.

While initially appearing to have transformed regulatees into rule-following robots, the outcome is in fact much worse, because external regulation transforms into internalised forms of control. The agency of the agent is lost in this translation, thereby reducing the regulatee into an object.

In an attempt to wrap up this paper, I draw an analogy to the Kessler Effect to emphasise that new technologies can precipitate diminishing affordances, and that the new paradigms that follow may have lasting consequences that become costly and difficult to change.

3. Legal disruption as a function of time-frame and rate of change

Before delving into how different flavours of legal disruption arise from the Change-Stability Matrix, I would like to draw attention to the two common denominators that underlie this typology: time-frame and rate of change.

It may be rather obvious that there are issues of scale that hang over notions of change and stability because these notions are inherently referential. As Chuck Palahniuk wrote in 'Fight Club': 'On a long enough time line, the survival rate for everyone drops to zero'.[10] Similarly, on a long enough time line, everything looks stable, stagnant, even eternal. Yet, if we zoom into the time line and focus on the minutiae, everything looks turbulent and erratic.[11]

The time-frame thus determines the rate of change, since the rate of change is a function of change over time. More crucially, however, the

---

[10]Chuck Palahniuk, *Fight Club* (Vintage, 2003) 17.

[11]Perhaps a good way to visualise this is to look at the stock market and the difference between a minute-by-minute view to a historical annual overview.

time-frame affects the *perception* of the rate of change and therefore the *experience* of disruption.

For legal disruption, perception and experience are foundational because what the rate of change really measures are: the *difference* between expectation and manifested reality (in absolute terms, in the actual plotted positions in space) and the *divergence* between expectation and manifested reality (in terms of trajectories and trends). Taking these together, legal disruption can be captured in the distance between legal expectations, which are relatively linear with a slow rate of change; and technologically driven sociotechnical changes, which may be non-linear and have higher, and perhaps erratic, rates of change. This distance may be exacerbated by coherentist legal mindsets,[12] by legal developmental responses to the disruptive moment,[13] or by Levels 0–1 thinking,[14] which all seek to absorb changing conditions into linear and incremental legal responses.

An analogy can be drawn from buffer solutions in chemistry, which are aqueous solutions that are capable of resisting significant changes in pH level upon the addition of relatively small amounts of acid or alkali. For our purposes, each buffer has a set capacity in the amount of acid or alkali it can neutralise, beyond which the further addition of acids or bases will lead to significant changes in the pH of the solution. The point for legal disruption is that doctrinal attempts to close or minimise the distance between legal doctrine and sociotechnical change in the real world may be successful within law's buffering capacity, but such approaches may lead to sudden shocks or steep rates of change over short time frames as the law's capacity to absorb or neutralise further changes abruptly runs out.

One final point on the distance between legal expectation and manifest reality is that the absolute difference between the two might arise simply as a function of a small amount of divergence taking place over a long time frame. Thus, one does not need to buy the idea that expectation is linear while sociotechnical change is non-linear for legal disruption to occur. Rather, legal disruption will be inevitable in situations where there are differences in the rate of change between legal expectation and sociotechnical realities. As long as their trajectories are not parallel, there will be a cross-over point given sufficient time, and therefore there will be divergence.

This value-neutral approach indicates that there may be an under-explored class of legal disruption where manifest realities turn out to be

[12]Brownsword, 'Law Disrupted, Law Re-Imagined, Law Re-Invented' (n 2).
[13]Liu and others (n 2) 233–42.
[14]Liu and Maas (n 4) 8–9.

underwhelming.[15] Colin Picker has charted what might be considered as pre-emptive attempts to regulate for putative technological developments that have not come to fruition.[16] One interpretation of such anticipatory regulatory endeavours is that there is legal adequacy and therefore no problem because legal disruption only occurs where sociotechnical affordances exceed legal expectations. Yet, such legal overshooting of contemporary sociotechnical capabilities may not be so innocuous: it may lock in certain presumptions that may not turn out to be true; and it may give the appearance that certain subject areas have been addressed and resolved even where subsequent developments take significantly different form.[17] These can become significant problems given that law and regulation progress by a process of accretion that limits future legal and regulatory responses to the 'adjacent possibles'[18] that branch off from these points of departure and thereby restrict a more open search of the potential response space. In the context of the Collingridge dilemma,[19] pre-emptive attempts at regulation necessarily suffer from the information problem, but narrow the cones of possibility and plausibility in terms of regulatory responses around inaccurate projections of what the problems posed will be.

This final point suggests that not all forms of legal disruption will arise from ever growing opportunities through expanded affordances. While I hope to elaborate on this point below in relation to stagnation, and through the example of the Kessler Effect,[20] it is worth bearing in mind that technological advancement is only one avenue to legal disruption.

4. The Change-Stability Matrix

As we have suggested elsewhere, 'something has begun to change in change'.[21] In order to develop this observation further in the context of

[15]That is, where the available affordances prove to be less spectacular than expected. Fictively, 'Back to the Future II' highlights this well with the flying cars, hover boards, weather control and other fantastic technologies widely available on 21 October 2015.

[16]Colin B Picker, 'A View from 40,000 Feet: International Law and the Invisible Hand of Technology' (2007) 23 *Cardozo Law Review* 149, 194–97. These include the Deep Sea Bed Mining provisions of the Law of the Sea, and the Outer Space Treaty.

[17]For example, the family of bilateral Strategic Arms Reduction Treaties between the United States and former Soviet Union that may be overshadowed by the subsequent emergence of other nuclear powers such as China and the need for at least trilateral nuclear arms control agreements.

[18]Stuart A Kauffman, *At Home in the Universe: The Search for Laws of Self-Organization and Complexity* (Oxford University Press, 1995); Steven Johnson, *Where Good Ideas Come From: The Seven Patterns of Innovation* (Penguin, 2011).

[19]David Collingridge, *The Social Control of Technology* (Frances Pinter, 1980).

[20]Steve Olson, 'The Danger of Space Junk' (1998) *The Atlantic*, www.theatlantic.com/magazine/archive/1998/07/the-danger-of-space-junk/306691/ (accessed 21 December 2021).

[21]Liu and Maas (n 4) 1. See also, Daniel Deudney, 'Turbo Change: Accelerating Technological Disruption, Planetary Geopolitics, and Architectonic Metaphors' (2018) 20 *International Studies Review* 223; Hartmut Rosa, *Social Acceleration: A New Theory of Modernity* (Columbia University Press, 2015).

legal disruption, it may be useful to add an extra dimension to the analysis of change and stability. Doing so yields the Change-Stability Matrix (Table 1).

The result is that four different types of change can be identified: Changing *change* (Turbulence); Changing *stability* (Phase transition); Stable *change* (Incremental innovation); and Stable *stability* (Stagnation). These different types of change have different relationships with the notion of disruption, thereby engendering different flavours of legal disruption.

Before proceeding to elaborate upon these flavours of legal disruption, I should note that the Change-Stability Matrix provides four stylised types of change and these can obviously be nested within each other.[22] For example, phases of turbulence can be found within periods of stagnation, and phase transitions can occur within broader incremental innovations. But these are observations only on the type of change as such, and can at best provide guidance as to what to expect depending on what quadrant we think we are in.

By itself, however, it cannot speak directly to disruption even though it may be tempting to map the two 'changing' quadrants to disruptive changes at the top, and the two 'stability' quadrants at the bottom as the opposite of disruption. Why is this? Surely turbulence and phase transitions are clear cut examples of disruption in action?

The concept of legal disruption is *relational*. There must be a baseline *expectation* that provides the benchmark against which we are measuring the *experience* of manifest reality. If we are expecting turbulent times, and it turns out that our period is indeed a rocky one, it may well be that the difference both in absolute terms and in the divergence trajectories is smaller than if we were expecting turbulent times but ended up instead in a stagnant world.

Underscoring this relational aspect of legal disruption, however, results in a caricature because the very notion of turbulence is characterised not only by instability, but also by *unpredictability*. Thus, the point about turbulence for legal disruption may not be that it is changing change as such, but rather that it is change that cannot be anticipated or absorbed by legal principles and processes. As Daniel Deudney has suggested in relation to a different, yet aligned, approach to change:

> The features of turbo change – rapid rate, large magnitude, high complexity, significant novelty, and disruptiveness – *make foresight of directions, assessment of consequences, and explanations of patterns very difficult.*[23]

While Deudney situates disruptiveness as a factor driving turbo change, I would suggest that (legal) disruption is instead the product of the features that produce turbo change. In other words, rapid rate, large magnitude,

[22] This may be a different way of approaching the relationship between time frame and rate of change discussed above.
[23] Deudney (n 21) 226. Emphasis added.

Table 1. The Change-Stability Matrix.

	Change	*Stability*
Changing	Changing *change* **Turbulence**	Changing *stability* **Phase transition**
Stable	Stable *change* **Incremental innovation**	Stable *stability* **Stagnation**

high complexity, and significant novelty interact to produce conditions of turbo change, and turbo change as a phenomenon makes foresight of directions, assessment of consequences, and explanations of patterns very difficult. It is this difficulty of looking into and understanding the future that undergirds legal disruption.

In short, even if we expect turbulent times and prepare for it, what form that turbulence will take, how it perturbs societal dynamics, and how to understand the ramifications will all contribute towards legal disruption. For now, it seems as though certain types of change, or change possessing certain characteristics, are likely to drive legal disruption. Yet, looking at the type of change, or the characteristics of that change, is insufficient to ground an understanding of ensuing legal disruption because legal disruption is relational.

5. Legal disruption in the Change-Stability Matrix

In an attempt to excavate the relational dimension of legal disruption, we can make a new iteration of the Change-Stability Matrix that emphasises the relationship between *technologically-driven change* and *legal expectations* (Table 2).[24]

From this Matrix, we can identify four different types of relationship between technologically driven change and legal expectations. Changing *change* leads to turbulent disruption; changing *stability* leads to transitional disruption; Stable *change* leads to incremental development, and Stable *stability* leads to continuity.

Thus, legal disruption appears to only be a possibility in the top two quadrants featuring changing conditions, while legal sufficiency seems to occupy the bottom two quadrants that are characterised by being stable. *This is consistent within the context of technologically-driven change and legal expectations since legal disruption occurs where legal expectations do not map to manifested realities.*

Yet, such an approach is overly simplistic for at least two reasons. First, the bottom two quadrants characterised by legal expectations might set up conditions for subsequent legal disruption.[25] As *expectations*, these two

[24]By technologically-driven, I do not mean a purely techno-deterministic account.
[25]We had previously identified the 'Default' response to legal disruption arising from resistance to change, erroneous identification of a disruptive moment, and in the aftermath of Legal Displacement

Table 2. Legal disruption in Change-Stability Matrix.

	Change	*Stability*
Changing **Experiences** Drivers of Change: Realisation and Exploitation of Affordances[a]; Social Organisation; Technological Development.[b]	Changing *change* **Turbulent disruption** Complex, interactional, emergent Chaotic	Changing *stability* **Transitional disruption** Paradigm shifts; Phase transitions Step-change
Stable **Expectations** Stabilising legal responses: Legal coherentism[c]; Law of the Horse.[d]	Stable *change* **Incremental development** Undulating, smooth change Linear with low gradient	Stable *stability* **Continuity** Resistance to change Linear with negligible gradient

[a]Liu and others (n 2) 226–32.
[b]Or taken together as sociotechnical change Lyria Bennett Moses, 'Regulating in the Face of Sociotechnical Change' in Roger Brownsword, Eloise Scotford and Karen Yeung (eds), *The Oxford Handbook of Law, Regulation and Technology* (Oxford University Press, 2016).
[c]Brownsword, 'Law Disrupted, Law Re-Imagined, Law Re-Invented' (n 2).
[d]Frank Easterbrook, 'Cyberspace and the Law of the Horse' (1996) *University of Chicago Legal Forum* 207.

quadrants are attempts to absorb or accommodate technologically driven changes within the parameters and frameworks of the contemporary legal system. These may be insufficient or incomplete, thereby building up a pressure or predisposition towards a future disruptive moment. Insofar as these legal expectations fail to functionally describe technologically driven changes, they increase the instability of the system which then heightens the probability for subsequent change.

Second, this Matrix at best captures a snapshot of time and progression. This can be seen in juxtaposition to David Collingridge's approach to the social control of technology:

> The root of the manifest difficulties with which the control of technology are beset is that our technical competence vastly exceeds our understanding of the social effects which follow from its exercise. For this reason, the social consequences of a technology cannot be predicted early in the life of a technology.[26]

While Collingridge sets this out as a dilemma, we can more usefully think about this as a timeline trajectory of how a technology produces problems during its integration with society. Thus, rather than first posing an information problem arising from the impossibility of predicting the social consequences of deploying a technology into society, and then switching to present a power problem due to the difficulties of implementing necessary

(essentially where the regulatory activity takes place in realms other than the law, thereby lessening reliance upon the law for regulatory purposes). Liu and others (n 2) 240–42.

[26]This is the 'information problem' of the Collingridge dilemma (the other limb of the dilemma, the 'power problem', posits that once the undesirable consequences of the technology are discovered or become apparent, the use of that technology has become woven into the political, economic, and social fabric that makes change extremely difficult). Collingridge (n 19) 11.

changes, this timeline emphasises the shifting problem portfolio arising from the relational dynamics between technologically driven change and legal expectation.

In other words, for the purposes of legal disruption, what Collingridge sets up as the information problem is really a mismatch between technologically driven change and legal expectation because new affordances are opened up, recognised, and exploited by that technology in ways that differ from the baseline of legal expectations. *What can be understood as uncertainty, opacity, unpredictability, or unforeseeability can be reframed as the obsolesce of expectation.*

Contextualising legal disruption within the life cycle of a technology enables movement between the different quadrants of the Legal Disruption Change-Stability Matrix. As a technology matures and becomes woven into the fabric of society, its impact becomes increasingly foreseeable and expectations calibrate with manifest realities. This shift along the spectrum from the information problem end of the spectrum towards the power problem end thus corresponds with a move from the changing quadrants to the stable quadrants. Indeed, if we buy into Collingridge's dilemma, we might expect that a new technology progresses from turbulent disruption upon its introduction and initial exploitation, towards incremental development and continuity as the attendant problems become apparent and better understood, and as responsive regulation is deployed.

Yet, this progression overlooks transitional disruption arising from changing *stability*, which looks like phase transitions or paradigm shifts,[27] whereby periods of stability are punctuated by significant and sudden changes. The novelty of new technologies, new combinatorial configurations of existing technologies,[28] and even new forms of social organisation that arise around these new possibilities opened up by new technologies,[29] eventually become mundane as their capabilities become woven into the fabric of society and their exploitation becomes more settled. Indeed, the novelty must be absorbed and neutralised in part through regulation for effective exploitation.

Until this point, however, I have just been reiterating in broad brush strokes what is already well-known. So what might the Legal Disruption Change-Stability Matrix add to our understanding of legal disruption? And how might it help us to identify, articulate, and frame problems that elude other approaches?

[27]Thomas S Kuhn, *The Structure of Scientific Revolutions* (University of Chicago Press, 1970).

[28]Erik Brynjolfsson and Andrew McAfee, *The Second Machine Age: Work, Progress, and Prosperity in a Time of Brilliant Technologies* (W W Norton & Company, 2014).

[29]See for example in relation to energy capture, Ian Morris, *Foragers, Farmers, and Fossil Fuels: How Human Values Evolve* (Princeton University Press, 2015). Indeed, significant shifts in the constellation of values underpinning a society may be considered as evidence for such stabilisation.

Here we move to the third and fourth lines in the quadrants. Turbulent disruption is characterised by complexity, and is therefore interactional generating chaotic emergent outcomes. Transitional disruption describes step-changes: paradigm shifts and phase transitions whereby sudden shocks lead to a different form of order. Incremental development concerns smoother, undulating forms of change; continuity involves resistance to change. Both the latter involve low to negligible rates of change implied by being characterised by stability. But all engage in different relationships with the concept of legal disruption.

6. Salience and invisibility: turbulent disruption vs. transitional disruption

The relationship between turbulent disruption and transitional disruption requires unpacking, which may usefully be done through the idea of technological transparency, that technology becomes invisible with familiarity while simultaneously mediating our experiences and creating our worlds.[30] The difference between turbulent disruption and transitional disruption can be simplified as that between salience and invisibility.

Turbulent disruption is jarring: it defamiliarises us by confronting us with realities that radically depart from our expectations. In doing so, it renders salient hitherto invisible presumptions, principles, and processes and allows us to hold them up for analysis and scrutiny. Examples include whether AI applications could or should be capable of enjoying intellectual property protections for their creative output, or criminally liable for harmful behaviour. Contemporary legal doctrinal analysis would indicate that only natural persons are in a position to enjoy legal rights and incur legal liabilities. Yet, the liminality of AI applications between agent and object at least raises the question as to whether such legal positions are justified, and encourage analogies and distinctions to be made with regards to legal persons and whether the doctrinal positions should be re-evaluated or altered.

The result is that turbulent disruption provides us with an alternative vantage point that allows us to see the partiality, indeed the arbitrariness, of legal doctrinal positions. What we choose to do in response to seeing lacunae and limitations in the law constitutes the vast majority of legal research with regards to new and emerging technologies, and with the idea of legal disruption to date. In short, turbulent disruption enables us to see more clearly, and facilitates deeper insight into arbitrariness of the law.

[30]Yoni Van Den Eede, 'In Between Us: On the Transparency and Opacity of Technological Mediation' (2011) 16 *Foundations of Science* 139; Susser (n 5).

The more pernicious form of invisible legal disruption has largely eluded academic attention, and can be situated largely within the idea of transitional legal disruption in the Legal Disruption Change-Stability Matrix. Where turbulent legal disruption emphasises the distance and divergence between expectations and realities, transitional disruption blurs the two together with the result that things appear normal, or at least more smooth and continuous. Transitional disruption does this blinkering, maybe even blinding, by immersing us into a new world: laws, regulations, rights and obligations, and norms and values, adapt around us thereby helping us to quickly habituate to the changes. In a sense, this is trite because this is just a different way of saying that technology changes the world around us, or that there are revolutionary technologies that transform society, and that we get used to it. An example of transitional disruption is to understand:

> [I]nformation technology as a set of tools that increasingly mediates everyday experience. Digital platforms are more like eyeglasses than magnifying glasses – technologies one wears and forgets about rather than those one picks up and puts to use … They attend not to the eyeglasses themselves, but to what they can see *through* them. It is only when something goes wrong – when one *cannot* see through the glasses because they get dirty or break – that we notice the technology itself.[31]

Yet, rather than being transparent (or merely corrective) eyeglasses, information technology mediation is instead distorting, deceiving, and disorienting. Rather than provide a sharpened view of the world, we are instead presented with an individualised, dynamically adaptive picture that primarily serves the interests of the corporate platforms.[32] The transitionally disruptive aspect of information technology, driven by AI and big data, enhance the hiddenness objection to influence and set the scene for manipulation instead by rendering the legal disruption itself invisible.[33]

7. From influencing decision-making to designing regulation

But manipulation does not seem to be the end of the story here, even though the confluence of AI and XR does effectively hide the influence, and thus

---

[31] Susser, Roessler and Nissembaum (n 5) 33. Emphasis original.

[32] Julie E Cohen, *Between Truth and Power: The Legal Constructions of Informational Capitalism* (Oxford University Press, 2019). The broader point here is that the mediation is executed for ulterior motives, not necessarily corporate or profit-driven. Indeed, the regulatory pressures made possible here would be such a motive, but one which is certainly not captured by the corporate angle; Shoshana Zuboff, *The Age of Surveillance Capitalism: The Fight for a Human Future at the New Frontier of Power* (Profile Books, 2019).

[33] Indeed, manipulation can be defined as: 'imposing a hidden or covert influence on another person's decision-making'. Susser, Roessler and Nissembaum (n 5) 26.

distinguish it from persuasion and coercion.[34] I argue that this is because the manipulator takes on the mantle of the regulator,[35] or that the regulator gains the effective methods of the manipulator. This is because the outcome is effective and stable behavioural influences that are neither captured by the concepts of manipulation nor regulation, and thus the impact of the confluence of AI and XR is not recognised.[36]

The point here is that forms of influence, be it persuasion and coercion or manipulation, are understood to affect *singular instances of decision-making*; regulation as I see it, however, structures more *stable forms of behaviour* of the regulatee. With regard to decision-making, Daniel Susser and colleagues suggest:

> [T]here are two ways of influencing another person's decision-making: change the options available to the other person (their decision space) or change how they understand their options (their internal decision-making process).[37]

What this focus on decision-making overlooks, however, are internalised forms of influence which fly under the analytical radar because these *appear to originate* from within the agency and autonomy of an 'autonomous agent' even if their true source was external to that agent. An analogy can be drawn from how a virus hijacks the replication machinery and metabolism of a host cell to produce new copies of the virus, at a cost to that host cell. Under this analogy, the extracellular, viral, origin of the behaviour of the host cell is clear, but the replication behaviour of the host cell appears to be internally driven. Yet, when it comes to external influence and human decision-making and human behaviour, however, the origins are complex and opaque.[38] The narrow focus on decision-making alone overlooks internalised influences that shape an individual's identity and outlook which in turn is manifested in that individual's behaviour.

Indeed, Roger Brownsword has proposed precisely this prospect:

> Finally, in a third-generation regulatory environment, regulators would go beyond traditional normative signals and design of products and places by incorporating the regulatory design within regulatees themselves (for example, by controlling their genetic coding). Where design is embedded in regulatees in such a way that it channels their behaviour, it is likely to be much less apparent to regulatees that they are being regulated – if the

[34] For the distinction between persuasion, coercion, and manipulation, hinging upon hiddenness, see Ibid, 13–17.

[35] Not in the legal institutional sense of regulator, but rather one who has significant control over the behaviour of the regulatee.

[36] On the need for legal recognition to transform mere harm and damage into injury, see Scott Veitch, *Law and Irresponsibility: On the Legitimation of Human Suffering* (Routledge-Cavendish, 2007).

[37] Susser, Roessler and Nissembaum (n 5) 14.

[38] See respectively, Daniel Kahneman, *Thinking, Fast and Slow* (Penguin, 2012); Robert M Sapolsky, *Behave: The Biology of Humans at Our Best and Worst* (The Bodley Head, 2017).

> design is reliable, regulatees will simply behave (like products) in accordance with their specification.[39]

Thus, rather than engage in first generation normative signalling (equivalent to decision-making and manipulation), or second generation design of products and places (approximating coercion), the third generation of regulation effectively designs the regulatees themselves. From this perspective, there are two different aspects that distinguish first and second generation regulatory environments from the third: that the former are both external contextual influences and involve one-off situations. Whether regulation is done through normative signalling or through environmental design, regulatee behaviour is influenced by an external regulator in a specific context. Absent such signalling or design by the regulator, the regulatee might well behave in a different way which suggests that the regulation has somehow bent the path of regulatee behaviour. Yet, in the third generation where the regulation has been embedded within the regulatee, there is no such friction or conflict between the contextual demands of the signal or design, and as such, the regulatee would behave in a similar manner even if those external contexts were removed. This effectively takes us beyond the realm of manipulation and into regulatee design and engineering, a transformation that erases agency and autonomy in the process.

This, I argue, is the transitional legal disruption triggered by AI and XR. It is one that is difficult to identify and articulate because we have simply been dumped into a new world (or transitioned to the third generation in Brownswordian parlance) but still rely upon the conceptual framework that structured our understanding of the old world (or helped us to understand Brownsword's first and second generations of regulatory environments). We still think that there is such a thing as regulation: that there is a regulator and regulatee, and that the former influences the latter by delineating the decision space and by shaping the decision-making processes. But as we have seen, third generation incorporation is an altogether different prospect, and yet this seems to have occurred through a transitional rather than a turbulent form of legal disruption.

But how does AI and XR take us out of the old paradigm and into the new?[40] I suggest that this arises from the differential nature of the affordances provided by AI and XR. These technologies: centralise power for the regulators; remove the normative basis of the regulation; alter the logic of regulating; and entrench this paradigm in the process. The regulatees suffer from a divide-and-conquer strategy insofar as their experiences, indeed their worlds, become tailored and therefore individuated such that grievances

[39] Brownsword, 'In the Year 2061' (n 7) 30–31.

[40] I would like to thank Victoria Sobocki for numerous discussions on these topics.

do not gain the momentum necessary to foment the social movements that have historically driven progressive change and revolution. The loss of the normative basis of regulation, as well as its contemporary purposes, untether the rationale and restraint upon regulation from the principles of the rule of law, thereby transforming regulation into mere control. Finally, insofar as the regulation is incorporated into the regulatee and becomes a part of their identity or shapes their outlook, subsequent change becomes very difficult because the behaviour according to the interwoven regulation objective appears and subjectively feels like an exercise of the regulatee's autonomy and agency.

8. Differential affordances between regulator and regulatee: into Roger Brownsword's third generation of regulatory environments

In the original Legal Disruption article, we argued that legal disruption arises from new affordances opened up or unlocked by new technologies, and whether and how these affordances are recognised and exploited.[41] While this approach helped to account for the different ways in which new technological developments could trigger legal disruption in general, it has proven to be an overly simplistic account since affordances are far from being neutral and evenly distributed. Situating affordances within the discussions on different ways of 'doing regulation' opened up by new technologies suggests that new technologies afford the regulator ever greater regulatory capability and power.[42]

Lawrence Lessig had highlighted the possibility through his 'pathetic dot' theory of regulation:[43]

> This general point is about the limits on law as a regulator and about the techniques for escaping those limits. This escape, both in real space and in cyberspace, comes from recognizing the collection of tools that a society has at hand for affecting constraints upon behavior. Law in its traditional sense – an order backed by a threat directed at primary behavior – is just one of these tools. The general point is that law can affect these other tools – that they constrain behaviour themselves, and can function as tools of the law. The choice among tools obviously depends upon their efficacy. But importantly, the choice will also raise a question about values.[44]

41 Liu and others (n 2) 224–32.

42 We had hinted at this in the original Legal Disruption article: 'In the Legal Displacement response category, the problem encapsulated in the disruptive moment is not that new technological innovations create affordances that challenge the substance of existing law (as under Legal Development), but rather that they create new affordances *for* the regulators producing and enforcing the law'. Ibid, 242. Emphasis original.

43 Lawrence Lessig, 'The New Chicago School' (1998) 27 *The Journal of Legal Studies* 661.

44 Lessig, 'Law of the Horse' (n 6) 502.

We will return to the observation concerning values, since one of the differentiating factors between turbulent and transitional legal disruption is that the latter moulds the value structure around the change, thereby minimising its impact.

That Lessig made these observations in response to Frank Easterbrook[45] in relation to the burgeoning field of cyberlaw suggests that it is not only AI and XR that grounds re-examination into law and regulation, by which we mean constraints on behaviour. Indeed, non-legal and non-normative means of constraining behaviour involve: regulatory modalities of architecture/code;[46] technological management;[47] hypernudging;[48] and behavioural manipulation;[49] amongst others.[50]

So what does AI and XR add to this discussion, and how does it change the nature of regulation to make it tantamount to control? Lessig had observed that the different regulatory modalities could be thought of as tools to affect behaviour, but thinking about it in terms of affordances and signifiers,[51] reveals the shortcoming of the tool analogy. A tool can be thought of as an object that can extend an agent's ability to modify features of its environment, so Lessig is not wrong to think of other regulatory modalities as tools for constraining behaviour, and indeed it may be the correct way to think about Brownsword's first generation of regulatory environment involving normative signalling.

Yet, when design begins to dominate the regulatory environment in the shift to Brownsword's second generation, appeal to affordances and signifiers comes to the fore. Design dictates what is or is not possible, in the technological management sense where undesirable behaviour is collapsed into impossible behaviour.[52] But the difference between affordances and signifiers can be gleaned in the context of technological management because the possibility of desire, contrary to the aims of the regulator, remains: it is just that the execution of that desire – the behaviour expressing that desire – becomes impossible. One way of putting this is that even in the second

[45]Frank Easterbrook, 'Cyberspace and the Law of the Horse' (1996) *University of Chicago Legal Forum* 207.

[46]Lawrence Lessig, *Code: And Other Laws of Cyberspace, Version 2.0* (Basic Books, 2nd Revised edn 2006); Lessig, 'Law of the Horse' (n 6); Lessig, 'The New Chicago School' (n 43).

[47]Roger Brownsword, 'Lost in Translation: Legality, Regulatory Margins, and Technological Management' (2011) 26 *Berkeley Technology Law Journal* 1321; Brownsword, 'In the Year 2061' (n 7); Roger Brownsword, 'Technological Management and the Rule of Law' (2016) 8 *Law, Innovation and Technology* 100.

[48]Karen Yeung, '"Hypernudge": Big Data as a Mode of Regulation by Design' (2017) 20 *Information, Communication & Society* 118.

[49]Susser (n 5); Susser, Roessler and Nissembaum (n 5); Susser, Roessler and Nissenbaum (n 5).

[50]See also for example, Edward Bernays, *Propaganda* (Ig Publishing, 2004); Kathleen Taylor, *Brainwashing: The Science of Thought Control* (Oxford University Press, 2006).

[51]'Affordances determine what actions are possible. Signifiers communicate where the action should take place'. Donald A Norman, *The Design of Everyday Things* (MIT Press, 2013) 13.

[52]'With technological management, the regulatory signals are radically disrupted; there is no option other than "compliance" ... Prescription and prohibition were replaced with impossibility; and both prudential and moral signals were overtaken by a signal that said to regulatees, "you cannot do this; you really cannot do this"'. Brownsword, 'In the Year 2061' (n 7) 6. Emphasis original.

generation of designed regulatory environments, regulation is symptomatic in that it constraints regulatee behaviour but leaves the motivational core of the regulatee intact. The regulatee may wish to act differently, but does not have the means at her disposal to do so in the context of that specific regulatory environment.

What does this have to do with affordances and signifiers? Geo-fencing golf courses and technologically immobilising golf carts may constitute highly effective technological fixes,[53] but the signifiers remain obvious, and the affordances are tantalising. The signal to the regulatees remain because, but for the technological fix, the regulatee would still joy-ride the golf carts. So, if in this example, the would-be joy-riders were able to hack the geo-fence or disable the immobilisation device, the technological fix would be thwarted and the original problem would re-emerge. The golf cart still affords joy-riding, and the signifiers as to how to manoeuver that cart still remain.

In Brownsword's third generation, it is not the regulatory environment that is designed and engineered, but the regulatee herself. Again, this goes beyond persuasion and coercion, and manipulation, because it is not a one-off decision that is being influenced because these concepts concern interventions in an individual's decision-making processes. This goes to the motivational core of the regulatee, affecting her very identity and outlook, and therefore alters the affordances and signifiers present in her world. In the golf cart example, incorporating the regulation into the regulatee would negate the need for first generation normative signalling or second generation regulatory environment design because the regulatee's desire to joy-ride a golf cart (affordance removal), or the perception that golf-carts can be the joy-ridden (signifier removal), may be eliminated.

9. Signifier awareness and recognition is crucial for the regulatee

In summary, new technologies expand the range of affordances for the regulator by broadening the toolbox of regulatory modalities at her disposal. More critically, however, is the regulatee's control over the signifiers in a designed environment or product because as Don Norman observed,

> an affordance exists whether or not anyone ever notices it. To the designer, *if affordances are not known, then they might as well not exist*. In other words, the designer is primarily concerned with *perceived* affordances; the perception is critical.[54]

[53]Ibid, 5–6.

[54]Donald A Norman, *Living with Complexity* (MIT Press, 2016) 228. First emphasis added, latter emphasis original.

In this context, Don Norman emphasises relationship between the designer and the affordances and signifiers that are present or absent in their design as a means of raising designer awareness of the impact and usability of their designs.

For our purposes of regulation and manipulation, however, I argue instead that the presence and awareness of signifiers for *users and for third parties* is paramount. Regulatee behaviour can be influenced far upstream from the ordinary locus where decision-making is analysed. By interfering with the design of signifiers, regulators and manipulators can simply render invisible the opportunities for behaviour that are afforded by a designed product or place, or conversely hide the forces that constrain the range of regulatee behaviour. A regulatee will simply not know that there are affordances present in the environment if these are not made explicit in a designed world.

This differs from classic choice architecture in behavioural economics because the focus there is primarily on nudging decisions: decisions are made between explicitly presented options where the decision is influenced by being foregrounded or marginalised. Here, it is the hiddenness of possibility that guides decision-making. Yet, all this might not seem to differ from changing the decision space of a regulatee.[55] Introducing the nuance of affordances and signifiers into our understanding of the decision space in which a regulatee operates reveals that there are different ways in which this space is sculpted or shaped. The absolute limits of the decision space would presumably involve what that space is ultimately able to support or afford, but the signifiers emphasise that only a subset of the full range of possibilities can be perceived, recognised, and acted upon. Thus, influencing behaviour through changes in the decision space then can involve actual changes to the affordance, but critically, it can also be manipulated more subtly and thoroughly through changes in the signifiers. A regulatee cannot behave in ways that the environment does not support (affordances), but equally cannot behave in ways that the regulatee does not realise are possible (signifier).

The distinction between affordances and signifiers holds significant ramifications for regulating behaviour in the context of AI and XR, because the ability to configure signifiers provides opportunities to 'overlay' additional forms of architectural regulation or technological management 'on top' of the full range of possibilities that are afforded by the product or place. Signifiers can provide information to certain individuals or groups enabling them to act differently within a certain common context, in which in theory at least all individuals have the same capability. Examples of this include coded or hidden messages that remain in plain

---

[55] Susser, Roessler and Nissembaum (n 5) 14.

sight.[56] As such, regulation through affordances remains uniform and undistinguished, but the use of signifiers by regulators can facilitate or exacerbate discrimination because different behaviours can be elicited from different people. Perhaps the best example of this is the Easter Egg hunt portrayed in Ernest Cline's *Ready Player One*, in which players in a shared virtual world put together clues and behave in ways as to reveal the Eggs.[57] While the Eggs afford discovery by anybody inhabiting that virtual world, it is the signifiers that serve to distinguish those who are able to unlock their location and safeguards.

To contextualise this in Roger Brownsword's golf cart example, the full range of driving behaviours that are afforded by the base technology of a golf cart comprise of the full decision space open to the regulatee (there are limitations as to what one can physically do with a golf cart). The geo-fencing and immobilisation technologies that Brownsword gives us as examples of technological management can be thought of as the regulator altering the affordances of the golf cart, thereby artificially circumscribing the range of activity afforded by the golf cart. Altering the signifiers is also another way of artificially circumscribing the range of affordances presented by the golf cart, for example by hiding or coding a disabling switch for the geo-fence and immobilisation device, by deviating from standard control interfaces, or by providing instructions in different languages.

This shows how regulatory affordances can be nested within each other, and where the regulator can intervene in terms of technological management. The technological specifications of the base golf cart set the broadest range of affordances (for example acceleration rate, top speed, engine power, and wheel clearance). The geo-fencing and engine immobilisation technology can be added on top of the basic golf cart for more control. Finally, variations can be overlaid on top through signifiers that allow for those in 'the know' to use the golf cart in ways that are not accessible to those who are not able so to perceive (for example to remove certain restrictions or enable a turbo mode). The ability for XR mediation serving up individually tailored perceptions readily reveals how such technologies can enable fine-grained and dynamically adaptive forms of imperceptible control.

Finally, the psychological dimension of signifiers needs to be emphasised. While both affordances and signifiers are designed into products and places, affordances are held in common to all who interact with or use them while signifiers lend an additional psychological dimension or cognitive

[56]Laurence Cawley, 'Your Pavement Squiggle Markings Decoded' *BBC News* (4 April 2014), www.bbc.com/news/magazine-26745534 (accessed 18 January 2022); See for example, Chris Baraniuk, 'The Secret Codes You're Not Meant to Know' *BBC Future* (17 December 2015), www.bbc.com/future/article/20151217-the-secret-codes-youre-not-meant-to-know (accessed 18 January 2022).

[57]Ernest Cline, *Ready Player One* (Broadway Paperbacks, 2011).

component. Thus, signifiers can be used to tailor and target regulation as a more nuanced means of technological management.

The upshot is that with affordances and signifiers becoming a part of the regulator's toolbox, especially through AI and XR, there is the prospect for unidirectional behavioural interventions to be imposed absent the need for a shared normative framework. Attention needs to be drawn to the one-way nature of these forms of technological management and the fact that they are informed by an instrumentalist mindset. Taken together, these entrench the new paradigm of regulation by removing the prospect for challenges to the new regulatory regime either through recourse to a shared ethical or normative framework or through feedback and oppositional mechanisms that are available in normative regulatory regimes.

10. Regulatee design and engineering through AI and XR

Bringing AI and XR back into this conversation illustrates in practice how this might work. While the pivot from concerns over AI making decisions about us, to influencing our decision-making processes is still relatively fresh,[58] there are well-known examples where big data and algorithmic processing have been combined to influence both individual and collective decision-making.[59] These generally exploit cognitive and emotive vulnerabilities as leverage points for influencing decision-making and thereby behaviour.[60] In essence, AI and big data provide insight an individual's psychological constitution with increasing accuracy and timeliness, thereby pinpointing leverage points to maximise the impact of influence, whether it is manipulation or regulation. As such, the basic problem involves interference with decision-making processes, and AI and big data provide the means to do this. Yet, introducing new affordances might feed-back and alter the basic problem itself, not least by providing granularity and context to a hitherto abstract debate.

How XR plays into this has received less attention, but its prospect for shaping and structuring human behaviour (rather than the mere influence made possible by AI and big data) occupies a different realm. A useful point of departure is John Danaher's distinction between: 'The technological vision of VR holds that a *virtual reality* is a *computer-simulated reality.* A virtual reality *life* is, consequently, one that is lived inside such a simulation'; and 'The anthropocentric vision of VR … as something that is made possible by the human mind, sometimes assisted by culture and technology, and with much deeper roots in the human condition' in the context of Virtual Reality

[58]Susser (n 5).
[59]Susser, Roessler and Nissembaum (n 5) 4–12.
[60]Richard H Thaler and Cass R Sunstein, *Nudge: Improving Decisions about Health, Wealth, and Happiness* (Yale University Press, 2008); Kahneman (n 38).

(VR).[61] Thus, while VR connotes a simulated reality in our technologically driven age which we actively inhabit only by immersion through a physical interface, VR can also be understood as a product of our imagination and thus a function of our minds.[62]

Rather than distinguish between the technological vision and the anthropocentric visions of VR, I argue that we should treat these as *nested* realities, not unlike a 'Matryoshka Doll'. By this I mean that the anthropocentric vision of VR is both the prerequisite for, and the vantage point from which we engage in, the technological vision of VR. Simply put, we need a mind, a consciousness, as the baseline foundation from which to experience technologically simulated forms of virtual reality.

Yet, the two visions of VR become enmeshed because of this 'nestedness', which I argue facilitates the flows of experience between the two. Effectively, this breaks down barriers of the self by establishing a smooth conduit to the world. The accessibility to the mind is facilitated by this 'nestedness' of realities that is highlighted by the distinction of VR as technological and anthropocentric.

While all this is pretty straight-forward it is a necessary bridge to connect the regulatory effects of XR and the characteristics of the regulatee. The keystone of this argument comes from Anil Seth's recent work which posits the brain as a prediction machine, and the processes of perception as a 'best-guess' as to what is taking place in the environment.[63] Inverting the intuitive understanding of perception as bottom-up feature detection,[64] Seth advances the notion of perception instead as being *controlled hallucination*:[65]

> [T]he brain is constantly making predictions about the causes of its sensory signals … These signals serve as *prediction errors* registering the difference between what the brain expects and what it gets at every level of processing. By adjusting top-down predictions so as to suppress bottom-up prediction errors, the brain's perceptual guesses maintain their grip on their causes in the world. In this view, perception happens through a continual process of *prediction error minimisation* … We never experience sensory signals themselves, we only ever experience interpretations of them.[66]

[61] John Danaher, 'Virtual Reality and the Meaning of Life' in Iddo Landau (ed), *The Oxford Handbook of Meaning in Life* (Oxford University Press, 2022). Emphasis original.

[62] As John Danaher puts it: 'André Nusselder (2014), for example, points out that ever since we have had the power of symbolic thought we have had to power to live in two worlds: the virtual world created by our minds and the physical reality in which we are embodied.' Ibid, referring to André Nusselder, 'Being More Than Yourself' in Mark Grimshaw (ed), *The Oxford Handbook of Virtuality* (Oxford University Press, 2014).

[63] Seth illustrates this idea with several convincing examples, Anil Seth, 'Your Brain Hallucinates Your Conscious Reality' (TED2017, April 2017), www.ted.com/talks/anil_seth_your_brain_hallucinates_your_conscious_reality (accessed 16 January 2022).

[64] Anil Seth, *Being You: A New Science of Consciousness* (Faber and Faber, 2021) 76–81.

[65] Ibid, 82–95. Emphasis original.

[66] Ibid, 82–83. Emphasis original.

This dynamic feedback between what the predictions that the brain projects in advance and what sensory input subsequently hones illustrates how incredibly vulnerable we are to our sensations. These sensations literally shape what we perceive, and in shaping our perceptions, cues us to particular understandings of the world by shaping our expectations and outlook. Seth sums it up:

> The immersive multisensory panorama of your perceptual scene ... is a reaching out from your brain to the world, a writing as much as a reading. The entirety of perceptual experience is a neuronal fantasy that remains yoked to the world through a continuous making and remaking of perceptual best guesses, of controlled hallucinations.[67]

The reason that I dwell at length on the idea of perception as a feedback loop between the brain's predictions and subsequent sensory corrections is that this approach blurs any distinction between subjective experience and objective realities.[68] Add to this the fact that sensation occurs before perception, and therefore prior to cognitive and deliberative processes that undergird analysis and critical thinking, and we can see that these sensory influences can pervade the self without engaging in any rational processes. Taken together, these reveal that we are more vulnerable to XR influences than we could otherwise have recognised.

Put differently, if perception was merely bottom-up feature detection then the implication is that the perceiver can be an independent entity who merely receives incoming sensory information from an outside world. Perception in this model implies that there is a barrier that separates the perceiver from what is being perceived, essentially reducing perception to observation. The difference between the observer and the perceiver is not so much that the observer is immune from external influences through what is being observed. Rather, the observer is able to bring their full self to bear on what is being observed, which implies that cognitive and analytical capabilities remain intact and can be used to critically evaluate the observations.

The prediction error minimisation model of perception, however, *adapts* the perceiver to the incoming sensory input, thereby moulding the perceiver through the very process of perception itself. Thus, this understanding of perception weaves sensory input into the fabric of the perceiver by calibrating projected expectations to experienced sensations. In the process of modulating the perceiver's expectations, the experience of *being* itself undergoes change:

> The self is not an immutable entity that lurks behind the windows of the eyes, looking out into the world and controlling the body as a pilot controls a plane.

---

[67]Ibid, 87.

[68]Indeed, it is the common agreement of our hallucinations that we call reality, see Ibid.

> The experience of *being me*, or of *being you*, is a perception itself – or better, a collection of perceptions – a tightly woven bundle of neutrally encoded predictions geared to keeping your body alive.[69]

If this is correct, then virtual reality should not be understood only as a means of generating worlds that we can observe, whether by machine or by mind, but rather as a way of subtly sculpting the identity and outlook of those who participate in those realities. Thus, VR opens the door for regulatee design.

Yet, all of this is complicated by the 'subjective stability of the self'[70] which 'fosters the false intuition that the self is an immutable entity, rather than a bundle of perceptions'.[71] In face of our perceptions changing who we are, we do not experience that change. This makes my argument difficult to comprehend, but even more difficult to relate to because this is not how we feel about our perceptions nor of our sense of self.

Objections might be raised that if perception has always involved the melding of the perceiver with the perceived, then the environment has always not only influenced regulatee behaviour, but also shaped regulatee identity and outlook. What is different with VR, and XR as we shall see below, is that: the barriers against altering that environment are lowered; support dynamically adaptive and individually tailored experiences; and enable fine-grained and direct control. This transforms the adaptive nature of perception into a susceptibility for regulatee design and engineering.

Under the technological vision of VR, an individual inhabiting the virtual world may be acutely aware of the simulated nature of that reality and likely took active and intentional steps to engage in that reality. With XR, and in particular Augmented Reality (AR) or Mixed, Merged, or Mediated, Reality (MR), the distinction between the physical analogue world and the digitally generated overlay mediating the perception of that world complicates matters significantly. Recalling the notion of technological transparency introduced above, we see the world through technological artefacts which become invisible to us despite such technological mediation potentially distorting, deceiving, and disorientating us through perceptual manipulation.

Under a bottom-up feature detection model of perception, such effects merely affect the observation of the world and may influence specific behaviours. Yet, under the prediction error minimisation model of perception, the identity and outlook of the perceiver is being altered by the dynamic feedback processes that calibrate perception with prediction.

The upshot is that XR is not merely a means of architectural regulation or technological management in the sense of asserting regulatory pressure

---

[69] Ibid, 154.
[70] Ibid, 168.
[71] Ibid, 169.

through environmental design. Rather, it can be understood as a means of sculpting the regulatee's internal identity through perceptual manipulation, design, and engineering because these influence the brain's prediction engine that generates both the subjectively experienced world and the regulatee's sense of self.

The difference between architectural regulation or technological management on the one hand, and regulation through the design and engineering of the regulatee on the other, is that the former is brittle because it is reliant upon the parameters of the environment remaining in place while the latter is robust to environmental changes or transfers between different environments. By weaving the regulation into the psychological constitution of the regulatee, the regulation not only accompanies the regulatee even in the absence of normative signals or technological management, but also informs regulatee behaviour in other spheres as well.

11. The regulatee as a rule-following robot?

To circle back to the beginning of this paper, I had suggested that legal disruption inheres within both the difference and the divergence between expectation and experienced reality. Just how far have we come from the familiar notions of normative legal principles and processes?

In a conference paper discussing the prospect for 'mechanical jurisprudence', Ian Kerr and Carissima Mathen delve into the distinction between 'rule-following' and 'behaviour according to the rules' originally proposed by Ludwig Wittgenstein.[72] In their view, rule-following is neither an internal process nor can be confirmed by reaching the correct outcome.[73] In addition, they argue that the nature of the rules must be normative, and that following a rule involves a 'social practice that surrounds its articulation, application and the responses that are made to it. To follow rules is to adopt a particular *form of life*'.[74]

Although both the context and the argument that Kerr and Mathen are making are different, there are lessons here for the transitional legal disruption that is taking place in the design and engineering of the regulatee through AI and XR. First, it is clear that the requirement that there be a normative basis for the rules falls away, along with the social practice surrounding rule-following,[75] because these forms of technologically driven regulation are non-normative. Thus, the legally disruptive transformation taking place

[72]Ian Kerr and Carissima Mathen, 'Chief Justice John Roberts Is a Robot' (2014) 23, https://robots.law.miami.edu/2014/wp-content/uploads/2013/06/Chief-Justice-John-Roberts-is-a-Robot-March-13-.pdf.

[73]'Likewise an AI might predict with perfect frequency the correct outcome in a mathematical series or respond correctly every time when generating legal outcomes – and yet the machine may only be *acting in accordance* with the rule rather than *following it*', Ibid. Emphasis original.

[74]Ibid, 25. Emphasis original.

[75]For the normative claim, see Ibid, 24–25.

here seems to be the substitution of rules with mere instructions. This is important because rule-following requires a social context, a normative underpinning, and a moral agent. Furthermore, because of the ambiguity of rules and the leeway of rule-following, there remains a large range of acceptably compliant behaviour. With non-normative architectural regulation or technological management, however, there is considerably less uncertainty about what behaviour is desired or permissible simply because these are the behaviours that are supported by the design of products and places.

The second lesson resides in the difference between behaviour according to the rules and rule-following. Behaviour according to rules implies a sort of external disciplining of a regulatee's behaviour: the idea is that there are external rules, and one's behaviour must simply align to their requirements. Rule-following on the other hand requires some sort of internalisation of the requirements imposed by the rule: 'Following a rule is analogous to obeying an order. One is trained to do so, and one reacts in a particular way'.[76] In this sense, rule-following can be thought of as weaving in normative demands into the fabric of the regulatee.

But Wittgenstein continued by asking: 'But what if one person reacts to the order and training *thus*, and another *otherwise*? Who is right, then?'[77] It is here that we can clearly see the difference between rule-following and regulatee design and engineering. Within normative rule-based regulatory orders, regulatees may have incorporated and internalised the rules, be appropriately socialised and 'live' those rules, but their subsequent behaviour may still vary. Rather than asking who is right or wrong with regards to their rule-following behaviour in cases of divergent behaviour, I argue that it is the very possibility for rule-following variance that stands out and demands attention. Assuming that the rule-following is conducted faithfully and authentically, what rule-following reveals is the presence of an autonomous agent. Rule-following thus involves normative demands that are signalled and communicated to a socialised agent, who then behaves autonomously and authentically. Variance in rule-following behaviour can thus be considered as a litmus test for the presence of autonomy and agency within a regulatory system. In this sense, a regulatory system can be understood as one which sets the parameters for the cones of future possibility and plausibility and which provide more well-worn paths within the remaining range of freedom.

Conversely, with non-normative forms of architectural regulation and technological management, environmental design significantly curtails the range of possible behaviours, and conceptually at least, reduce these cones of future possibility to narrowly defined lines of possible behaviour. I argue

[76] Ludwig Wittgenstein, *Philosophical Investigations* (GEM Anscombe, PMS Hacker and Joachim Schulte trs, Blackwell, 2009) 88e.

[77] Ibid. Emphasis original.

here that with the regulatory design of products and places, regulatee autonomy and agency vanish because desirable/undesirable behaviours become collapsed into possible/impossible behaviours. Yet, even in these instances, only objective or external forms of agency and autonomy are removed because it is only the range of possible action that has been subjected to control. Subjective or internal forms of agency and autonomy can, under forms of architectural regulation and technological management, remain in the desire to decide or act differently even in the absence of supporting affordances or apparent signifiers.[78] To use the golf cart example again, regulatee desire to joy-ride can remain even where those carts have been technologically immobilised. In summary, regulation through environmental design restricts autonomy of behaviour but does not necessarily affect the internal desires of an agent.

This is why it is especially pernicious to regulate through the design and engineering of the regulatee herself, and why these forms of regulation are not appropriate analogies to regulation through architectural or technological means. The possibilities of influencing sensory inputs in a dynamically adaptive fashion can shape perceptions, and perceptions in turn shape the regulatee. Rather than curtailing the expression of an agent's autonomy, it is the restriction *within* what used to be the autonomy of the regulatee that prunes variance.

The upshot here is that forms of regulation involving the design and engineering of the regulatee cannot be considered as regulation, but instead have become transformed into control. The consequence, I argue, is that the regulatee has been transformed into object which is shaped by the controller. Referring back to Anil Seth's objection to drawing an analogy between the self and the body with the pilot and the plane,[79] it may now be that there is an autopilot in charge. Rather than being rule-following robots, we as former regulatees, may be reduced instead to automatons behaving in accordance with how we are controlled.

12. Concluding thoughts: diminishing affordances and an analogy with the Kessler Effect[80]

I have painted a rather grim picture of how new and emerging technologies might be used to shape our perceptions and experiences, through the examples of AI influencing our decision-making processes and with XR creating virtual worlds and mediating our interactions with the physical world. When these influences are strained through the prism of

[78] In reality, this will not be so clear cut because an agent would gradually become conditioned or acclimatised to the range of behaviours that their world supports. For example, we do not lament our limited agency because we cannot time-travel or fly unaided because these are things that our world does not afford us.

[79] Seth, 'Your Brain Hallucinates' (n 67) 154.

[80] I owe this idea to Hjalte Osborn Frandsen.

contemporary neuroscientific insights, we are able to see that in shaping our perceptions, it is the very identity of the self and our outlook that are being crafted through this influence and mediation.

If legal disruption does indeed inhere within the distance and divergence between expectations and experience, however, it becomes clear that any initial wave of turbulent disruption will eventually become transitional disruption (with the main difference between transitional disruption and incremental development or continuity being the preceding shift in paradigm).

Yet, there may be an additional layer of disruption taking place as a result of what AI and XR are specifically capable of. This is because of the ability to use AI in a way to shape expectations (insofar as decision-making and other cognitive processes can be influenced through its applications), and because of the possibility of shaping experiences through XR (because of its applications creating virtual worlds that we inhabit or mediate our interaction and experience of the physical world), the very means by which we gauge and access (legal) disruption can be recalibrated by the very technological means that drive that (legal) disruption in the first place. If this is correct, AI and XR technologies both drive significant changes in terms of affordances and signifiers of disruption itself because these technologies control both our prior expectations and subsequent experiences of the world. We might think of this as a form of meta-disruption affecting our very ability to assess and analyse disruptive influences and impacts.

But to draw this paper to a close, I would like to explore the idea of diminishing affordances that runs contrary to the narrative that new and emerging technologies offer ever expanding opportunities, and therefore continually undergird an expanding array of affordances.[81] The idea here is that incremental developments appear to provide ever greater progress in expanding our capabilities and control, but run the risk of triggering a tipping point which makes future technological progress and enjoyment more difficult.

This idea is easiest to illustrate by analogy with the Kessler Effect because it is tangible and intuitive.[82] The Kessler Effect raises the concern that future space activities will be more difficult or impossible because of an orbital debris belt or cloud that would surround the earth (diminished affordances). This debris field would be the result of human activity in space (incremental technological progress): intersecting satellite orbits result in a finite probability of satellite collisions and these collisions would in turn produce a

[81]While this narrative is most explicit with the Techno-Optimists, the purpose of developing technology intuitively appears to be to enable us to do more things.

[82]Donald J Kessler and Burton G Cour-Palais, 'Collision Frequency of Artificial Satellites: The Creation of a Debris Belt' (1978) 83 *Journal of Geophysical Research: Space Physics* 2637. For a discussion, see a 2009 discussion by Donald Kessler available at: https://web.archive.org/web/20100527195029; http://webpages.charter.net/dkessler/files/KesSym.html. For a dramatisation, there is an exciting sequence in the film, Gravity (2013). A different way of illustrating this would have been through runaway anthropogenic climate change, but this example suffers from a lack of ready visualisation.

number of fragments that have a probability of triggering further satellite collisions. The ensuing collisional cascade has the potential to render large swaths of Low Earth Orbit functionally unusable and to make the exploration of outer space more difficult if not impossible.[83] Furthermore 'Kessler showed mathematically that once a certain amount of mass, known as the critical mass, is put into a particular orbit, collisional cascading begins even if no more objects are launched into that orbit'.[84] Thus, while the risks build incrementally, there is a threshold after which the system tips into an altogether different equilibrium even where no further action is taken.

What does this have to do with AI, XR, regulation, or governance? Roger Brownsword has argued that there should be regulatory responsibility for maintaining the commons in the midst of re-imagining and re-defining the law in the aftermath of legal disruption: 'For regulators, the equivalent injunction [to the Hippocratic Oath] should be, first, to ensure that no harm is done to the generic conditions that underpin the lives and prospects of their regulatees'.[85] What I argue that the Kessler Effect analogy shows is both the unique importance of preserving the commons and that the loss of the commons conditions may come about more as emergent outcome rather than by design or negligence.

The imagery of the earth literally being encased within a cloud of our own junk that traps future generations on its surface may provide the necessary visual metaphor to the imperceptible effects of architectural regulation and technological management. We can see the advances in AI and XR as potentially caging our minds and locking in this state into the future. Roger Brownsword has emphasised that it is 'not that human *existence* is compromised but that human *agency* is compromised' in the transition from normative law to instrumental technological management,[86] but this is neither easy to see nor to grasp. Finally, the Kessler Effect analogy also reframes the by-products of our technological pursuits as waste and pollution, which, given the contemporary climate crisis, connects the challenges in law and technology to the other existential risks of our time. Technological advances do not come for free, and while they often provide short-term benefits, the externalities accrue and are left to future generations to resolve. Yet, because these technological advances may curtail our range of affordances in the long-run – our very ability to do what may be necessary – it may be that these externalities will prove to be too costly or too difficult to overcome. These are effects that have generally been marginalised in discussions about (legal) disruption – that their effects may have self-entrenching qualities that resist subsequent

[83] Olson (n 20).
[84] Ibid.
[85] Brownsword, 'Law Disrupted, Law Re-Imagined, Law Re-Invented' (n 2) 21.
[86] Ibid, 22. Emphasis original.

change. At minimum, to effectively preserve the commons, we must be able to identify the challenges and opportunities raised by new technologies, to analyse the full range of legal disruption that these may trigger, and to chart the pathways by which this might occur.

Yet, beyond maintaining the commons, the concerns that I have raised in this paper suggest that we should also ground a requirement to maintain cognitive (System 2) and emotive (System 1) autonomy and assert freedom from external interferences. While this is obviously impossible in the abstract, especially in light of Anil Seth's model of perception as prediction error minimisation whereby we are continually sculpted by our sensations of the world, the new affordances opened by AI and XR technologies present genuinely novel challenges that require recognition and response before the problems proliferate and become permanent features. Similar to germline genetic modifications where alterations are passed down the generations and justify prohibition where this involves human DNA, the spectre of regulatee design and engineering through AI and XR presents similar issues of manipulation resonating down the ages. Unlike germline genetic modification, however, the use of AI and XR involve more subtle interventions, pursue other goals, and therefore their impact is more difficult to discern and to capture as harm. The upshot is that, in addition to recognising the novelty and severity of the challenges posed by AI and XR to the autonomy of the regulatee, we need to also emphasise the transitionally disruptive nature of these technologies. As a result, these features should be underscored in debates about how these technologies can be deployed, and about how these affect individual autonomy, societal structures, and indeed the axiological foundations that may be undermined through their deployment.

Disclosure statement

No potential conflict of interest was reported by the author(s).

Online content platforms, copyright decision-making algorithms and fundamental rights protection in China

Tianxiang He

ABSTRACT
Concentration of power in terms of user traffic and copyright content is most evident in content platforms in China. Such concentration has generated an unexpected impact on the way we understand and appreciate creativity, on copyright enforcement and determination of liability on content platforms, and on the regulation of the cultural market by the government. Specifically, the concentration of power in content platforms has not only curbed direct online piracies to a large extent but has also accelerated the fragmentation of copyright enforcement and spawned the need for algorithmic recommendation and filtering systems, which in turn has reinforced the cultural censorship system of China. This paper argues that the employment of algorithms by platforms must be treated with prudence: the algorithmic decision-making systems employed by platforms must be transparent as much as possible, and remedies must be provided for concerned users. The algorithms employed by content platforms must be adjusted to reflect not just the interests of the platforms but also the public interest in accessing and delivering information and local policy considerations. This paper suggests that our regulatory framework should reflect the algorithmic turn of content platforms in its legal and non-legal instruments and alleviate their negative impact on society.

1. Introduction

One of the important functions of internet platforms in modern society is content distribution. Most of the contents being distributed on the platforms, such as graphics, messages, audios, and videos are not only vehicles that carry and disseminate information and knowledge but also potentially copyright works. When the trend of 'digitalisation of everything' became a real thing, the role of platforms as a critical public forum emerged as many public discussions surrounding the abovementioned contents are now moved online. There is a threat when the platforms are under supervision inequivalent to their power in controlling the intellectual activities that happen within.[1]

The concentration of power or high penetration rate is evident in the case of Chinese content platforms in recent years.[2] For example, in May 2021, it was recorded that integrated social platforms that disseminate various kinds of content, such as WeChat, have more than 1 billion monthly active users.[3] In comparison, the seventh place on the list, Zhihu, which is a knowledge-sharing platform similar to Quora, was only recorded to have around 30 million monthly active users in that month.[4] For video platforms, it was reported that in 2006, there were over 300 competing video-sharing websites in China.[5] In 2020, the market of video sharing in China is highly concentrated as the number of video platforms decreased dramatically due to fierce competition, and major platforms that attract the most traffic are all controlled by the so-called BAT (Baidu, Alibaba, Tencent) group.[6] For example, Tencent Video was recorded to have 397 million monthly active users in May 2021, whereas Xiaomi Video in the tenth place was only recorded to have around 12 million monthly active users in the same month.[7] This kind of concentration is also evident in music and literature platforms.[8]

Amongst all types of content platforms, the development of video platforms in China is most dramatic and can be characterised by the following changes. On the one hand, video platform services in China have now evolved from merely providing video streaming service into three distinct types of service: the first is the traditional type – on-demand video sharing

[1]The 'big platform' risk is also identified by the EU via its proposal of the The Digital Services Act (DSA). From the perspective of the EU, there are three major problems associated with uncontrolled big platforms, namely: fragmentation of the single market; risks to the safety of citizens and to their fundamental rights; and information asymmetries and ineffective oversight. See Aída Ponce Del Castillo, 'The Digital Services Act package: Reflections on the EU Commission's policy options' (2020) *ETUI Policy Brief, N°12/2020*, https://www.etui.org/sites/default/files/2020-09/The%20digital%20services%20act%20package.%20Reflections%20on%20the%20EU%20Commission%27s%20policy%20options-2-2020.pdf.

[2]According to Joshua Gans, the term 'content platform' means 'a standardized means of presenting information', and it apparently covers a wide range of platforms that provide information services such as Yelp and Google. See Joshua Gans, 'The Rise of Content Platforms', *Harvard Business Review*, Oct. 13, 2011, at https://hbr.org/2011/10/the-rise-of-content-platforms. This paper is focusing on content platforms that provide copyright works, such as YouTube.

[3]Data according to *iiMedia Polaris database*: http://bjx.iimedia.cn/app_rank.

[4]Ibid.

[5]Rui Zhang, 'Video Sharing Boom Grinding to a Halt', *China.org.cn* (July 6, 2007), http://www.china.org.cn/english/entertainment/216266.htm (accessed July 16, 2021).

[6]Zeping Ren, 'Internet Content Industry Report', *Evergrande Research Institute* (July 6, 2018)(任泽平，《互联网内容产业报告》，恒大研究院，2018年7月6日).

[7]Data according to *iiMedia Polaris database*: http://bjx.iimedia.cn/app_rank.

[8]For instance, while Kugou music attracted nearly 300 million monthly active users in May 2021, Imusic in tenth place only recorded 3 million monthly active users in the same month. Ibid.

or streaming service, in which three big platforms Tencent Video, YouKu and IQiyi are dominating the Chinese market.[9] The second type is the webcasting service, in which YY.com, Huya and Douyu are topping the list in terms of the number of visitors.[10] The third type is short video platforms, in which Douyin (known as Tiktok in overseas markets) and Kuaishou together have a market share of 62.7%.[11] But it should be noted that this classification is artificial as the merging trend of these forms are obvious: traditional platforms and even short video platforms have also entered the webcasting business. Integrated platforms, such as WeChat and Weibo, have also included webcasting and short-video services as part of their businesses.

The evolution of the video platform business also exemplifies the fundamental change in the pattern of consumption of copyright works in China, which is catalysed by the superabundance of copyright products due to easily accessible creative tools, super-fast network services, handy platforms for sharing contents and limited human ability in processing information. The change in the pattern of consumption has led to an attention or eyeball economy, in which only those copyright products that could attract attention will survive.[12] And what could attract attention can now be calculated using big data and algorithms, which in turn has caused many unexpected outcomes that have a profound impact on our legal system.

In order to find a solution for the abovementioned issue, this paper first examines the changes to the copyright ecosystem brought about by the concentration of power of platforms with section 2. Section 3 critically assesses the theoretical challenges of these changes to the regulatory framework of

[9]It is reported that in May 2021, the number of monthly active users on Tencent Video is 385 million, the number on Youku is 381 million and Iqiyi is 356 million. Ibid. The number of online video users is estimated to be 0.75 billion in the first half of 2019. CNNIC, 'The 44th China Statistical Report on Internet Development', *CNNIC* (August 2019), http://www.cac.gov.cn/pdf/20190829/44.pdf (accessed July 16, 2021).

[10]According to the 2020 report by MobTech, the market share of YY.com alone in the entertainment webcasting market is 40% in March 2020 and it has more than 10 million active monthly users. In comparison, dozens of other entertainment webcasting platforms occupy another 30% with an average of 1 million active monthly users. For game webcasting platforms, Huya and Douyu together represent 80% of the market and collectively own 56 million monthly active users in the same month. See MobTech, '2020 China Webcasting Industry Insights', *Mob.com* (May 21, 2020), https://www.mob.com/mobdata/report/95 (accessed July 16, 2021). YY.com's monthly active users recorded in May 2021 have risen to nearly 25 million, and that number for Huya and Douyu together is nearly 50 million. See iiMedia database (n 3).

[11]See MobTech, '2020 China Short Video Industry Insights' (October 27, 2020), https://view.inews.qq.com/a/20201027A0FO5B00 (accessed July 16, 2021).

[12]'As this report has shown, faced with an overwhelming array of choices and guided by menus, digital rankings and suggestions calculated by algorithms, they (consumers) increasingly pick from just a few of the most popular items.' See 'The battle for consumers' attention: Forget the long tail', *Economist* (February 9, 2017), https://www.economist.com/special-report/2017/02/09/the-battle-for-consumers-attention (accessed July 16, 2021); see also Tim Wu, *The Attention Merchants: The Epic Scramble to get Inside Our Heads* (Vintage 2016) 6.

platforms and copyright works in China. The last section presents the recommendations and the conclusion.

2. Concentration is changing the copyright ecosystem

2.1. Curbing direct piracy in video platforms

In general, one of the beneficial aspects of concentration of power in platforms is that it helps to destroy direct physical piracy such as pirated DVDs and even digital piracy to a large extent.[13] This is understandable as when more licenced works are introduced to major platforms, and the easier the consumers can access copyright works in terms of price and convenience, the less likely that they will seek the burdensome, hard-to-locate, and often low-quality piracy copies outside these platforms.[14] For most direct piracies being uploaded to these platforms, quite often filtering technologies were employed to decrease piracy,[15] and that potentially pushed them into less visible sites.

As for China, it is impossible and unreasonable for video platforms to obtain all available copyrighted audiovisual products in practice. The reasons for that may include market considerations (the data analysis tells them not to introduce some titles that are destined to fail in the Chinese market) and content censorship (heterodox audiovisual works that failed the censorship requirements of the Chinese government).[16] As a result, direct online piracy will remain visible but will be kept at a low rate, as

---

[13]Eric Priest observed that when the market became mature, the video platforms in China took proactive measures to purge 'their services of unlicensed content' and sought 'exclusive licenses from copyright owners.' See Eric Priest, 'Copyright Extremophiles: Do Creative Industries Thrive or Just Survive in China's High-Piracy Environment' (2014) 27 *Harvard Journal of Law & Technology* 467; Jyh-An Lee also points out that '[c]onsumers now can rarely see infringing content for free on the major video-streaming websites' due to the update of platform commercial models. See Jyh-An Lee, 'Tripartite perspective on the copyright-sharing economy in China' (2019) 35 *Computer Law & Security Review* 434, 452; Of course, the existence of powerful legal measures is also indispensable. See Vincent Brodbeck, 'Using the Carrot, Not the Stick: Streaming Media and Curbing Digital Piracy in China' (2013) 19 *Boston University Journal of Science & Technology Law* 127, 155 ('[A] law like IPRED … coupled with the release of legal streaming content services such as Netflix, Spotify, and Hulu could jolt the populous away from piracy and toward legitimate practices.').

[14]It was reported that, according to the existing copyright infringement cases in China, the piracy copies have moved from big video platforms to subtler distribution channels, and the video files distributed are often attached with illegal advertisements, watermarks and links. See Jiaxin Liu, 'Is Sharing Piracy Links an Infringement?', *Beijing Daily* (March 4, 2021), http://www.legaldaily.com.cn/Finance_and_Economics/content/2021-03/04/content_8447487.html （刘佳欣，《"分享"盗版链接侵权吗》，北京日报，2021年3月4日).

[15]The most famous example is the Youtube Content ID system. See Youtube, 'Using Content ID', *Youtube*, https://support.google.com/youtube/answer/3244015?hl=en (accessed July 16, 2021).

[16]For a detailed account of content censorship in China, see Tianxiang He, 'Control or Promote? China's Cultural Censorship System and its Influence on Copyright Protection' (2017) 7(1) *Queen Mary Journal of Intellectual Property* 96 (hereinafter 'Control or Promote'); for the transnational enforcement issue in China, see Tianxiang He, 'The Big 'Ban' Theory and Piracy: Which Way Forward for Effective Transnational Copyright Enforcement Policy in China?' (2019) 66 *Journal of the Copyright Society of the U.S.A.* 161–190 (hereinafter 'The Big 'Ban' Theory and Piracy').

most copyrighted audiovisual works are already available on major Chinese video platforms, thanks to the internationalisation process. Of course, exceptions still exist: when the supply is not there, or even when there is just a time lag between the jurisdictions in which the copyright owners choose to distribute their audiovisual works, piracy may thrive.[17]

2.2. Facilitating partial copying

The concentration of platforms has brought in consumer traffic, and the current commercial model of most video platforms is to reward those contents that can generate traffic. As previously discussed, direct piracy in big Chinese platforms is no longer visible. Opportunists then turned on a massive scale to partial copying activities facilitated by easily accessible editing tools, as the legal determination of infringement of these cases is often complex and not straightforward. They take segments from existing hot titles and upload remixed content to the video platforms to reach a wider audience. Here the video platforms have provided copyright infringements with the perfect stage to perform in an online world, and concentration is making this kind of copyright infringement more visible.

In practice, uploads that involve direct and partial copying activities posed big challenges to copyright policing and enforcement in platforms, as the transaction costs became unbearable when the number of infringements approaches infinity.[18] One of the solutions is to shift the pressure to platforms via secondary infringement. Compared with users, platforms are an easy target with a deep pocket, and they did aid copyright infringers to some extent. The DMCA safe harbour rules were then proposed by the US and commonly accepted by most countries to add a degree of certainty.[19] Moreover, in order to attract copyright owners and to reduce litigation risk, and with the confidence provided by the 'smart' algorithm, major platforms have employed filtering technologies pairing with the matching database provided by the copyright owners to pre-emptively identify the infringing contents so as to avoid secondary copyright infringement claims.

[17]The most recent example is the new Disney movie 'Mulan'. See Matt Haldane, 'Piracy hurt Disney's Mulan in China in 1999, and it appears to be happening again', *SCMP* (September 16, 2020), https://www.scmp.com/abacus/culture/article/3101525/piracy-hurt-disneys-mulan-china-1999-and-it-appears-be-happening (accessed July 16, 2021); similar intention was identified by a 2011 GfK report on 'generation file-share' and 'self-serving consumers' groups, claiming that they were interested in accessing foreign copyright works before their official launch in UK. See GfK NOP, 'Qualitative research into online digital piracy', *Ofcom* (August 2011), https://www.ofcom.org.uk/__data/assets/pdf_file/0023/41387/gfk.pdf (accessed July 16, 2021).

[18]Tim Wu, 'Tolerated Use' (2008) 31 *Columbia Journal of Law & the Arts* 617, 629.

[19]For a fair account of the safe harbour rules and its recent development, see Jie Wang, *Regulating Hosting ISPs' Responsibilities for Copyright Infringement: The Freedom to Operate in the US, EU and China* (Springer 2018).

However, platforms are not equal in an economic sense. While major platforms have money and the bargaining power to employ screening technologies and negotiate a bulk licence from copyright owners to cover all activities that happen in their platforms so that infringement litigations can be by and large avoided,[20] small platforms do not have similar resources. They will have to depend on the safe harbour rules to protect themselves or employ third-party filtering companies to do the job, such as ACRCloud.[21] Nevertheless, there are some serious risks associated with these technological measures in detecting partial copyright infringements, which are addressed in section 3 of this paper.

2.3. 'information cocoons' and the shrinking pool of choices

The concentration of power in platforms has empowered them not only to filter copyright infringement contents but also to identify the next blockbusters with technological aids. But it is clearly an issue if content platforms have developed to a stage that massive users are gathered in it,[22] and the platforms apply algorithms on big data of their users' online activities to predict user preferences,[23] as utilitarianism cannot be the sole standard for deciding what goods shall be pushed to or even made for their users. In this respect, we should recall how Sandel elaborates Mill's account of higher pleasures by comparing the works of Shakespeare and the Simpsons: 'we judge *Hamlet* as great art not because we like it more than lesser entertainments, but because it engages our highest faculties and makes us more fully human.'[24] It will then be a technological risk if the predicted user preference will determine platform purchase, promotion, and even production of copyright works.[25] Accordingly, the concentration of power in platforms may lead to fewer choices or even convergence in audiovisual works production

[20] These licences are referred to as 'second level agreements'. See Yafit Lev-Aretz, 'Second Level Agreements' (2012) 45 *Akron Law Review* 137.

[21] 'It (ACRCloud) can quickly match a target song's "fingerprint" or ID — key acoustic features like the tempo and tones of a piece — with a reference database of millions of tracks.' See Rita Liao, 'How China's ACRCloud detects copyrighted music in short videos', *Techcrunch* (August 13, 2020), https://techcrunch.com/2020/08/12/acrcloud-profile/ (accessed July 16, 2021).

[22] The estimated monthly active user in Tencent Video in May 2021 alone is nearly 400 million, almost one third of China's population. CNNIC (n 9).

[23] 'The online platforms' algorithms for recommending music based on previous selections (Spotify is a good example of these practices) emphasizes the superstar effect.' See Manuel Pacheco Coelho and José Zorro Mendes, 'Digital music and the "death of the long tail"' (2019) 101 *Journal of Business Research* 454, 459.

[24] Michael Sandel, *Justice: What's the right thing to do?* (Penguin 2009) 56.

[25] The three Chinese giant video platform Youku, Iqiyi and Tecent Video all initiated their own production project in recent years, and it was reported that the total percentage of own production versus purchased production in these three platforms is 65%. See Hanci Chen, 'Own production accounts for 65%, the copyright purchases of video platforms are not that high anymore', *Yicai* (May 21, 2019), https://www.yicai.com/news/100195956.html (accessed July 16, 2021)(陈汉辞，《自制剧占比65%，视频网站版权采购没那么烧钱了》，第一财经，2019年5月21日).

and generate 'information cocoons.'[26] Accordingly, when people are gathering in big video platforms, and those tailor-made hot titles are introduced and fed to the users within, there will be less chance for the public to be attracted by the long tail,[27] as users' attention is often scarce[28] and can easily be manipulated.[29] This trend is exemplified by a rapidly growing 'fragment' market segment of the copyright works market.

2.4. The fragmentation of exploitation of copyright works

The concentration of power in platforms has also led to changes in consumption patterns and fragmentation of exploitation of copyright works. As discussed above, the 'superstar effect' could be enhanced by the employment of algorithms and big data. The potentially infringing but hard-to-regulate partial copying activities also help to spotlight the highlights of copyright works. Due to the interactive nature of online communication, voices and opinions about consumers' preferences with regard to copyright products provided by the video platforms were spitted out and were collected and received by platforms and copyright owners as data. It has then spawned a hatchery for new ways of exploration of the copyright works that could be developed into submarkets. For example, webcasting and short video markets were discovered when the view statistics of related videos went viral. Moreover, the existence of affordable, even free creative tools and applications and super-fast internet services has provided the means for consumers to explore and test the water in a 'prosumer' era.[30]

The concentration of power in platforms has led to the subdivision of the copyright market and further concentration of users. Moreover, these submarkets, such as webcasting and short-video platforms, are firmly connected with extracts of copyright works (such as extracts of movies, songs and games). The protection model then changed from protecting the whole

[26]Sunstein defines information cocoons as 'communications universes in which we hear only what we choose and only what comforts and pleases us'. See Cass Sunstein, *Infotopia: How Many Minds Produce Knowledge* (OUP 2006) 9. But scholars also believe that there is little empirical evidence to support the concern. See Frederik J. Zuiderveen Borgesius et al. 'Should We Worry About Filter Bubbles' (2016) 5 *Internet Policy Review* 1.

[27]Anderson argues that niche products and out of popularity products can collectively represent a substantial market that rivals or exceeds the current hits, provided that the distribution channel is large enough. See Chris Anderson, *The Long Tail: Why the Future of Business is Selling Less of More* (Hyperion 2006). However, if consumers' attention is determined by algorithms or the supply is super abundant, then it will be hard for them to discover the tails. This can be referred to as the 'Tyranny of Choice'. See Mark Mulligan, 'The Death of the Long Tail: The Superstar Music Economy', *MIDiA* (July 14, 2014), https://www.midiaresearch.com/reports/the-death-of-the-long-tail (accessed July 16, 2021).

[28]Simon Herbert, 'Designing Organizations for an Information-Rich World' in Martin Greenberger (ed.), *Computers, Communication, and the Public Interest* (The Johns Hopkins Press) 40–41.

[29]Persson Petra, 'Attention Manipulation and Information Overload' (2018) 2 *Behavioural Public Policy* 78.

[30]Alvin Toffler, *The Third Wave: The Classic Study of Tomorrow* (Bantam 1st ed. 1984) 11 ('... Third Wave civilization begins to heal the historic breach between producer and consumer, giving rise to the "prosumer" economics of tomorrow.').

work (such as in the early days of the traditional platforms, the job was to prevent the distribution of pirated or unauthorised copies) to protecting extracts of the work, no matter how short and how insignificant they are. This has generated big challenges to our copyright jurisprudence.

2.5. Stronger but subtler governmental control on illegal contents

One of the significant side effects of the concentration of power in platforms in China is that it makes it easier for the government to control and wipe out illegal and heterodox contents. In China, video platforms are not only regulated by the Copyright Law of China (CLC) and related regulations via courts, but also by market and cultural regulations administered by regulatory bodies such as the State Administration for Market Regulation (SAMR) and Minister of Culture and Tourism of China (MCT), which all contain strict censorship requirements for video platforms.[31] The filtering technologies can be easily employed to identify illegal and heterodox contents.[32] This is also evident in third-party filtering services such as the Video Content Moderation service powered by Huawei Cloud.[33] With powerful support from filtering technologies, the Chinese government could exert more precise control over the contents being distributed among major platforms via its content censorship requirements. But the vagueness of the censorship criteria[34] and the opacity of the technical process have cast doubts on whether the pre-emptive filtering mechanism will have negative impacts on the fundamental rights of users.

3. Theoretical challenges to the legal system

As discussed above, what can be expected is that at least in major platforms, direct copying is rarely seen, which is especially so when the filtering technologies were employed by platforms to detect copyright infringements. Instead, the partial copying of contents, which is subtler and hard to judge whether it constitutes copyright infringements due to the ambiguity of the exceptions/fair use standards in the copyright laws of most jurisdictions, is more commonly observed. A thriving practice of partial copying in the

[31] For a detailed discussion about these censorship rules, see He, 'Control or Promote' (n 16); see also Priest (n 13).

[32] A prominent example is the popular Chinese mobile app WeChat. According to the findings of Knockel and Xiong, 'content filtering on WeChat is non-transparent, as no explicit notice is given to users when content is filtered and the original content remains visible to the user that sent or posted it'. See Jeffrey Knockel and Ruohan Xiong, '(Can't) Picture This 2: An Analysis of WeChat's Realtime Image Filtering in Chats' *The Citizen Lab* (15 July 2019), https://citizenlab.ca/2019/07/cant-picture-this-2-an-analysis-of-wechats-realtime-image-filtering-in-chats/ (visited 8 June 2020).

[33] 'What is Video Analysis Service?' *Huawei Cloud* (February 1, 2021), https://support.huaweicloud.com/productdesc-vas/vas_01_0001.html (accessed July 16, 2021).

[34] He, 'Control or Promote' (n 16) 84.

form of user-generated contents (UGCs)[35] and the related submarkets have not only raised the concern of large-scale copyright infringements from copyright owners but have also generated new revenue streams and allured platforms to make special arrangements with the big copyright conglomerates to reap the profits. However, these arrangements are theoretically flawed.

3.1. Shall we protect every use of a copyrighted work?

UGCs that partially copy others' works vary in the degree of copying. According to copyright jurisprudence, whether the parts borrowed amount to a 'substantial part' or 'substantial taking' is crucial in deciding whether a copyright infringement occurs.[36] Accordingly, if the borrowing is considered not substantial, then it will not be deemed a copyright infringement. However, what amounts to 'substantial' is often a tricky question for all courts around the world, especially for cases of audiovisual remixes. The practical result is that, except for cases in which the whole work is taken without emendation, the assessment is in general a case-by-case one[37] and platforms are not the suitable judge for that.[38]

The filtering technologies that are addressed in later parts of this paper aside, one of the notable solutions that the platforms adopted to avoid copyright infringement claims is the so-called 'second level agreements' that are defined as 'a preemptive licence obtained by UGC platforms owners in order to ratify the mass usage of copyrighted content by their users.'[39] This kind of practice is accepted by many major Chinese video platforms such as Youku and Tudou as well.[40] Under this setting, copyright owners as partners of the

[35]The term UGC was frequently referred to by copyright scholars, but it is never a homogeneous subject matter. See e.g., Daniel Gervais, 'The tangled web of UGC: Making copyright sense of user-generated content' (2009) 11 *Vanderbilt Journal of Entertainment & Technology Law* 841 ('[T]here is no such thing as "user-generated content."').

[36]See Melville B. Nimmer & David Nimmer, *Nimmer on Copyright* § 13.03[A][2] (rev. ed. 2018); see also William Cornish, David Llewelyn and Tanya Aplin, *Intellectual Property: Patents, Copyright, Trade Marks and Allied Rights* (9 edn, Sweet & Maxwell 2019) 474-476.

[37]See the discussion on 'thin' copyrights by *Nimmer*, where it is claimed that '[t]he measure of how substantial a "substantial similarity" must be may vary according to circumstances' and 'if substantial similarity is the normal measure required to demonstrate infringement, "supersubstantial similarity" must pertain when dealing with works subject to only "thin" protection.' See Nimmer & Nimmer, Ibid, at 13-69.

[38]It is intrinsically not a percentage assessment. For works that represent significant creative effort, even copying a single line could amount to infringement. The famous US precedents include *Heim v. Universal Pictures Co.*, 154 F.2d 480 n.8 (2d Cir, I 946); *Exxon Corp. v. Exxon Ins. Consultants Int'l. Ltd.* [1981] 2 All E.R. 495. In EU, it was ruled by CJEU in the *Infopaq* case that an 11-word extract of a newspaper article may reflect 'intellectual creation' hence could be considered as copyright protected. See Case C-5/08, *Infopaq Int'l A/S v. Danske Dagblades Forening* [19 July 2009] ECR I-6569. However, for the 'thin' copyrights it may require 'supersubstantial' similarity to establish infringement. See Nimmer & Nimmer, Ibid, at 13-69.

[39]Lev-Aretz (n 20) at 152.

[40]Tianxiang He, 'Study on the Copyright Pre-Licence of the Audio-visual Sharing Platforms: Taking the New Copyright Business Method of YouTube as an Example' (2012) *Intellectual Property*, no.10,

platforms will then enjoy unprecedented control over contents that copied their copyright works: any use of partners' copyright materials in UGCs uploaded to the platform will be deemed licenced and partners will have the discretion to detain, remove, or even supersede the video creators' right to enjoy the advertisement revenues.

The licencing model mentioned above is beneficial to copyright owners, video platforms and users to a certain degree, as it helps to reduce transaction costs and litigation risks and to increase the variety of works.[41] A similar model is also advocated by the EU Digital Single Market Directive as well.[42] But its downsides are also obvious. Besides the awkward status of users inside the second level agreements, its non-inclusiveness and the potential augmentation of the current uncertainty surrounding a fair use analysis for the uploaded contents,[43] the greater risk lies in the fact that the model enables copyright owners to reap what they did not sow in the name of copyright protection. As discussed above, copyright over a certain work only protects the author's expression of intellectual creation. However, not every part of a copyrighted work is protected. In the case of audiovisual UGC, even if a UGC uses frames from a movie or cartoon, it will not trigger copyright issues unless the parts used are considered substantial.[44]

The question is: can big copyright owners single out a segment of a copyrighted work and claim independent protection? In the classic UK case *Ladbroke*, Lord Reid mentioned that 'it may sometimes be a convenient shortcut to ask whether the part taken could by itself be the subject of copyright,'[45] which seems to signal a positive answer. However, Lord Reid went on to indicate in the judgment that 'the more correct approach is first to determine whether the plaintiffs' work as a whole is 'original' and protected by copyright, and then to inquire whether the part taken by the defendant is

---

pp. 90–96 (何天翔：音视频分享网站的版权在先许可研究——以美国YouTube的新版权商业模式为例，《知识产权》，2012年第10期，第90-96页).

[41] Lev-Aretz (n 20) at 166-168.

[42] See Article 17 of the Directive (EU) 2019/790 of the European Parliament and of the Council of 17 April 2019 on copyright and related rights in the Digital Single Market (DSM Directive).

[43] Lev-Aretz (n 20), at 168-172.

[44] In the UK, it was held that taking a single photograph of a substantial part of one frame of a film, or a photograph capturing a substantial part of a momentary display on a television, infringes copyright. See *Spelling Goldberg v BPC Publishing Ltd* [1981] RPC 225. However, it was later held that a frame of a film, not being a photograph, is not a substantial part of a film. See *Football Association Premier League Ltd v QC Leisure & Ors* [2008] EWHC 1411 (Ch). In China, the debate also exists. In a case ruled by Hangzhou Internet Court in 2017, the court held that a single frame of a film could demonstrate the recorder's selection and arrangement with regard to composition and brightness hence it could be original and protected as photographic works. See *Xinli Television Cultural Investment Co. Ltd. v Yangzhou Shengji and Zhejiang T-mall* [2017] Hangzhou Internet Court, Z8601MC. No.2296. However, in another case ruled by the Beijing Chaoyang District Court in the same year, it was held that the snapshot as a frame of a film is part of that film and cannot be considered as an independent photography work. See *Dongyang Le Shi Hua Er Co., Ltd. v. Douban.com* [2017] Beijing Chaoyang District Peoples' Court, J0105MC No.10028.

[45] *Ladbroke (Football) Ltd. v. William Hill (Football) Ltd.* [1964] 1 W.L.R. 273 at pp. 276/7.

substantial.'[46] Of course, for separatable joint authorship audiovisual works such as movies,[47] the answer is not that straightforward. In many jurisdictions, some of the components of a movie, such as soundtracks, characters' images and subtitles are all deemed separatable copyright pieces and can be enforced independently. It is just that the law has made a special arrangement designating the director and producer as the copyright owner of the whole work.[48] Accordingly, it is justified for the author of a separatable component to enforce her copyright if that component alone is included in a UGC. But for the director and producer of the whole film, using that component is not necessarily infringing the whole work unless it amounts to a substantial taking of the whole movie. This is even more so when the borrowing does not concern those separatable parts. As a result, the copyright enforcement on video platforms by big copyright owners is questionable if the claims are based on these separatable parts and they are considered insubstantial in terms of the whole movie.

That said, as Feist confirms, 'Not all copying, however, is copyright infringement.'[49] This fragmentation of exploitation of copyright works I described above echoes with Hannibal Travis's concern about 'micro-copyright' enforcement by big copyright owners: it is on the one hand not fair for individual, family and small business copyright owners as the big copyright owners 'earn additional profit that they do not need' based on fragments of copyright works they own while the former earn little income from their intellectual labours,[50] on the other hand, it is not justified for the latter to reap from UGCs that used insubstantial parts of a copyrighted work.[51] But when platforms widely employ second-level agreements plus filtering technologies to

---

[46]Ibid.

[47]In China, CLC art 14 provides that 'if a work of joint authorship can be separated into independent parts and exploited separately, each co-author shall be entitled to independent copyright in the parts that he has created, provided that the exercise of such copyright does not infringe upon the copyright in the joint work as a whole'.

[48]CLC art 17 provides that 'The copyright of cinematographic works and TV play works in audio-visual works shall be enjoyed by producers, but screenwriters, directors, photographers, lyricists, composers, and other authors shall enjoy the right of signature and have the right to obtain remunerations as agreed upon in the contracts signed with producers ... The authors of script, music, and other works that may be used separately shall have the right to separately exercise their right of copyright.' The situation in other authors' rights regime like Germany is similar. See Pascal Kamina, *Film Copyright in the European Union* (Cambridge University Press, 2016) 170.

[49]*Feist Publications, Inc., v. Rural Telephone Service Co.,* 499 U.S. 340, 361 (1991).

[50]See Hannibal Travis, *Copyright Class Struggle: Creative Economics in a Social Media Age* (Cambridge University Press, 2018), 104-105.

[51]For example, in a 2018 case regarding fanfiction of the works of a reputable Chinese writer, the Chinese court ruled that although the fan author has used dozens of character names derived from the plaintiff's works, their characteristics, relationships, and the background design were deliberately altered. Therefore, they were not substantially similar to the original and thus not a copyright infringement case. See *Jin Yong v. Jiang Nan* [2016] Guangzhou Tianhe District People's Court Y0106MC No. 12068. Rebecca Tushnet also opined that the '[e]verybody pays for everything' scenario enabled by large-scale compulsory licencing raises 'the possibility of potentially infinite demands for compensation.' See Rebecca Tushnet, 'Copy This Essay: How Fair Use Doctrine Harms Free Speech and How Copying Serves It' (2004) 114 *Yale Law Journal* 535, 590.

address their copyright concerns, the risks of overcompensation and suppression of free speech would become real if no corrective measures are in place.

3.2. Should the algorithm rule?

The second level agreements are not enforceable without an efficient mechanism to detect potential copyright infringements. Video platforms nowadays have employed filtering technologies similar to Youtube's Content ID system to detect potential infringing content.[52] Although China does not impose a positive obligation on platforms to employ filtering technology for the moment,[53] the EU DSM Directive has taken a U-turn by requiring platforms to 'make, in accordance with high industry standards of professional diligence, best efforts to ensure the unavailability of specific works and other subject matter for which the rightsholders have provided the service providers with the relevant and necessary information.'[54] Even though the DSM Directive does not explicitly provide that the employment of filtering technology is mandatory, the limitations such as '[making] best efforts to obtain an authorisation' and 'high industry standards of professional diligence' suggest that, in practice, the filtering technology is almost the only choice.[55] Moreover, the introduction of algorithmic rules into the filtering system has raised many theoretical challenges to our copyright jurisprudence.

To start with, technology development is pushing the copyright culture towards a licenced one. In the pre-digital era, it will be practically impossible for the copyright owners to enter the 'free zones' enjoyed by individuals.[56] Even in the early years of the internet age, there is still a de facto

---

[52]Giancarlo F. Frosio, 'Why keep a dog and bark yourself? From intermediary liability to responsibility' (2017) 26 *International Journal of Law and Information Technology* 1, 32.

[53]In China it was provided that ' … [w]here a network service provider fails to conduct proactive examination regarding a network user's infringement of the right of dissemination on information networks, the people's court shall not determine on this basis that the network service provider is at fault', according to Article 8 of the Provisions of the Supreme People's Court on Several Issues concerning the Application of Law in Hearing Civil Dispute Cases Involving Infringement of the Right of Dissemination on Information Networks 2020. The US also provides that an online entity has no duty to 'monitor[] its service or affirmatively seek[] facts indicating infringing activity, except to the extent consistent with a standard technical measure.' See 17 U.S.C. § 512(m)(1).

[54]Article 17, DSM Directive. The EU has changed its previous attitude as demonstrated in Article 15 of the Directive 2000/31/EC of the European Parliament and of the Council of 8 June 2000 on certain legal aspects of information society services, in particular electronic commerce, in the Internal Market (Directive on electronic commerce).

[55]'However, if large platforms do not come up with any innovative solutions, they may end up opting for filters. Such filters are indeed already used by the big companies!' See 'Questions and Answers on issues about the digital copyright directive' *European Parliament* (March 27, 2019), https://www.europarl.europa.eu/news/en/press-room/20190111IPR23225/questions-and-answers-on-issues-about-the-digital-copyright-directive (accessed July 16, 2021).

[56]Edward W. Ploman & L. Clark Hamilton, *Copyright: Intellectual Property in the Information Age* (Routledge & Kegan Paul. 1980), 197.

'enforcement equilibrium'[57] or a 'giant grey zone' of enforcement[58] that prevents total enforcement from happening, as the cost and benefit analysis of enforcing directly against the primary infringer, the users, will hinder most copyright owners from doing so.[59] However, technological advancements today have enabled copyright owners to exert control over almost every use of their copyright works.

On the one hand, online uploads to major platforms will be governed by algorithms in filtering and matching systems.[60] Almost every piece uploaded to these platforms that contains pre-existing copyright segments could be identified and put in the hands of partner copyright owners to decide whether further actions should be taken. As the existing copyright works and users concentrate on several major platforms, the impact will be greater as our daily life is inevitably intertwined with big and small platforms. As a result, everything we have uploaded is now traceable therefore theoretically enforceable.

On the other hand, the unfiltered UGCs containing pre-existing copyright segments and which are scattered in smaller platforms are targeted by copyright owners as well as by copyright trolls. A copyright troll is defined as 'a non-producer who merely has acquired the right to bring lawsuits against alleged infringers.'[61] Trolls threaten to file copyright infringement claims to induce rapid settlements against large groups of anonymous defendants without the intention of proceeding to trial on the merits.[62] Trolls today even employ technological measures to detect potential infringements. For example, the Visual China Group (VCG)–a China-based photo supplier established in 2000 and the exclusive distributor of Getty Images' library since 2006–alone brought 8,095 copyright cases against the unauthorised online use of photos and pictures over which it claimed ownership since

[57]The 'enforcement equilibrium' described by Balganesh is characterised by 'a systematic underenforcement of otherwise actionable claims … manifests itself in the creation of a balance between actionable claims of infringement that are actually enforced and actionable claims that are instead tolerated and treated as de facto noninfringing claims.' See Shyamkrishna Balganesh, 'The Uneasy Case against Copyright Trolls' (2013) 86 *Southern California Law Review* 723, 729.

[58]'There is a giant grey zone in copyright, consisting of millions of usages that do not fall into a clear category but are often infringing.' Wu (n 18) at 617.

[59]Tim Wu opined that the reasons for nonenforcement could include 'simple laziness or enforcement costs, a desire to create goodwill, or a calculation that the infringement … actually benefits the owner.' Ibid, 619.

[60]Frosio warned that 'intermediary responsibility does morph into algorithmic responsibility'. See Giancarlo F. Frosio, 'The Death of "No Monitoring Obligations": A Story of Untameable Monsters' (2017) 8 *JIPITEC* 199, 214; See also Matthew Sag, 'Internet Safe Harbors and the Transformation of Copyright Law' (2017) 93 *Notre Dame Law Review* 499, 543.

[61]*Malibu Media, LLC v. Does*, No. 12-2078, 2013 WL 3038025, at *1–2 (E.D. Pa. June 18, 2013).

[62]Luke S. Curran, 'Copyright Trolls, Defining the Line Between Legal Ransom Letters and Defending Digital Rights: Turning Piracy into a Business Model or Protecting Creative from Internet Lawlessness?' (2013) 13 *John Marshall Review of Intellectual Property Law* 170, 172; For a detailed discussion on the copyright trolling matter, see Balganesh (n 57).

2014. It has also launched its online tracking system called 'Hawk Eye' to detect the unauthorised use of its photos online.[63]

It is obviously a trend that copyright owners are encroaching upon the 'free zone' once enjoyed by the public with the expansion of copyright and the employment of tracking technologies. We used to share scrapbooks and video recordings with friends physically in a pre-internet era, and today we are doing the same thing by sharing UGCs online. It is no doubt that the impact of online sharing and copying activity is much greater and harder to control. But at the same time, it also has multiple speech values[64] and brings tremendous opportunities that are not available in the pre-internet era to both copyright owners and users.[65] As a result, copyright owners are hesitant to sue individuals directly and turn to platforms hosting these contents via the route of secondary infringement. It is a fact that the safe harbour rules are very useful in solving online disputes, but the establishment of the primary infringement is not always certain in cases where only a small part of copyright work was borrowed, as it concerns the determination of substantial borrowing and fair use that shall be determined by courts rather than by platforms. The safe harbour mechanism plus the filtering technology is thus in fact empowering the platforms to adjudicate whether a copyright claim is justifiable. Of course, one would argue that besides the notice-takedown mechanism, there are corrective measures such as counter-notice and even litigation, but for most cases in the grey area, users will tend to compromise, even if their use can eventually be justified. Moreover, empirical findings confirm that, even during the years in which the traditional notice-takedown procedures are dominating, the counter notice mechanism is seldom used.[66] Indeed, scholars recorded a drastic increase in notice-takedown requests in recent years,[67] and most of these notices were sent by agents rather than by copyright owners

[63]Shangguan Data, '2279 Litigations a Year, How Has the 'Visual China' Become Rich using Litigations', *The Paper* (15 April, 2019), https://www.thepaper.cn/newsDetail_forward_3296223 (visited 8 June 2021)(上观数据，《一年2279场诉讼，"视觉中国"是如何靠打官司发家致富的》，澎湃，2019年4月15日).

[64]Tushnet argued that even 'ordinary copying serves multiple speech values, from simple access to self-expression to political persuasion.' See Tushnet (n 51) 546.

[65]Wu (n 18) 619; see also Tianxiang He, *Copyright and Fan Productivity in China: A Cross-jurisdictional Perspective* (Springer Singapore. 2017) 113-114.

[66]Jennifer M. Urban, Joe Karaganis & Brianna L. Schofield, *Notice and Takedown in Everyday Practice* (The American Assembly 2016) 44–46 ('by all accounts, the actual use of counter notices is extremely infrequent. Only one respondent among both service providers and rightsholders reported receiving more than a handful per year. Many—including some large services handling thousands of notices per year —reported receiving none.').

[67]Daniel Seng, 'The State of the Discordant Union: An Empirical Analysis of DMCA Takedown Notices' (2014) 18 *Virginia Journal of Law & Technology* 369, 389–390 ('Google receives a very large number of takedown notices. From 67,571 notices in 2011, this number jumped sixfold to 441,370 notices in 2012.'). The author of this paper checked the LUMEN database (https://www.lumendatabase.org/), and it is recorded that from July 29, 2020 to July 29 2021, the number of takedown notices received by Google LLC is 2766,221, almost fivefold of the number in 2012 indicated by Sen.

themselves.[68] Predictably, when filtering systems can decide pre-emptively what can be published on their platforms, the negative impact will be even more significant.

Next, the employment of filtering algorithms by platforms has in practice empowered them to take over the role of the court in deciding massive copyright infringement cases that used to be in the grey area. This practice is undermining the enjoyment of users' exceptions and limitations.[69] It looks like the workload of the courts is reduced as these cases were 'solved', but in fact this practice is detrimental to the copyright system. For one thing, in many big platforms such as YouTube, filtering technology can not only help to identify suspected uploads but will also give the copyright partners the power to decide whether to share the advertisement revenues of the videos or block or remove the content even before they appear in the platforms. In the case of partial copying UGCs, the identification of potentially infringing contents itself is problematic if the finding of fair use is not covered by the algorithms of the filtering system,[70] and it is also doubtful whether algorithms can take over that judgement properly.[71]

Keeping a 'free zone' or the 'enforcement equilibrium' for users is very crucial, as pursuing every ambiguous case of infringement has the potential to discourage new creativity while doing little to protect the copyright holder's legitimate interests.[72] Moreover, the copyright owner's decision will interfere with the secondary creator's creative choice: the latter will soon learn from their decision about what is preferred by the copyright owner and what is not, rather than what is allowed by the law. As the decision is based on the algorithm's matching result, it is without solid legal grounds and is taking advantage of the fact that most users tend to stay away from trouble. This has potentially made the fair use judgement by the court secondary or even insignificant as cases are 'solved' before they went to the court.

In all, the second level agreements between copyright owners and major platforms help to build the matching database, and then the safe harbour

---

[68]A 2016 empirical study shows that, among the samples collected, 91.8% of the notices were sent by agents. In comparison, only 7.5% of these notices were sent by copyright owners themselves. See Urban, Karaganis & Schofield (n 66) 84.

[69]Leron Solomon, 'Fair Users or Content Abusers? The Automatic Flagging of Non-Infringing Videos by Content ID on Youtube' (2015) 44 *Hofstra Law Review* 237.

[70]Guobin Cui has summarized the current content filtering systems based on intelligent content analysis methods. Basically, it is a matching system that compares the uploaded content with a pre-set database provided by copyright partners. In other words, the filtering system in the current level is incapable of making fair use judgements. See Guobin Cui, 'On the Content Filtering Obligations of the Internet Service Providers' (2017) *China Legal Science* no.2, 215, 217 (崔国斌, 《论网络服务商版权内容过滤义务》, 中国法学, 2017年第2期, 第217页).

[71]See Zoe Carpou, 'Robots, Pirates, and the Rise of the Automated Takedown Regime: Using the DMCA to Fight Piracy and Protect End Users' (2016) 39 *Columbia Journal of Law & the Arts* 551, 564-582. For a detailed discussion about this issue, see Peter Yu, 'Artificial Intelligence, the Law-machine Interface, and Fair Use Automation' (2020) 72 *Alabama Law Review* 187.

[72]Balganesh (n 57) 730.

rules plus the filtering technologies are in fact allowing the copyright conglomerates to reap the benefits of grey area uses that were not possible before. This new practice will greatly limit users' creative choices and impair their freedom of speech.

3.3. Challenges to freedom of speech and privacy

The extra power given to copyright owners to block content using the filtering technologies provided by the platforms is also a threat to users' fundamental rights, such as freedom of speech[73] and privacy.[74] With the 'successful' application of voluntary filtering measures on major platforms, it is expectable that the measures will be a good tool to detect heterodox or harmful contents and to access personal data. Jack Balkin has warned us of the danger of 'collateral censorship', in which the government could achieve its censorship goals via its regulation of agents such as platforms,[75] as 'rules imposing civil and criminal liability on distributors could have the same censorial effect.'[76]

It is also a responsibility for the Chinese platforms to censor a wide variety of other content, including politically heterodox materials, pornographies, terrorist-related content, etc.,[77] and now that comes with the filtering system as well. The author identifies three concerns where platform filtering measures in China may be considered detrimental:

The first concern is the overly powerful algorithm. Just like the copyright owners, the Chinese government finds it difficult to regulate illegal online contents without the help of platforms as the resources and users are concentrated nowadays. Moreover, as the censorship requirement comes directly from the government as administrative orders, the pressure is more imminent therefore the filtering is more strictly enforced compared with copyright filtering requests. Specifically, not only keyword scan but also OCR scan for photos and pictures, audios, and even videos will be employed by the platforms to detect heterodox literal materials.[78] And it not only concerns the

[73] The CJEU upheld this position in the *Netlog* case. C-360/10 *Belgische Vereniging van Auteurs, Componisten en Uitgevers CVBA (SABAM) v. Netlog NV* [2012] ECLI:EU:C:2012:85, § 55.

[74] The ECJ identified this risk in a 2014 judgement. See C-314/12 *UPC Telekabel Wien GmbH v. Constantin Film Verleih GmbH et al* (2014) ECLI:EU:C:2014:192 § 50.

[75] Jack M. Balkin, 'Old-School/New-School Speech Regulation' (2014) 127 *Harvard Law Review* 2296, 2309.

[76] Michael I. Meyerson, 'Authors, editors, and uncommon carriers: Identifying the speaker within the new media' (1995) 71 *Notre Dame Law Review* 79, 116.

[77] He, 'Control or promote' (n 16) 74.

[78] It was reported that 'WeChat (the most popular chat app in China) uses two different algorithms to filter images in Moments: an OCR-based one that filters images containing sensitive text and a visual-based one that filters images that are visually similar to those on an image blacklist.' See Jeffrey Knockel, Lotus Ruan, Masashi Crete-Nishihata, and Ron Deibert, '(Can't) Picture This: An Analysis of Image Filtering on WeChat Moments', *The Citizen Lab,* 14 August 2018, available at https://tspace.library.utoronto.ca/bitstream/1807/94801/1/Report%23112--Can%27t%20Picture%20This.pdf (visited 8 June 2021).

publicly disseminated materials such as normal uploads, but it also applies to private chats between individuals.[79] That means the coverage of the filtering technology for censorship is much wider than its copyright version. However, it was also reported that the current filtering mechanism employed by platforms such as WeChat is not that intelligent, and due to cost–benefit considerations, computationally expensive filtering technologies will not be applied to all activities within the platform.[80] But as the censorship requirement gets stricter and the costs of surveillance go down over time, it is to be expected that more sophisticated content will be included in the censor list sooner or later.

Another concern is the over-censor issue. When the power is shifted from the government to the platform, the risk of excessive self-censorship will arise.[81] As the secondary executor, platforms can only grasp the degree of tightness of the ambiguous policy requirement by their daily business exchange with the government. Of course, when they underestimate the tightness of the policy they will be punished.[82] Platforms will then set the threshold higher to avoid potential risks. But users' freedom of speech will suffer if their legitimate contents are caught by the system.

A related issue is that the platforms are using different mechanisms and technologies to nudge.[83] For example, WeChat has been filtering different content uploaded by its users since the beginning. But recently, researchers found that WeChat employed technologies to make sure that, when an individual publishes a 'WeChat Moment' and the content uploaded is caught by the system, the sender will not be notified, but only the sender can see the 'published' content.[84] And most importantly, these mechanisms often come unnoticed (such as limiting the network traffic of certain content so that others cannot view them) or in the disguise of profit calculation (such

---

[79] See Knockel and Xiong (n 32).

[80] Ibid.

[81] Balkin (n 75); See also *Delfi AS v. Estonia* N 64569/09 (ECHR, 16 June 2015) § 110, Joint Dissenting Opinion of Judges Sajò and Tsotsoria § I.2 ('Because A (platform) is liable for someone else's speech, A has strong incentives to over-censor, to limit access, and to deny B (user)'s ability to communicate using the platform that A controls. In effect, the fear of liability causes A to impose prior restraints on B's speech and to stifle even protected speech.').

[82] It was reported that video platforms such as Youku and Iqiyi received administrative punishments from the government for leaking illegal contents. Manzi Zhang, 'Youku and Iqiyi received administrative punishments due to illegal activities', *Xinhua News* (August 7, 2020), http://www.xinhuanet.com/legal/2020-08/07/c_1126339683.htm (accessed July 16, 2021)(张漫子, 《"优酷""爱奇艺"因违法违规行为受到行政处罚》, 新华网, 2020年8月7日).

[83] '[A] nudge is any factor that significantly alters the behaviour of Humans, even though it would be ignored by Econs.' Richard H. Thaler and Cass R. Sunstein, *Nudge: Improving Decisions about Health, Wealth, and Happiness* (Yale University Press, 2008) 8.

[84] A prominent example is the popular Chinese mobile app WeChat. According to the findings of Knockel and Xiong, 'content filtering on WeChat is non-transparent, as no explicit notice is given to users when content is filtered and the original content remains visible to the user that sent or posted it.' See Knockel and Xiong (n 32).

as YouTube's Advertiser-friendly content guidelines)[85] or self-protection. Although it is also a fact that new technologies such as real-time webcasting will make the pre-publication censorship much harder, it is to be expected that the loophole will soon be filled by other new censor methods too. Just like Julie Cohen has indicated, 'compromises that involve voluntary filtering shift much day-to-day authority over interdiction of information flows to platforms and at the same time make interdiction decisions more difficult to contest.'[86]

The third concern is the limited choice of users. The censorship requirement in China is imposed by the government via laws and regulations on all platforms. Hence the users' platform shopping power is greatly limited: once internet users find a platform that is lenient or insensitive towards certain illegal content and they switch platforms, then censorship problems will soon become obvious in that platform. The latter will have to enforce more rigidly or self-censor contents even without a direct order from the government. All these have increased the platforms' willingness to avoid risks in subtler ways.

In sum, the new algorithmic censor tools will make the abridgement on freedom of speech imperceptible, and unlike copyright cases, many cases are without proper notice and even if noticed, remedies are often not available.

4. Solutions: the way forward

The concentration of platforms seems like an irreversible trend, and the disruptive power of new technologies is unleashed. But just as Cheng Han Tan indicates, '[h]umankind's ability to adapt will allow it over time to react and shape technology to its optimal use.'[87] But the solutions proposed must be carefully designed to reflect the policy needs and should not be limited to legal measures. The current algorithmic ruling in platform copyright enforcement is a clear example of a Law 2.0 scenario termed by Roger Brownsword, in which the 'technologies are being employed as tools that are designed to assist with a rule-based regulatory enterprise.'[88] Will a Law 3.0 era come anytime soon, in which 'technical solutions and technological management are becoming the default strategy and not just something to be considered alongside a rule-based approach'?[89] By then, the solutions might lie

---

[85]According to this guideline, a list of topics is deemed 'not suitable for ads'. If certain content falls into the list, no monetary rewards can be received by the YouTuber who posted it. 'Advertiser-friendly content guidelines', *YouTube Help*, https://support.google.com/youtube/answer/6162278?hl=en (visited 8 June 2020).

[86]Julie E. Cohen, 'Law for the Platform Economy' (2017) 51 *U.C. Davis Law Review* 133, 175.

[87]Cheng Han Tan, 'The Online World and the Offline World' in Simon Chesterman (ed.), *Data Protection Law in Singapore – Privacy and Sovereignty in an Interconnected World* (Academy Publishing, 2018) 80.

[88]Roger Brownsword, *Law 3.0: Rules, Regulation, and Technology* (Routledge, 2020) 35.

[89]Ibid, at 36.

in the technology itself. But the case of copyright enforcement implies that the process might be very long, as the determination of infringement and fair use is complex and algorithms at the current level are not capable of delivering a satisfactory answer.[90] The solution proposed by this paper turns on complementing second level agreements and regulating algorithms.

4.1. Complement the second level agreements

The second level agreements are the contractual foundation of the filtering mechanisms. But the doctrine of privity has decided that these agreements will not bind the users if they are not the negotiating parties. To strengthen its positive effects, the following measures must be taken:

Making transparency of the agreement terms that concern platform users as a statutory requirement could be a solution. This can provide users with the required legal certainty. After all, if terms such as coverage of the copyright works concerned and the agreement duration can be revealed, platform users could then evaluate the risk associated with their uploads; the public will also be able to exert pressure on unjustified terms.[91] Content platforms could either publicise the agreement terms with a separate page or alert the users about the abovementioned terms in their users' agreements. Moreover, a clear statement of platform users' legal rights and obligations under the pact[92] or at least a revocable exemption statement that explains copyright owners' enforcement strategies[93] could be included in the users' agreements as well. This will fill the missing link by binding users to the parties of the second level agreements and providing them with complete information about the agreement terms that concern users.

4.2. Regulate algorithms

Even if the contractual foundation is established, the employment of filtering measures by platforms is still problematic: the users may not enjoy the vast freedoms provided by the second level agreements when the copyright owners have the power to control the uploaded contents after receiving the filtering results. Moreover, the user preference prediction problem also requires further regulation.

With regard to the issue of fragmentised copyright enforcement, several measures must be taken to restore the balance. What needs to be emphasised is that enforcement by copyright owners should be supported, especially in the

[90] See Dan Burk and Julie Cohen, 'Fair Use Infrastructure for Copyright Management Systems' (2001) 15 *Harvard Journal of Law & Technology* 41, 55-57.

[91] Lev-Aretz (n 20) at 184.

[92] Ibid, 185.

[93] He (n 65) at 207.

case of full-scale copying. Notice-takedown procedures are still very much useful, but filtering technology can certainly provide additional support in this scenario. However, the author supports voluntary rather than mandatory filtering obligations for platforms, not just because it is more coherent with fundamental rights protection,[94] but also because it could accommodate different types of authors and it is more feasible in terms of cost.[95] But the author argues that for those platforms that employ filtering measures, whether partial copying cases amount to infringement cannot be simply decided by percentages. Measures must be taken at different levels of the filtering process in order to achieve a balanced result. The law should intervene when a platform utilises copyright filtering technologies.

Specifically, before a matching database is provided to the filtering mechanism of a platform by its copyright partners, it is necessary for both the platform and copyright owners to ascertain that only copyright works enjoyed by the latter are included. This will require due diligence checks from the platforms' side and liability for false claiming from the copyright owners' side. The exclusion of all public domain and third-party copyright items and parts of an item in the matching database can thereby increase the precision rate of the matching result.

After a matching database is provided or certain works not provided but the infringement risk is already obvious like a red flag so that the filtering mechanism is triggered, it is necessary to refine the filtering mechanism to create a more balanced environment that could protect not only the economic interests of the copyright owners but also the interests related to users.

For one thing, filtering technology is needed but the parameter should be carefully set. Only those UGCs that substantially copied and distributed the copyright works should be filtered. But there is no consensus about the clear boundary that a part can be considered substantial even among the courts within one jurisdiction. Theoretically speaking, if a single frame of a movie cannot be excluded as a substantial part, then basically every derivative work of a movie will be covered. The author suggests that the trigger point should be set above the controversial cases. Accordingly, the focus should be on the unique contribution from the user rather than how much has been borrowed from a single work. A UGC could possibly contain a full song as the background music but with many creative inputs in the video setting. A commentary video may as well contain 90% borrowed segments

[94]Frosio (n 60) at 212.

[95]The CJEU upheld this opinion in the *Netlog* case (n 73) § 46; See also Chris Sprigman & Mark Lemley, 'Why Notice-and-Takedown Is a Bit of Copyright Law Worth Saving', *Los Angeles Times* (21 June, 2016), https://www.latimes.com/opinion/op-ed/la-oe-sprigman-lemley-notice-and-takedown-dmca-20160621-snap-story.html (visited 8 June 2021); Cui has indicated that different service providers could share the R&D cost of the system, so it is not a problem. Cui (n 70) at 225-226. But the author believes that the competing nature among platforms will prevent that from happening, as the filtering system is a real competitive edge.

from a certain movie. The system must be able to point out the percentages of the matched parts and the unmatched parts. For instance, if the unmatched part is more than 10% and the length of the matched parts from a single source is not unjustifiably long, then the UGC should be excluded and further examined by human staff. Of course, guidance from previous court practices should be sought to come up with detailed rules with regard to the exact percentage, as the situation may change should the type of work concerned be different.

For another thing, after the filtering system delivers a result, uploaders should receive a detailed notice immediately, indicating the rationale behind the decision and the remedies. Specifically, as most algorithms employed by platforms are mainly focusing on similarity rates resulting from a matching process, it is feasible to require platforms to disclose or explain the algorithmic decisions.[96] For example, information regarding the requests from the copyright owners, the parameters used by the algorithm, the matching results and their percentages, similar cases, the record of correct and error rates, and supporting judgements from Chinese courts should be shared with the concerned users.[97] Moreover, in order to prevent abuse of copyright by owners, the notice should also include an introduction of copyright exceptions in layman's terms. This educational function could encourage more users to make use of the remedies available under the filtering system.[98] If the user is not happy with the result, an easy-to-use counter-notice system must be available.

For the issue of concentration of power, extra responsibilities shall be placed on major platforms. This suggestion echoes the proposed EU Digital Services Act (DSA), in which online platforms, especially big online platforms bear more obligations such as transparency and code of conduct than small platforms.[99] Of course, the determination of big or major platforms shall be carefully designed, either determined on the basis of years of service or annual turnover or the number of users covered.[100] In other words, we need to make sure that concentration will not lead to

---

[96]The requirement for transparency of algorithms employed is justifiable in the case of content platforms as their decisions are not just concerning their business but also affecting the public with regard to accessing information and knowledge and expressing ideas.

[97]These are all considered 'subject-centric explanations' termed by Edwards and Veale that are 'more about building a relationship between these tools and their users or decision subjects that can provide "meaningful" explanation'. See Lilian Edwards and Michael Veale, 'Slave to the Algorithm? Why a 'Right to an Explanation' Is Probably Not the Remedy You Are Looking For' (2017) *Duke Law & Technology Review* 18, 58-59.

[98]Solomon (n 69) at 262-263.

[99]See Section 3, Section 4 of Proposal for a Regulation of The European Parliament and Of the Council on a Single Market for Digital Services (Digital Services Act) and amending Directive 2000/31/EC, European Commission, Brussels, 15.12.2020 COM(2020) 825 final.

[100]The DSA defines 'very large online platforms' as 'online platforms which provide their services to a number of average monthly active recipients of the service in the Union equal to or higher than 45 million'. See Article 25, Ibid.

unfair competitive advantages of major platforms and abridgement of fundamental rights. While in the US, the concerns are mostly about the overly powerful platforms in controlling news, political discourses and our personal lives,[101] currently, the big Chinese platforms are by and large still playing the role of an agent in carrying out the tasks of the government. But still, there is a risk that the platforms may take advantage of the ambiguity of the government censorship policy to suppress or help third parties to suppress their business opponents. Accordingly, certain measures must be taken to regulate platforms' filtering activities. For that purpose, no matter the filtering act concerns copyright works or illegal materials, big platforms should disclose the details of the filtering and censorship mechanisms and provide adequate remedies for the affected users. In addition, codes of conduct issued by the government could also serve as a tool to enhance transparency to make sure that no hidden nudges that will hamper the rights of the users are employed by the big platforms.[102]

A multi-level regulatory framework is also needed to tackle the potential 'information cocoon' problem related to the users' consumption pattern of copyright works reinforced by algorithms. The platforms should take the initiative to update the concerned algorithm so that it will not make recommendations merely based on user portraits using data provided by users. Specifically, they should update their recommending algorithms so that the recommendations made could not only include contents that suit the users' tastes but also professional content that is of value to them.[103] However, the content platforms may have little incentive to push for it as it is against their economic interests. Accordingly, besides self-regulation initiatives by the content platforms,[104] as an ancillary mechanism, the law should intervene and monitor the design and application of algorithms by content platforms to avoid bias.[105] This paper suggests that platforms that

---

[101] Tim Wu, *The Curse of Bigness Antitrust in the New Gilded Age* (Columbia Global Reports 2018) 133.

[102] Peter Yu, 'The Algorithmic Divide and Equality in the Age of Artificial Intelligence' (2020) 72 Florida Law Review 368-370.

[103] Facebook indicates that it uses thousands of ranking signals in its News Feed ranking algorithm. Accordingly, selecting different ranking signals could have different impacts over users. See Akos Lada, Meihong Wang and Tak Yan, 'How machine learning powers Facebook's News Feed ranking algorithm' *Facebook Engineering* (January 26, 2021), https://engineering.fb.com/2021/01/26/ml-applications/news-feed-ranking/ (accessed July 16, 2021).

[104] Peter Yu argued that intelligent platforms should build inclusivity, intervenability, and interoperability into their platform design. Intervenability means that the 'operators of intelligent platforms' should be 'ready to intervene when things go wrong.' See Peter Yu, 'Beyond Transparency and Accountability: Three Additional Features Algorithm Designers Should Build into Intelligent Platforms' (2020) 13 Northeastern University Law Review 285.

[105] The European Data Protection Board opined that '[c]ontrollers should carry out frequent assessments on the data sets they process to check for any bias, and develop ways to address any prejudicial elements, including any over-reliance on correlations' and these assessments or audits require 'regular reviews of the accuracy and relevance of automated decision-making, including profiling … not only at the design stage but also continuously'. See European Data Protection Board, 'Guidelines on automated individual decision-making and profiling for the purposes of Regulation 2016/679'

employ algorithms for user-affected decision-making should register with related government authorities and endure their regular inspections.[106] In addition, the concerned parties should be well informed. As a technical solution, algorithms could also be employed to decide the disclosure of other algorithms.[107] The government authorities should also open channels to receive user complaints, and penalties should apply to platforms that fail to adjust their abnormal decision-making algorithms when detected.

5. Conclusion

Concentration is most evident in the content platforms in China. When contents and users have gathered in several big platforms, direct piracy became distinct on these platforms due to the adoption of higher copyright policing standard and the employment of filtering technologies. Concentration in big platforms has also led to the fragmentation of exploitation of copyright works, whereby partial copying activities become the new normal. While fighting piracy on platforms remains a hot topic among different jurisdictions, the employment of algorithms to detect and block partial copying contents should be inspected: copyright enforcement is a mixture of 'right and wrong' decisions due to the conflicting interests concerned and, hence, it requires a dynamic balancing of them. For China, there is no single correct answer as to the finding of fair use of similar cases as the judicial attitude changes with national policies.[108] Filtering mechanisms can no doubt boost the efficiency of copyright infringement prevention, but they can also potentially jeopardise the fundamental rights of platform users when applied wrongfully.

In a Law 2.0 era, we have already made the decision to adapt our copyright laws to the platform economy: laws were changed, and new rules were designed to guard the new industry. DMCA is a clear example. But these rules are running the risk of being superseded by new creative tools and filtering technologies. However, Law 3.0 is yet to come in content filtering: the ambiguity of the originality standard and the flexibility provided by the copyright exceptions to accommodate a mixture of conflicting interests

---

European Commission News Room (6 February), https://ec.europa.eu/newsroom/article29/redirection/document/49826 (accessed July 16, 2021).

[106]The inspections are not necessarily ex-post in nature, they could also include 'regulatory sandboxes' such as those commonly seen in the Fintech industry, in which regulations and innovative technological applications are tested by interested parties such as the regulators, users and platforms in controlled environments. See Michael Piri, 'The Changing Landscapes of Fintech and Regtech: Why the United States Should Create a Federal Regulatory Sandbox' (2018) 2 *Business and Finance Law Review* 233.

[107]Fabiana Di Porto and Marialuisa Zuppetta, 'Co-regulating algorithmic disclosure for digital platforms' (2021) 40 *Policy and Society* 272, 285-288.

[108]See Tianxiang He, 'Transplanting Fair Use in China? History, Impediments and the Future' (2020) *The University of Illinois Journal of Law, Technology & Policy* 359.

have jointly determined that there is no definitive answer to each infringement case, and different jurisdictions may render different answers when certain factors are weighed more heavily in one jurisdiction than in others. This has decided the voluntary nature of the employment of filtering algorithms and will greatly hinder the 'takeover' process of filtering algorithms in determining copyright infringements. For the moment, we need to make sure that the filtering mechanisms are carefully designed and useful not just for wealthy platforms and copyright owners but also for users. In China, users are under double scrutiny from copyright and censorship angles. It is therefore crucial for the law to mandate transparency for machine-made decisions to the best we can: the more information we provide to the users, the greater chance we can assuage the concerns of the public about black box decisions and build the trust for future algorithmic decision-makers. Until then, society should monitor algorithm owners' behaviour and provide instant functioning remedies for the concerned users.

Acknowledgement

Earlier versions of this paper were also presented and discussed at the "EUPLANT Agora" which was organized at Tsinghua University in January 2022. The author is grateful to Guobin Cui, Wenwei Guan, Shujie Feng and other participants for their valuable comments and suggestions. The author acknowledge the support of City University of Hong Kong Strategic Research Grant: "Copyright or Copywrong? Piercing the Veil of the Private Copyright Enforcers in Chinese Courts" (7005571/SLW).

Disclosure statement

No potential conflict of interest was reported by the author(s).

Algorithmic bias and the New Chicago School

Jyh-An Lee

ABSTRACT

AI systems are increasingly deployed in both public and private sectors to independently make complicated decisions with far-reaching impact on individuals and the society. However, many AI algorithms are biased in the collection or processing of data, resulting in prejudiced decisions based on demographic features. Algorithmic biases occur because of the training data fed into the AI system or the design of algorithmic models. While most legal scholars propose a direct-regulation approach associated with right of explanation or transparency obligation, this article provides a different picture regarding how indirect regulation can be used to regulate algorithmic bias based on the New Chicago School framework developed by Lawrence Lessig. This article concludes that an effective regulatory approach toward algorithmic bias will be the right mixture of direct and indirect regulations through architecture, norms, market, and the law.

1. Introduction

Advances in artificial intelligence (AI) algorithms have led to unprecedented progress in data analytics and pattern recognition. Today AI systems are increasingly deployed in both public and private sectors to independently make complicated decisions with far-reaching impact on individuals and the society. While these AI algorithms have become an unprecedentedly efficient and effective tool for identification and assessment, many of them are biased in the collection or processing of data, resulting in prejudiced decisions based on demographic features, such as race, ethnicity, gender, religion, and so on. Some scholars claim that the algorithmic biases in various AI applications have become one of the most urgent and important issues faced by contemporary society.[1] Even tech giants taking the lead in global AI development cannot avoid problems of algorithmic bias created

[1]See, e.g. Harry Surden, 'Artificial Intelligence and Law: An Overview' (2019) 35 *Georgia State University Law Review* 1305, 1335.

by their own AI systems. For example, in November 2017, Google Translate produced sexist translation from Turkish into English.[2] The Turkish 'O bir doctor' was translated as '*he* is a doctor', whereas 'O bir hemşire' led to '*she* is a nurse'.[3] However, the single-third person pronoun 'O' in Turkish does not mark for gender.[4] This was because the AI in Google Translate learned from the pattern, including gender and occupations, from billions of bilingual texts on the Internet.[5] Moreover, Amazon discontinued its AI-based recruitment system in late 2018 because the system was found biased against women by giving low ratings to resumes with terms, such as 'women's' in the applications for technical positions.[6] Based on the pattern of a decade's worth of resumes from people applying for jobs at Amazon, the company's recruitment AI algorithm taught itself to favour male, which was the gender of most applicants.[7] These are just a few of many examples of how AI embodies biases that have significantly affected our society.

While bias is not a new problem in human society, the deployment of AI in crucial decision making magnifies pre-existing bias or even creates new types of it. In recent years, AI algorithms have been widely deployed to determine the allocation of various resources, such as finance, recruitment, and admissions to educational institutes. When important societal processes such as voting, policing, and sentencing, become increasingly AI-based, these biases are not only technical and social problems, but also legal ones. If technologies in effect displace the values in laws, such as fairness and anti-discrimination, lawmakers need to decide whether and how to reclaim the values displaced.

This article uses Lawrence Lessig's theories of 'code is law' and 'new Chicago School' to understand the ongoing debate concerning AI bias and the dynamic factors reducing or reinforcing algorithmic bias. Part 2 of the article explains how biases are generated by AI algorithms. Algorithms' biases occur because of the inadequate quality and quantity of data, the existing bias in current social structure, or the model design of the algorithms. Part 3 analyses factors that affect algorithmic bias based on the New Chicago School framework of architecture, norms, and market developed by Lessig. Part 4 examines how the law can regulate algorithmic bias through direct regulation and indirectly by regulating architecture, norm,

[2] Nikhil Sonnad, 'Google Translate's Gender Bias Pairs 'He' with 'Hardworking' and 'She' with Lazy, and Other Examples' (*Quartz*, 30 November 2017), https://qz.com/1141122/google-translates-gender-bias-pairs-he-with-hardworking-and-she-with-lazy-and-other-examples/?mc_cid=f851a23312&mc_eid=aac87b70fb.

[3] Ibid.

[4] Ibid.

[5] Ibid.

[6] Jeffrey Destin, 'Amazon Scraps Secret AI Recruiting Tool That Showed Bias Against Women' (*Reuters*, 10 October 2018), www.reuters.com/article/uk-amazon-com-jobs-automation-insight/amazon-scraps-secret-ai-recruiting-tool-that-showed-bias-against-women-idUKKCN1MK08K?edition-redirect=uk.

[7] Ibid.

and market. With this analytical framework, this article argues that current literature in law focuses too much on the legal obligation of transparency and explainability. It fails to provide a holistic viewpoint that includes indirect regulation through the other three modalities of regulation. Given the inherit limitation of the legal obligation in transparency and explainability, policymakers should take a multifaceted legislative approach to algorithmic bias. Part 5 concludes.

2. Bias generated by AI algorithms

Algorithmic biases might originate from the quality of data used to train the AI system, the type of machine-learning method chosen, and the design of the algorithms.[8] A selection bias occurs when the input data does not accurately represent the population or context being analysed.[9] From a statistical viewpoint, the training dataset fails to represent a random sample from the population.[10] This problem exists especially when certain datasets are easier to access for the AI systems but they are not produced based on rigorous statistical standards.[11] This kind of bias is well illustrated in Amazon's recruitment AI algorithm mentioned above, which failed to incorporate sufficient female applicants' data. It has been reported that Apple credit card approval process and the decision of its credit line exhibited similar biased outcomes against female applicants.[12]

Bias also occurs when AI algorithms learn from the data that reflect existing structural inequalities in the society.[13] The outcome from these algorithms will then reinforce undesirable biases and stereotypes.[14] Even if the AI algorithm is not designed to consider sensitive characteristics, such as gender and race, some other correlated features may be used as proxies, which lead to similar biases.[15] Although AI can possibly identify correlations

[8]See, e.g. Boris Babic et al., 'When Machine Learning Goes Off the Rails' (*Harvard Business Review*, January 2021), https://hbr.org/2021/01/when-machine-learning-goes-off-the-rails; Miriam C Buiten, 'Towards Intelligent Regulation of Artificial Intelligence' (2019) 10 *European Journal of Risk Regulation* 41, 51–53; Stefan Feuerriegel et al., 'Fair AI: Challenges and Opportunities' (2020) 62(4) *Business & Information Systems Engineering* 379, 381.

[9]See, e.g. Akter et al., 'Algorithmic Bias in Data-Driven Innovation in the Age of AI' (2021) 60 *International Journal of Information Management* 1, 1; Buiten (n 8) 51; Bernhard Waltl, 'Explainability and Transparency of Machine Learning in ADM Systems' in Roland Vogl (ed), *Research Handbook on Big Data Law* (Edward Elgar, 2021) 350.

[10]See, e.g. Akter et al. (n 9) 5.

[11]Eirini Ntoutsi et al., 'Bias in Data-Driven Artificial Intelligence Systems—An Introductory Survey' (2020) 10(3) *WIREs Data Mining & Knowledge Discovery* 1, at 4.

[12]Subrat Patnaik, 'Apple Co-founder Says Apple Card Algorithm Gave Wife Lower Credit Limit' (*Reuters*, 11 November 2019), www.reuters.com/article/us-goldman-sachs-apple-idUSKBN1XL038.

[13]See, e.g. Buiten (n 8) 51–52; Frank Pasquale, *New Laws of Robotics: Defining Human Expertise in the Age of AI* (Harvard University Press 2020) 119; Akter et al. (n 9) 1; Ntoutsi et al. (n 11), 3.

[14]See, e.g. Michael Li, 'Addressing the Biases Plaguing Algorithms' (*Harvard Business Review* 13 May 2019), https://hbr.org/2019/05/addressing-the-biases-plaguing-algorithms.

[15]See, e.g. Buiten (n 8) 53; Waltl (n 9) 342.

between different variables, it cannot recognise causal connections. For example, because neighbourhoods in the United States (U.S.) are sometimes correlated with race, using 'neighborhood of residence' as a proxy when developing an algorithm for a loan decision may lead to racial biases and controversies.

Another common origin for bias is the problematic design of the algorithm, which usually leads to over-generalisation or correlation fallacy.[16] Although AI can identify some patterns from the underlying data, it does not understand social context. A notable example is the commercial prediction algorithm, Optum, which helps U.S. hospitals to identify and help patients with significant health needs. Hospitals and health insurers use Optum to identify high-risk patients by looking at their medical histories and their medical expenses, and to detect who need more resources to manage their health. However, because less money was spent on black patients who have the same level of need as white patients, Optum incorrectly determined that black patients were healthier than equally sick white patients.[17] This bias occurred because Optum did not understand that black patients were more concerned about the rising insurance fee resulting from the medical treatment they received, and therefore health costs from insurance data were not a proper measure for health needs.[18]

3. The New Chicago School approach to algorithmic bias

Lawrence Lessig advocates for the New Chicago School approach by arguing that behaviour is regulated by four types of constraint: architecture, social norms, market, and the law.[19] These four modalities of regulation, or multiplicity of constraint, operate together to shape human behaviour.[20] This part analyses how AI bias is regulated by these modalities of regulation other than the law.

3.1. Architecture

Lessig defines architecture as 'nature' of things, referring to the features of the world made or found by human beings.[21] Architectures regulate behaviours by restricting or enabling them via their nature. In the digital environment, code, including the pervasive software and hardware, is the architecture embedding certain values that regulates

---

[16] See, e.g. Akter et al. (n 9) 8–9.

[17] Ziad Obermeyer et al., 'Dissecting Racial Bias in an Algorithm Used to Manage the Health of Populations' (2019) 366 *Science* 447, 449–451.

[18] Ibid, 452–453.

[19] Lawrence Lessig, 'The New Chicago School' (1998) 27 *Journal of Legal Studies* 661, 662–665.

[20] Ibid, 663.

[21] Lessig (n 19) 666.

behaviour.[22] This is the 'code is law' theory. Algorithmic biases occur because of the selection of data or the design of the algorithms. While these biases lead to discrimination in important social activities, such as hiring, healthcare, insurance, or even criminal justice, the data and algorithms generating these biases present noticeable regulatory power. In this sense, 'code is law' theory provides a proper lens to understand the legal implications of algorithmic biases.

Lessig has cautioned that regulation by code is not as transparent as regulation by law.[23] Users of technology are normally not aware of the fact that their behaviours are constrained by the code.[24] They 'experience these controls as nature'.[25] The danger of such code regulation is that it embodies values that significantly affect our life but is not subject to any public scrutiny. This transparency problem of code regulation becomes more serious in AI algorithms. AI applications sometimes covertly amplify social biases with the pretence of objectivity.[26] However, humans can hardly understand AI's decision-making process and predict its outcome.[27] This 'black box' in machine-learning algorithms is inscrutable even for domain experts, especially algorithms incorporating deep-learning or neural-network approaches.[28] Consequently, this opacity obfuscates the discovery of how biases are generated during the operation of AI algorithms.[29] When AI systems are making critical decisions in society, the incompatibility between its black-box nature and the value of due process in modern democracies becomes salient.[30]

To address the 'black box' problem in machine learning, a very common proposal is to push toward more transparency or to implement the principle of explainable AI (XAI) in algorithmic design, a suite of machine-learning techniques that produces more explainable models for humans to understand.[31] XAI allows users to check whether the algorithmic decisions are

---

[22] Lawrence Lessig, 'The Law of the Horse: What Cyberlaw Might Teach' (1999) 113 *Harvard Law Review* 501, 509.

[23] Lawrence Lessig, *Code Version 2.0* (Basic Books, 2006) 138.

[24] See, e.g. Jyh-An Lee and Ching-Yi Liu, 'Forbidden City Enclosed by the Great Firewall: The Law and Power of Internet Filtering in China' (2012) 13 *Minnesota Journal of Law, Science & Technology* 125, 138.

[25] Lessig (n 23) 138; Lessig (n 22) 535, 541.

[26] Karl Manheim and Lyric Kaplan, 'Artificial Intelligence: Risks to Privacy and Democracy' (2019) 21 *Yale Journal of Law & Technology* 106, 111.

[27] Yavar Bathaee, 'The Artificial Intelligence Black Box and the Failure of Intent and Causation' (2018) 31 *Harvard Journal of Law & Technology* 889, 905; Manheim and Kaplan (n 26) 111; Meg Leta Jones and Elizabeth Edenberg, 'Troubleshooting AI and Consent' in Markus D. Dubber et al. (eds) *The Oxford Handbook of Ethics of AI* (Oxford University Press, 2020) 367.

[28] Arun Rai, 'Explainable AI: From Black Box to Glass Box' (2020) 48 *Journal of the Academy of Marketing Science* 137, 137; Waltl (n 9) 344.

[29] Rai (n 28) 137.

[30] Manheim and Kaplan (n 26) 157.

[31] See, e.g. Amina Adadi and Mohammed Berrada, 'Peeking Inside the Black-Box: A Survey on Explainable Artificial Intelligence (XAI)' (2018) 6 *IEEE Access* 52138; Alejandro Barredo Arrieta et al., 'Explainable Artificial Intelligence (XAI): Concepts, Taxonomies, Opportunities and Challenges Toward Responsible AI' (2020) 58 *Information Fusion* 82, 83.

fair and unbiased[32] by creating the visibility of how an AI system makes decisions and predictions and the possibility to detect flaws in training data and architecture of the algorithms.[33]

However, the principle of XAI cannot be easily adopted in all types of AI algorithms. With their nested non-linear structure, deep-learning or neural network algorithms normally need to sacrifice transparency and interpretability for prediction accuracy.[34] That is because neural network algorithms are ordinarily not programmed with specific rules that define predictions from the input.[35] These algorithms can automatically find relevant criteria and their decision structures therefore cannot be evaluated.[36] While such machine learning can relieve programmers from writing complicated instructions for computers, its identification of subtle relationships in data might be beyond human's understanding.[37] Explainabilty would then lead to inaccuracy in these deep learning algorithms.[38] Some scholars even argue that a black box model with supra-human accuracy should be compulsory in certain medical fields,[39] rather than being forced to become explainable. Some studies have shown that while it is not technically or economically possible to require ex ante interpretability from deep neural networks, it is often possible for their developers to identify ex post input variables that lead to specific outcomes.[40] However, from a technical viewpoint, the trade-off between explainability and accuracy is always a difficult choice.[41] Therefore, while XAI principle may help decrease algorithmic biases, it is still technically challenging to balance the transparency and accuracy of certain AI algorithms.

Moreover, as mentioned above, a large portion of AI biases result from incomprehensive datasets fed to the learning algorithms. Therefore, data is a major part of the architecture to ensure fair decision making in the AI systems. The fundamental way to solve the problem arising from data is to produce a 'balanced dataset' so that discrimination in the algorithmic outcome can be avoided.[42] AI developers should avoid features such as

[32]Philipp Hacker et al., 'Explainable AI under Contract and Tort Law: Legal Incentives and Technical Challenges' (2020) 28 *Artificial Intelligence and Law* 415, 429.
[33]Ibid, 429.
[34]See, e.g. Babic et al. (n 8); Heike Felzmann et al., 'Transparency You Can Trust: Transparency Requirements for Artificial Intelligence Between Legal Norms and Contextual Concerns' (2019) *Big Data & Society*, https://doi.org/10.1177/2053951719860542; Rai (n 28) 138.
[35]See, e.g. Buiten (n 8) 50.
[36]See, e.g. Waltl (n 9) 344.
[37]Andrew D. Selbst and Solon Barocas, 'The Intuitive Appeal of Explainable Machines' (2018) 87 *Fordham Law Review* 1085, 1094.
[38]See, e.g. Buiten (n 8) 58; Hacker et al. (n 32) 422.
[39]Hacker et al. (n 32) 423.
[40]Ibid, 417.
[41]Selbst and Barocas (n 37) 1110–1111.
[42]Ntoutsi et al. (n 11) 3.

race, gender or religious affiliation, and other attributes that are highly correlated with these sensitive features.

3.2. Norms

There has been rapid development in norms concerning AI ethics. To address the problem of AI bias, there has been a movement in both professional communities and the business sector promoting fairness, accountability, explainability, and transparency in machine learning.[43] The Institute of Electrical and Electronics Engineers (IEEE) published a study, *Ethically Aligned Design,* in which a number of principles, such as human rights, transparency, and accountability, were listed to address the problem of bias generated by AI algorithms.[44] High tech giants, such as Google,[45] IBM,[46] and Microsoft,[47] also released similar AI ethical principles. Several government agencies have published ethics guidelines for more neutral applications of AI as well. For example, the European Commission (EC) published *Ethics Guidelines for Trustworthy AI* in 2019.[48] In October 2020, the European Parliament endorsed the Framework of Ethical Aspects of Artificial Intelligence, Robotics and Related Technologies.[49] The Monetary Authority of Singapore released ethical principles concerning AI and data analytics in the financial sector.[50] The Canadian government also announced major principles in deploying AI in the public sector.[51]

While the above-mentioned AI principles have drawn wide attention from both academia and industries, they have been criticised for being too imprecise, vague abstract, and non-binding.[52] Some research even suggests that the effectiveness of these AI ethical codes is almost zero.[53] Therefore,

---

[43]See, e.g. Pasquale (n 13) 120.

[44]IEEE, *Ethically Aligned Design* (2019) 18–35, https://standards.ieee.org/content/dam/ieee-standards/standards/web/documents/other/ead1e.pdf?utm_medium=undefined&utm_source=undefined&utm_campaign=undefined&utm_content=undefined&utm_term=undefined.

[45]Google, *Artificial Intelligence at Google*, https://ai.google/principles/.

[46]IBM, *AI Ethics*, www.ibm.com/cloud/learn/ai-ethics.

[47]Microsoft, Responsible AI, www.microsoft.com/en-us/ai/responsible-ai?activetab=pivot1:primaryr6.

[48]European Commission, Directorate-General for Communications Networks, Content and Technology, *Ethics guidelines for trustworthy AI*, Publications Office, 2019, https://data.europa.eu/doi/10.2759/177365.

[49]European Parliament, Framework of Ethical Aspects of Artificial Intelligence, Robotics and Related Technologies (20 October 2020), www.europarl.europa.eu/doceo/document/TA-9-2020-0275_EN.html.

[50]Monetary Authority of Singapore, 'Principles to Promote FEAT in the Use of AI and Data Analytics in Singapore's Financial Sector' (2018), www.mas.gov.sg/~/media/MAS/News%20and%20Publications/Monographs%20and%20Information%20Papers/FEAT%20Principles%20Final.pdf.

[51]Government of Canada, 'Responsible Use of Artificial Intelligence (AI)' (12 October 2021), www.canada.ca/en/government/system/digital-government/digital-government-innovations/responsible-use-ai.html.

[52]See, e.g. Inga Strümke et al., 'The Social Dilemma in Artificial Intelligence Development and Why We Have to Solve It', (2021) *AI & Ethics*, https://doi.org/10.1007/s43681-021-00120-w.

[53]Thilo Hagendorff, 'The Ethics of AI Ethics: An Evaluation of Guidelines' (2020) 30 *Minds & Machines* 99, 108.

commentators regard these principles 'toothless'[54] and IEEE has called for clearer legal standards to implement these principles, especially those concerning accountability of algorithmic bias.[55] Compared to the law, norms suffer the disadvantage that they are less clear in terms of boundary and liability.[56] Moreover, an obvious limitation for business norms promoting AI ethics is that companies will not promote norms that benefit the society but put them at a disadvantage compared to their competitors.[57] It is not surprising that some companies use these AI principles for public relations purposes[58] whereas others may even manipulate these principles for their own profit concerns.[59] After all, the norm supreme above all others in the business sector is to maximise shareholder's value or profit.[60] Where companies strive to deploy AI systems, their reasons are also profit-based.[61] Therefore, norms concerning AI ethical principles are not entirely effective in eliminating undesirable algorithmic biases.

3.3. Market

The market is the main driving force for businesses to develop and use AI. It also affects how businesses approach algorithmic biases. There are different market forces shaping business activities. Firms have incentives to strategically manipulate the algorithmic decision-making process if doing so entails more profit generation.[62] Some social media platforms use algorithmic biases to lock in their users or even manipulate their psychology and behaviour. In this sense, the market is encouraging the production of algorithmic bias.

Nevertheless, market forces driving for more ethical use of AI also develop rapidly. According to Capgemini Research Institute's 2019 survey of 4,400 consumers across six countries, sixty-two percentage indicated that they would place higher trust in a company whose AI interactions they perceived as ethical.[63] Around sixty percentage of the consumers suggested that they would be more loyal to the company and share their positive experience

---

[54] Anaïs Rességuier and Rowena Rodrigues, 'AI Ethics Should Not Remain Toothless! A Call to Bring Back the Teeth of Ethics' (2020) 7(2) *Big Data & Society*, https://doi.org/10.1177/2053951720942541.
[55] IEEE (n 44) 19, 29, 40, 103.
[56] Jacqueline D Lipton, 'What Blogging Might Teach About Cybernorms' (2010) 4 *Akron Intellectual Property Journal* 1, 6.
[57] See, e.g. Strümke et al. (n 52).
[58] Hagendorff (n 53) 108.
[59] See, e.g. Rességuier and Rodrigues (n 54).
[60] See, e.g. Mark J. Roe, 'Political Preconditions to Separating Ownership from Corporate Control' (2000) 53 *Stanford Law Review* 539, 554–555.
[61] Hagendorff (n 53) 108.
[62] Selbst and Barocas (n 37) 1093.
[63] Capgemini Research Institute, 'Organizations Must Proactively Address Ethics in AI to Gain the Public's Trust and Loyalty', 5 July 2019, www.capgemini.com/wp-content/uploads/2019/07/2019_07_05_Press-Release_Ethics-in-AI-_EN.pdf.

with friends and family.[64] Based on the finding of this research, companies do have an incentive to develop more ethical AI and avoid possible biases in their algorithms so that they can gain trust from consumers. Furthermore, more start-up companies have developed new business models to provide services to certify AI products and processes free from bias, prejudices, and unfairness.[65] Google also offers AI ethics services assisting its clients to examine multiple dimensions of their AI applications, ranging from the data used to train systems to how these systems work to their impact on society.[66] The demand for such ethical or relevant certification services reveals that market competition can also be a positive force alleviating algorithmic biases.

4. Law

While many have argued that legislation is necessary to reduce algorithmic biases,[67] it has been controversial regarding what is the best legal approach to this issue. Lessig distinguishes the New Chicago School from the old school by arguing that law can not only regulate behaviour directly but also regulate it indirectly by regulating market, architecture, and norms.[68] He contends that modern regulation is a mix of these direct and indirect aspects.[69] This argument provides a novel angle to analyse existing laws and legislative proposals concerning algorithmic bias.

4.1. Direct regulation

The most straightforward way for lawmakers to address the algorithmic bias is to regulate the behaviour of an AI developer or data processor directly. The law may forbid automated decision making and require human intervention. In *State v. Loomis,* the Wisconsin Supreme Court ruled that when deciding on a sentence, a human judge could consider the scores produced by COMPAS, a risk-assessment algorithm developed by a private company.[70] That was because the sentence was still decided by the judge, instead of the AI algorithm.[71] This human intervention rule was later adopted in Article 22(1) of the European General Data Protection Regulation (GDPR), which provides the data subject with right to object to 'a decision based solely on automated processing, including profiling, which produces legal effects

[64]Ibid.
[65]Babic et al. (n 8).
[66]Ibid.
[67]See, e.g. Strümke et al. (n 52).
[68]Lessig (n 19) 666.
[69]Ibid, 666–667.
[70]881 N.W.2d 749 (Wis. 2016).
[71]Ibid, 753.

concerning him or her or similarly significantly affects him or her'.[72] The objection right in GDPR has been transplanted in the recent Chinese Personal Information Protect Law (PIPL), which similarly provides data subjects with the right 'to reject the decision made by the personal information processor only through automatic decision-making'.[73] The objection right in Article 22(1) of GDPR is waivable with the data subject's explicit consent.[74]

A more common legislative approach is to mandate certain information disclosure or transparency concerning the algorithmic process. In the above *State v. Loomis* case, the court rejected Loomis's challenge of using COMPAS in sentencing and explained that according to a *Wired* report, 'knowledge of the algorithm's output was a sufficient level of transparency'.[75] The idea to require transparency in algorithms was stipulated in the GDPR in a more detailed way. Article 13 of the GDPR obliges the data controller to provide the data subject with the 'information necessary to ensure fair and transparent processing', which includes 'meaningful information about the logic involved, as well as the significance and the envisaged consequences of such processing for the data subject' in the case of 'automated decision-making, including profiling'.[76]

When a data controller is exempted from Article 22(1) of GDPR, Article 22(3) requires that the controller 'shall implement suitable measures to safeguard the data subject's rights and freedoms and legitimate interests'. In discussing Article 22(3), Recital 71 of the GDPR states that the safeguards should, inter alia, include 'the right ... to obtain an explanation of the decision reached after such assessment'. However, since the recital is not binding, most scholars agree that it cannot be a legal basis for a right to an explanation.[77] Article 22 together with Recital 71 has affected Article 24 (3) of the recent Chinese PIPL, which likewise provides the data subject with the 'right to request the personal information processor to provide explanation' if he or she believes that 'the automatic decision making has a significant impact on his or her rights and interests'.[78]

Article 15(1)(h) of the GDPR stipulates that in the case of automated processing in the context of Article 22(1), the controller must provide

[72]GDPR, art. 22(1).
[73]PIPL, art. 24(3).
[74]GDPR, art. 22(2).
[75]Jason Tashea, "Courts Are Using AI to Sentence Criminals. That Must Stop Now" (*Wired*, 17 April 2017), www.wired.com/2017/04/courts-using-ai-sentence-criminals-must-stop-now.
[76]GDPR, art. 13(2).
[77]See, e.g. Bryce Goodman and Seth Flaxman, 'European Union Regulations on Algorithmic Decision-making and a Right to Explanation' (2017) 38(3) *AI Magazine* 50, 53–54; Andrew D Selbst and Julia Powles, 'Meaningful Information and the Right to Explanation' (2017) 7(4) *International Data Privacy Law* 233, 235; Sandra Wachter et al., 'Why a Right to Explanation of Automated Decision-making Does Not Exist in the General Data Protection Regulation' (2017) 7(2) *International Data Privacy Law* 76, 79–81.
[78]PIPL, art. 24(3).

'meaningful information about the logic involved'. It has been debated by scholars that whether this information only includes the general structure of the model, explanations about individual decisions, or the weight of each variable.[79]

4.2. Indirect regulation

Indirect regulation means law constrains behaviour through regulating market, code, or norms. In other words, law uses the regulatory power of other modalities of regulation.[80] The New Chicago School views these other modalities as objects of law's regulation.[81] Based on this understanding, the law can regulate algorithmic bias via market, code, and norms.

4.2.1. Law and market

Law can constrain behaviour through the creation of new market demand. To address the problem of algorithmic bias, some propose a new auditing requirement in the law for AI systems to detect potential biases before these systems are used. This requirement can be found in the Algorithmic Accountability Act, which was introduced to the U.S. House of Representatives in 2019.[82] The idea of such proposals is to reduce algorithmic biases through the creation for a new market for AI auditing.

In fact, some scholars have argued that algorithmic audit is the best way to safeguard against bias generated from the automated decision-making.[83] In recent years, some auditing techniques have been developed to successfully identify algorithmic bias across various industries.[84] Although algorithmic audits may be voluntarily conducted by AI development companies or their clients without the law,[85] the law might help to further strengthen the effectiveness of such auditing.

While the GDPR has authorised government authorities to conduct data auditing to combat algorithmic discrimination in opaque AI systems,[86] a more effective auditing approach might be requiring accounting firms or other private accredited professional organisations to conduct the

[79]See, e.g. Gianclaudio Malgieri and Giovanni Comandé, 'Why a Right to Legibility of Automated Decision-making Exists in the General Data Protection Regulation' (2017) 7(6) *International Data Privacy Law* 243, 246–247; Selbst and Powles (n 77) 241; Wachter et al. (n 77) 83.
[80]Lessig (n 19) 666.
[81]Ibid.
[82]H.R.2231 - Algorithmic Accountability Act of 2019, 116th Congress of the United States (2019–2020).
[83]Bryan Casey et al., 'Rethinking Explainable Machines: The GDPR's "Right to Explanation" Debate and the Rise of Algorithmic Audits in Enterprise' (2019) 34 *Berkeley Technology Law Journal* 143, 152, 182.
[84]Casey et al. (n 83) 182.
[85]Wolfgang Hoffmann-Riem, 'Artificial Intelligence as a Challenge for Law and Regulation' in Thomas Wischmeyer and Timo Rademacher (eds) *Regulating Artificial Intelligence* (Springer, 2020) 19.
[86]Chapter 6, GDPR.

algorithmic audit. In that way, the law can promote algorithmic fairness through a new market of algorithmic auditing and the norms emphasising independence in the professional auditing community. The law does not necessarily need to make algorithmic auditing compulsory.[87] Instead, it may choose to encourage such auditing by limiting AI companies' liability or providing them with priority in government procurement projects or other public resources. Although it is still challenging to develop an effective auditing approach for algorithmic audits,[88] using the law to encourage the market to develop more comprehensive auditing techniques can certainly help alleviate the problem of algorithmic bias.

4.2.2. Law and code

The law may use code, or architecture, to bring about a regulatory change.[89] In other words, instead of regulating behaviour directly, the law can choose to regulate how algorithms are designed. GDPR has taken this 'data protection by design' approach in some of its rules.[90] Its Recital 71, according to which processing under Article 22, requires data controllers to 'use appropriate mathematical or statistical procedures for the profiling… and prevent, inter alia, discriminatory effects on natural persons on the basis of racial or ethnic origin, political opinion, religion or beliefs, trade union membership, genetic or health status or sexual orientation, or processing that results in measures having such an effect'.[91] This provision can be understood as law regulating the code by requiring the later to incorporate 'appropriate mathematical or statistical procedures'.

Another example of law's regulating code concerning AI algorithms is recent EC's proposal of the AI Act, which requires '[h]igh-risk AI systems shall be designed and developed in such a way to ensure that their operation is sufficiently transparent to enable users to interpret the system's output and use it appropriately'.[92] While there might be some controversy regarding to what extent a user can interpret the output from an AI system, this legislative approach aims to regulate behaviour via requiring interpretability in AI algorithmic design.

[87] Hoffmann-Riem (n 85) 19.
[88] Adriano Joshiyama et al., 'Towards Algorithm Auditing: A Survey on Managing Legal, Ethical and Technological Risks of AI, ML and Associated Algorithms', 15 February 2021, https://papers.ssrn.com/sol3/papers.cfm?abstract_id=3778998.
[89] Lessig (n 22) 512.
[90] Casey et al. (n 83) 179–183.
[91] GDPR, Recital 71.
[92] European Commission, Proposal for a Regulation of the European Parliament and of the Council, Laying Down Harmonised Rules on Artificial Intelligence (Artificial Intelligence Act) and Amending Certain Union Legislative Acts, 21 April 2021, art. 13(1), https://eur-lex.europa.eu/legal-content/EN/TXT/HTML/?uri=CELEX:52021PC0206&from=EN.

4.2.3. Law and norms

The relation between norms and law has been a major focus of the New Chicago School.[93] Although both business sectors and governments have advocated for principles regarding AI ethics, their motives for doing so are quite different. Businesses express their support for ethical AI development because they want to gain trust from their customers. Some even believe that by embracing AI ethical guidelines, AI companies are delivering a message to the policymakers that no legislation is needed in this area.[94]

Policymakers can incorporate non-legal norms to encourage or discourage certain behaviours.[95] As mentioned above, several government agencies have promoted norms based on ethical AI principles. In addition to stimulating the social awareness of algorithmic bias, these government initiatives are a foundation for the society to discuss the necessity and substance of future legislation. A noteworthy example is the European Union (EU)'s approach to AI legislation. Since the High-Level Expert Group set up by the EC first issued the *Ethics Guidelines for Trustworthy AI* in 2019,[96] the EU has published a series of principles associated with AI ethics,[97] which all become the basis of the EC's legislative proposal for a regulation on Artificial Intelligence, the so-called 'Artificial Intelligence Act' or 'AI Act', in April 2021.[98] This development illustrates how norms are codified in the law if they are able to penetrate into the consciousness of a large portion of the population,[99] and how governments promote social norms to build social consensus for future legislation.

Social norms are usually enforced through the social structure of a community where an individual lives,[100] and law can indirectly regulate behaviour through supporting this structure.[101] Given the pervasive deployment of AI and the increasingly critical bias problem, a plausible proposal is to use the law to establish professional societies for AI developers. The law can require all AI developers to join the society, and unethical behaviour could lead to disqualification from it.[102] One advantage of this proposal is that a professional society has more power than individual AI developers in insisting on AI principles against the employer's commercial interests. Furthermore, compared to the government or companies, a professional society can develop and enforce the AI ethics code through the pride of a

---

[93]See, e.g. Mark Tushnet, 'Everything Old Is New Again: Early Reflections on the "New Chicago School"' (1998) 1998 *Wisconsin Law Review* 579, 579.
[94]Hagendorff (n 53) 100.
[95]Tushnet (n 93) 581.
[96]European Commission (n 48).
[97]Part 3.2 of this article.
[98]European Commission (n 92).
[99]See, e.g. Cass R. Sunstein, 'Social Norms and Social Roles' (1996) 96 *Columbia Law Review* 903, 915.
[100]Lessig (n 19) 662; Lipton (n 56) 6.
[101]Ibid. at 669.
[102]Strümke et al. (n 52).

profession. The law can also mandate or encourage certification of AI ethics compliance developed by professional organisations, such as IEEE or International Organization for Standardization. With the support of the law, the community of professional AI developers can better work collectively toward more ethical AI development.

Law can also reinforce ethical AI applications through organisational structure and culture. Some commentators argue that companies' internal governance has failed to assure the fairness of AI decision making.[103] To address algorithmic bias and other relevant AI ethical issues, some companies have introduced AI ethics committees as an internal governance framework to examine how they design and implement AI systems.[104] Although these initiatives are profit-oriented with the view to mitigate business risks,[105] this is a positive development for more ethical and fair use of AI. The idea of an AI ethics committee comes from the legal requirement of the committee-based oversight for all research involving humans and vertebrate animals, which might lead to ethical concerns.[106] Currently, there has been no consensus on the composition of the committee, the scope of its review, and the level in the company. However, once more companies establish similiar committees in their organisations, the law might reinforce such ethics monitoring mechanism by making the committee a mandatory part of the corporate organisation.

The legal evolution of independent directors provides a good example for a possible future of AI ethics committees. Independent directors were viewed as a 'good governance' exhortation, which companies could adopt on a voluntary basis in the United States.[107] Companies had started to have more incentives to include independent directors in their boards since the Delaware courts applied the lenient 'business judgment rule' to board action undertaken by independent directors.[108] Gradually, independent directors have become a mandatory element of company and securities law, especially for public-listed companies.[109] The development of the independent director mechanism provides an insightful lesson for AI ethics committee. Policymakers may provide enterprises with some incentives for the

---

[103]Feuerriegel et al. (n 8) 383.

[104]See, e.g. Zara Stone, 'The Artificial Intelligence Ethics Committee' (*Forbes* 11 June 2018), www.forbes.com/sites/zarastone/2018/06/11/the-artificial-intelligence-ethics-committee/?sh=375a0baf1637; Steven Tiell, 'Create an Ethics Committee to Keep Your AI Initiative in Check'(*Harvard Business Review* November 2019), https://hbr.org/2019/11/create-an-ethics-committee-to-keep-your-ai-initiative-in-check.

[105]Tiell (n 104).

[106]Accenture and Northeastern University Ethics Institute, *Building Data and AI Ethics Committees* (2019) 7, www.accenture.com/_acnmedia/PDF-107/Accenture-AI-And-Data-Ethics-Committee-Report-11.pdf#zoom=50.

[107]Jeffrey Gordon, 'The Rise of Independent Directors in the United States, 1950-2005: Of Shareholder Value and Stock Market Prices' (2007) 59 *Stanford Law Review* 1465, 1468.

[108]Ibid.

[109]Ibid.

voluntary adoption of AI ethics committees, such as the reduction of legal liability for companies involved in litigation associated with AI ethics dispute or priorities in government's AI systems procurement. Once a critical mass of AI companies has instituted such an organisation design, the legislature can consider making it a compulsory governance mechanism under some circumstances.

4.3. Information disclosure and algorithmic bias

Most current laws and legislative proposals regulate algorithmic bias through different levels of information disclosure requirement. All direct and indirect regulations of algorithmic biases described above aim to provide more transparency or information about the automated decision-making process. Although the legal requirement of transparency and information disclosure will not directly eliminate algorithmic biases, they can certainly enhance the trustworthiness of AI systems and provide stakeholders with more opportunities to evaluate the validity and justifiability of the automated decision making.[110]

However, from a technical perspective, there are different possible explanations of transparency in AI systems.[111] From a legal viewpoint, there has been no consensus regarding what information should be disclosed, to what extent it should be disclosed, and how it should be disclosed required by the law.[112] Take the GDPR for example, scholars are still debating whether there is a right of explanation for data subject and whether the law requires an ex ante explanation of how the system functions, the so-called 'prospective transparency',[113] or an ex post explanation of each individual automated decision,[114] the so-called 'retrospective transparency'.[115] This article does not intend to join the legal debate regarding transparency, explainability, or interpretability. Instead, it aims to identify the key technical and legal challenges for using transparency as a major liability mechanism in regulating algorithmic biases.[116]

Scholars have argued that algorithms without explainability or transparency should be prohibited from making important decisions, such as credit rating.[117] If the policy goal is to avoid algorithmic biases, the

[110]Felzmann et al. (n 34).
[111]Nicholas Diakopoulos, 'Transparency' in Markus D. Dubber et al. (eds.), *The Oxford Handbook of Ethics of AI* (Oxford University Press, 2020) 200.
[112]See, e.g. Buiten (n 8) 45.
[113]Felzmann et al. (n 34).
[114]Maja Brkan, 'Do Algorithms Rule the World? Algorithmic Decision-Making and Data Protection in the Framework of the GDPR and Beyond' 27(2) *International Journal of Law and Information Technology* 91, 110–111; Selbst and Barocas (n 37) 1107–1108, 1122–1123.
[115]Felzmann et al. (n 34).
[116]Felzmann et al. (n 34).
[117]Waltl (n 9) 344.

transparency or disclosure requirement should allow stakeholders to trace back the factors or variables that lead to certain outcomes in the decisions.[118] In other words, stakeholders should be able to understand how changing a certain factor would affect the final decision. However, a legal requirement for algorithmic transparency is not a panacea to the issue arising from AI's 'black box' approach. While the costs in making training and testing data transparent might be acceptable to AI companies, transparency in AI's decision-making process is sometimes economically and technically infeasible for them. In addition to the technical dilemma between AI's accuracy and explainability, the law needs to consider whether individual users can really understand the legally required explanation. Stakeholders normally fail to understand how an algorithm makes certain decisions even if its source code is made available.[119]

Furthermore, although information disclosure or transparency can help stakeholders to identify possible algorithmic biases, this individual remedy is not a perfect solution. Transparency in algorithms will not necessarily lead to the knowledge about whether and how biases are generated from them.[120] Individual users may lack the capability to understand the complicated process in the AI systems even if they are provided with relevant information.

Moreover, with the logic and model processing details underlying the AI systems at hand, individual users may still fail to see the possible bias without a bird's eye view at the statistical scale.[121] However, legislators need to consider that one of the positive outcomes of legally required explanation is that it may eventually increase digital literacy of the public.[122] In other words, the law may help individual users to understand more about algorithmic decision-making processes and underlying variables as a result of adopting a reasonable scope of explanation or information disclosure obligation. This education function will partly help to resolve the algorithmic bias problem.

Imposing a transparency requirement on AI algorithms may create a tension within the legal system. Source code of computer programmes and other relevant information are trade secrets or confidential information in most jurisdictions. Therefore, disclosure of the algorithmic model and logic means the software proprietor needs to give up its trade secret over algorithms.[123] Policymakers need to consider to what extent that trade secret protection should compromise with policy concerns of transparency in algorithms.

While transparency in AI algorithms is desirable for stakeholders to understand whether and how biases come from, imposing a wild legal

---

[118]See, e.g. Felzmann et al. (n 34).
[119]See, e.g. Buiten (n 8) 54; Selbst and Barocas (n 37) 1094.
[120]Selbst and Barocas (n 37) 1094.
[121]Casey at el. (n 83) 181.
[122]Jones and Edenberg (n 27) 368.
[123]See, e.g. Diakopoulos (n 111) 200; Selbst and Barocas (n 37) 1092–1093.

requirement of transparency is certainly not a smart move. When considering such a requirement, legislators should contemplate what kind of transparency is most useful and technically available. If the policy goal is to maintain the fairness of algorithmic decision making, explainability or information disclosure is the means rather than the end.

Given the above-mentioned legal controversies over the definitions of explainability and transparency, policymakers should consider using indirect regulation to foster a more feasible and effective monitoring mechanism for AI algorithms. Through the new auditing market and professional AI developer societies introduced previously, a more practical code for AI governance can be possibly developed through private ordering. The law does not need to intervene in this unclear water with every detail. The successful development and wide application of the generally accepted accounting principles (GAAP) is such an example, where government can rely on this professional guideline developed through the collective action of professional bodies.

5. Conclusion

Biases have been part of human society for a long time and we can never eliminate them with the law and other modalities of regulation. With AI systems increasingly making various critical decisions in our society, algorithmic bias has been an important social and legal issue. Most current literature addressing the problem of algorithmic bias focuses on the direct regulation associated with users' right of explanation and AI operators' transparency obligation. Recognising the significance of this direct regulation, this article identifies the limitations of this approach and provides a different picture of regulating AI bias via code, norms, and market. The understanding of the interactions between these modalities will help policymakers ponder what is the best regulatory strategy against the fast-changing AI technologies and the subsequent bias problem. This article concludes that an effective regulatory approach toward algorithmic bias will be the right mixture of these modalities.

Acknowledgments

The author is grateful to Roger Brownsword, David Donald, and Tianxiang He for their insightful comments and suggestions. This article has also benefited from feedback provided in the Law, Technology, and Disruption Conference held by the City University of Hong Kong School of Law, and Technology and the Evolution of Law Seminar held by the Chinese University of Hong Kong Faculty of Law. The author also thanks Yangzi Li and Jingwen Liu for their research assistance.

Disclosure statement

No potential conflict of interest was reported by the author(s).

OPEN ACCESS

Intellectual property in digital agriculture

Anselm Kamperman Sanders

ABSTRACT
This article seeks to address the impact of digitisation of the agricultural market in assessing the market definitions in the context of potential harm to competition in this sector. In doing so, the emphasis will be on the role of trust, frontier technologies, and intellectual property in this market and the article asks the question how the transfer, processing, and analytics of data can be made broadly accessible to all stakeholders, while assessing regulation on the basis of competition law and the law against unfair competition.

1. Introduction

The 2021 *Compendium of Approaches to Improving Competition in Digital Markets*[1] collates the input of competition authorities of the G7[2] and invited guests,[3] and provides an overview of how different authorities are working to promote competition in digital markets. Frontier technologies play a key role in digital markets, where the use of data and the role of algorithms raise concerns about the exercise of market power in multisided markets,[4] where economic factors on one side of the business may be influenced by the conditions of competition on the other. This also allows companies at different levels of the supply chain to make vertical agreements. These markets are dominated by digital platforms in *inter alia* digital

[1]G7 United Kingdom 2021, *Compendium of Approaches to Improving Competition in Digital Markets* (29 November 2021). Available at https://www.gov.uk/government/publications/compendium-of-approaches-to-improving-competition-in-digital-markets.

[2]Canada, France, Germany, Italy, Japan, the United Kingdom and the United States, as well as the European Union.

[3]The UK invited Australia, India, South Africa and South Korea as guests.

[4]For a description of algorithms and dominance, see A. Kamperman Sanders, 'Competition and IP Policy for AI—Socio-economic Aspects of Innovation', in R. Hilti et al. (eds.) *Artificial Intelligence and Intellectual Property* (Clarendon Press, 2020).

advertising, app stores, and online marketplaces. Digital platform providers may thus offer free services provided to consumers that are subsidised by revenues earned by charging advertisers.[5] This market power translates in possibilities for data aggregation as a barrier to entry, self-preferencing, parity obligations (MFNs),[6] non-competes, information exchange or price fixing, abuse of superior bargaining position, and other conduct.[7] In these markets data is the key driver to compete and innovate, and the inability to access data thus becomes a barrier to entry into the digital economy.

One of the findings of the *Compendium* is that the existing enforcement by competition authorities of digital markets is challenging, as the effects in the market may be different from the price effects occurring in traditional markets and may require new theories of harm. Early attempts to address this issue are visible in the 10th Amendment to the German Competition Act (Gesetz gegen Wettbewerbsbeschänkungen, or GWB- Digitalisierungsgesetz), which created[8] new competences for the German Competition Authority (Bundeskartellamt) in the context of digital markets.[9] The new provisions[10] deal with digitisation and explicitly include the access to data relevant to competition as a factor for the assessment of a position of dominance and possibilities for abuse. Section 18(3)(2) dealing with market dominance adds 'access to data relevant to competition' on a par with the criterion of financial strength an undertaking can leverage. Similarly, Sections 18(3a) and 18(3b) GWB-Digitalisierungsgesetz[11] consider for the

[5]See in this regard the European Commission's Decision of 20 March 2019 no. 40111 in Case AT.39740 *Google Search (Shopping)*, available at https://ec.europa.eu/competition/elojade/isef/case_details.cfm?proc_code=1_39740; as well as that of the French Autorité de la Concurrence, Decision of 7 June 2021 no. 21-D-11, available in English at https://www.autoritedelaconcurrence.fr/en/decision/regarding-practices-implemented-online-advertising-sector .

[6]In this case platforms require that suppliers do not offer prices lower or terms better on other platforms or on their own websites. One needs to distinguish between 'narrow' and 'wide' parity clauses. 'Wide' clauses prevent a supplier from offering better terms elsewhere, while 'narrow' clauses prohibit a supplier to make better offers on its own website. See German Federal Court of Justice 18 May 2021, KVR 54/20 Booking.com's 'narrow price parity clauses', available in English translation at https://www.bundeskartellamt.de/SharedDocs/Meldung/DE/AktuelleMeldungen/2021/15_06_2021_Federal_Court_Booking.com.html; and C. Bergqvist, 'Discrimination and Self-favouring in the Digital Economy' (2020), paper presented at *The Challenges of Regulating and Enforcing Competition Law*, Bucharest 14–15 of November 2019.

[7](n 1), at 5–6.

[8]The '10. GWB-Novelle' entered into force on 19 January 2021, and incorporated the implementation of the ECN+ Directive (EU) 2019/1 of the European Parliament and of the Council of 11 December 2018 to empower the competition authorities of the Member States to be more effective enforcers and to ensure the proper functioning of the internal market, *OJ* L 11, 14.1.2019, p. 3–33.

[9]For a description of these new competences and definition of harm, see A. Kamperman Sanders, 'Data and Technology Transfer: Competition Law in the Fourth Industrial Revolution', in C. Heath, A. Kamperman Sanders & A. Moerland (eds.), *Intellectual Property and the Fourth Industrial Revolution* (Kluwer International, 2020), pp. 199–220.

[10]Entwurf eines Zehnten Gesetzes zur Änderung des Gesetzes gegen Wettbewerbsbeschränkungen für ein fokussiertes, proaktives und digitales Wettbewerbsrecht 4.0 (GWB-Digitalisierungsgesetz), available at https://www.d-kart.de/wp-content/uploads/2019/10/GWB-Digitalisierungsgesetz-Fassung-Ressortabstimmung.pdf.

[11]GWB-Digitalisierungsgesetz §18(3)(b) When assessing the market position of an undertaking acting as an intermediary on multi-sided markets, account should be taken in particular of the importance of the intermediary services it provides for access to supply and sales markets.

assessment of dominance whether undertakings can influence in multi-sided markets and networks,[12] and whether an undertaking is acting as intermediary in multi-sided markets. Furthermore, the (refusal to) supply of products or services may be abusive in the context of Section 19(4) GWB-Digitalisierungsgesetz, including 'access to data, networks or other infrastructure, the supply of which is objectively necessary in order to operate on an upstream or downstream market and the refusal to supply threatens to eliminate effective competition on that market.' Finally, a new provision in the form of Section 19a is foreseen to deal with 'Abusive Conduct of Undertakings with paramount significance for competition across markets'.[13]

Based on the new competences, the Bundeskartellamt initiated proceedings against Facebook,[14] Amazon, Google and Apple to determine whether

---

[12]GWB-Digitalisierungsgesetz §20 Prohibited Conduct of Undertakings with Relative or Superior Market Power

(3a) An unfair impediment [...] shall also be deemed to exist where an undertaking with superior market power on a market within the meaning of Section 18(3a) impedes competitors' independent attainment of positive network effects and thereby creates a serious risk of a considerable restriction of competition on the merits.

[13]GWB-Digitalisierungsgesetz §19a Abusive Conduct of Undertakings of Paramount Significance for Competition across Markets

(1) The Bundeskartellamt may issue a decision declaring that an undertaking which is active to a significant extent on markets within the meaning of Section 18(3a) is of paramount significance for competition across markets. In determining the paramount significance of an undertaking for competition across markets, particular account shall be taken of:
  1. its dominant position on one or more markets;
  2. its financial strength or its access to other resources;
  3. its vertical integration and its activities on otherwise related markets;
  4. its access to data relevant for competition;
  5. the importance of its activities for third parties' access to supply and sales markets and its related influence on third parties' business activities.

(2) In case of a declaratory decision pursuant to subsection 1, the Bundeskartellamt may prohibit such undertakings from
  1. treating the offers of competitors differently from its own offers when providing access to supply and sales markets;
  2. directly or indirectly impeding competitors on a market in which the respective undertaking can rapidly expand its position even without being dominant, provided that the impediment is likely to significantly obstruct the competitive process;
  3. creating or raising barriers to market entry or impeding other undertakings in another way by using data relevant for competition that has been collected from the other side on a dominated market, also in combination with other data relevant for competition from sources beyond the dominated market, or demanding terms and conditions that permit such use;
  4. making the interoperability of products or services or data portability more difficult and thereby impeding competition;
  5. informing other companies insufficiently about the scope, the quality or the success of the performance they provide or commission, or making it difficult in other ways for them to assess the value of this performance. This shall not apply where the conduct in question is objectively justified. In this respect, the burden of presenting facts and the burden of proof lie with the undertaking in question [...]

[14]See in this respect also the Bundskartellamt's decision B6-22/16 of 6 February 2019 against Facebook in respect of processing of user data, which enjoins Facebook from using terms and conditions by which the platform entitles itself to gather data from numerous sources outside the social network facebook.com without users' freely given consent to combine them with 'on-Facebook' data. Available at https://www.bundeskartellamt.de/SharedDocs/Entscheidung/DE/Entscheidungen/Missbrauchsaufsicht/2019/

the respective undertaking is of 'paramount significance for competition across markets'.[15] Furthermore, the Bundeskartellamt is currently also examining the Google News Showcase service, Google's data processing terms and the linkage between Oculus and the Facebook social network.[16] On 30 December 2021, the Bundeskartellamt found that Alphabet Inc./Google, including all its affiliated companies has an overriding importance for competition across markets within the meaning of Section 19a (1) GWB.[17] This means that based on this decision the Bundeskartellamt can now take action against specific anti-competitive practices by Google. This is not only attributed to the 80% share that Google has in terms of internet search engines, but also to the digital ecosystem Google can use to exert influence over other companies' access to its users and advertising customers (e.g. via Google Search, YouTube, Android, Play Store or its advertising services) and the fact that it can set rules and conditions for other businesses across markets. It is through this ecosystem that Google also has access to data relevant to competition. This decision will give the Bundeskartellamt five years to subject Google to special abuse control set out in Section 19(a)(2) GWB,[18] which will provide more leeway to pursue the investigations into Google's dataprocessing terms[19] and News Showcase Service[20] that are already underway.

The innovations in the German law now serve as a template for reform across the European Union, as well as for the European Commission

B6-22-16.pdf?__blob=publicationFile&v=8 (last accessed 31-12-2021); The German Federal Court of Justice has provisionally endorsed this decision, see https://www.bundesgerichtshof.de/SharedDocs/Pressemitteilungen/DE/2020/2020080.html.

[15]Bundeskartellamt, Press Releases concerning Facebook of 28 January 2021; concerning Amazon of 18 May 2021; concerning Google of 25 May 2021; concerning Apple of 21 June 2021, available at www.bundeskartellamt.de.

[16]Bundeskartellamt, Press Releases concerning Facebook of 28 January 2021; concerning Google of 25 May 2021; concerning Google News Showcase of 4 June 2021, available at https://www.bundeskartellamt.de/SharedDocs/Publikation/DE/Pressemitteilungen/2020/09_12_2020_Facebook_Oculus.pdf?__blob=publicationFile&v=5.

[17]Bundeskartellamt 30 December 2021 Decision B7-61/21, *Alphabet Inc./Google Germany GmbH*, available at https://www.bundeskartellamt.de/SharedDocs/Entscheidung/DE/Entscheidungen/Missbrauchsaufsicht/2021/B7-61-21.pdf?__blob=publicationFile&v=2.

[18]See (n 13) above.

[19]See Bundskartelallamt press release of 25 May 2021 concerning *Google's Data Processing Terms*: 'The Bundeskartellamt will examine whether Google/Alphabet makes the use of services conditional on the users agreeing to the processing of their data without giving them sufficient choice as to whether, how and for what purpose such data are processed (Section 19a(2) no 4a GWB).' Available at https://www.bundeskartellamt.de/SharedDocs/Meldung/EN/Pressemitteilungen/2021/25_05_2021_Google_19a.html;jsessionid=E85730C959D6DA2AABDFF59B6CFCDEE0.2_cid371?nn=3591568.

[20]See Bundskartelallamt press release of 4 June 2021 concerning *Google News Showcase Service*: 'Acting upon a complaint from Corint Media the Bundeskartellamt is now examining in this proceeding whether the announced integration of the Google News Showcase service into Google's general search function is likely to constitute self-preferencing or an impediment to the services offered by competing third parties.' Available at https://www.bundeskartellamt.de/SharedDocs/Meldung/EN/Pressemitteilungen/2021/04_06_2021_Google_Showcase.html;jsessionid=E85730C959D6DA2AABDFF59B6CFCDEE0.2_cid371?nn=3591568.

itself.[21] In particular, we should equate 'competition law' with the abuse of a dominant market position and 'the law against unfair competition' with unfair (anti-competitive) market practices. Whereas European competition law finds its roots in post Second World War ordo-liberalism that justifies state intervention to create a social free market economy, the law against unfair competition is of a more universal nature and is enshrined in the Paris Convention for the Protection of Industrial Property of 1883. Article 10*bis* of the Paris Convention with its general clause stating that: 'Any act of competition contrary to honest practices in industrial or commercial matters constitutes an act of unfair competition', provides the bedrock for the protection of a competitive market, and provides the glue between the laws of intellectual property and monopolies.[22]

This contribution seeks to address the impact of digitisation of the agricultural market in assessing the market definitions in the context of potential harm to competition in this sector.[23] In doing so, the emphasis will be on the role of trust, frontier technologies, and intellectual property in this market and the article asks the question how the transfer, processing, and analytics of data can be made broadly accessible to all stakeholders, while assessing regulation on the basis of competition law and the law against unfair competition.[24]

2. Digital agriculture

The use of frontier technologies in agri-business is transforming the sector to one of the most application-rich environments in terms of the deployment of mobile devices, robotics, drones, satellite imaging, artificial intelligence, and other automated processes. The use of and access to agricultural data in the agri-business sector is relevant to the entire value chain, from agro-

[21] See the EU's Digital Services Act package https://digital-strategy.ec.europa.eu/en/policies/digital-services-act-package.

[22] See in this respect the, to this day, influential treatise by R. Callmann, *The Law of Unfair Competition, Trademarks, and Monopolies* (Clark Boardman Callaghan, 1945), who presented a holistic view on free market regulation covering unfair competition, intellectual property, and anti-trust law. On one of the implications of a holistic approach for common law development see C. Wadlow, 'Rudolf Callmann and the Misappropriation Doctrine in the Common Law of Unfair Competition' (2011) 2 *Intellectual Property Quarterly* 110–153. On the historical link between intellectual property law and the law of unfair competition also see C. McManis and D. Friedman, *Intellectual Property and Unfair Competition in a Nutshell*, 7th edn. (West Publishing, 2012).

[23] See for example I. Graef, 'Market Definition and Market Power in Data: The Case of Online Platforms' (2015) 38 *World Competition* 473–505, available at https://papers.ssrn.com/sol3/papers.cfm?abstract_id=2657732.

[24] For alternative approaches see M. Jouanjean, F. Casalini, L. Wiseman, and E. Gray, *Issues Around Data Governance in the Digital Transformation of Agriculture: The Farmer's Perspective*, OECD Food Agriculture and Fisheries Papers, No. 146, (OECD Publishing, 2020), available at https://doi.org/10.1787/53ecf2ab-en (last accessed 31-12-2021); and S. van Erp, *All good things come to an end, but access remains* (Wolf Legal Publishing, 2021), available at https://papers.ssrn.com/sol3/papers.cfm?abstract_id=3939380, Valedictory Lecture of 23-09-2021 also available at https://www.youtube.com/watch?v=QjFYrrr7nro .

processing to retail, and post-sale traceability of agro-food products.[25] Data-driven expert systems can thus generate operational information on weather, climate, soil, pests, suitable crop varieties, and harvests, but also on facilitation of trade, transaction values, cross-border regulatory issues, logistics, processing, packaging, and sales of processed products.

In some ways, such information is encapsulated in trade marks, geographical indicators, sanitary and phytosanitary standards (SPS), or production and labelling requirements. The collected raw data, however, is not so easily categorised, as this takes place *remotely* by use of weather balloons, drones and satellites, and/or *in situ* by means of sensory devices and Internet of Things (IoT) or Artificial Intelligence of Things (AIoT, or edge computing) connected to farming machinery or placed in or around the farm itself, and/or *sourced* from aggregated and processed data-analytics expert systems comprising surveys, financial, market, sales, or bio-, and geo-environmental information. In all instances information on all matters related to data in agriculture (ag-data) is the driver for these services that are transforming agriculture.

3. Market concentration and issues of trust

For a farmer using machinery that is fitted with sensory devices and using agri-business data services, the sharing of farm data should yield benefits in production, compliance, and sales, but it should also be safe and equitable. The issue of trust in the data transfer transaction[26] thus becomes of the utmost importance,[27] as granting access to farm data to third parties may after all lead to a disclosure of trade secrets.[28] From a governmental perspective, however, such data-driven information systems can be used to deal with societally relevant questions on environmentally sound and sustainable food production, as well as the monitoring of regulatory standards. Farmers therefore may feel the impact of much more direct government intervention, both sectoral, but even at farm level. For a platform service aggregator, the ability to acquire, process and analyze data offers possibilities of delivering

[25]See in this respect also the Directive (EU) 2019/633 of the European Parliament and of the Council of 17 April 2019 on unfair trading practices in business-to-business relationships in the agricultural and food supply chain, (2019) OJ, L 111/59, available at https://eur-lex.europa.eu/legal-content/EN/TXT/PDF/?uri=CELEX:32019L0633&from=en.

[26]On the importance of trust in the fourth industrial revolution see A. Kamperman Sanders, 'Incentives and Obstacles to Innovation', in D. Prévost, I. Alexcovicová and J. Hillebrand Pohl (eds.), *Restoring Trust in Trade – Liber Amicorum for Peter van den Bossche* (Hart Publishing, 2019) 199–218.

[27]S. van der Burg, L. Wiseman, and J. Krkeljas, 'Trust in Farm Data Sharing: Reflections on the EU Code of Conduct for Agricultural Data Sharing' (2021) 23 *Ethics and Information Technology* 185–198, available at https://doi.org/10.1007/s10676-020-09543-1.

[28]For an overview of the protection of trade secrets in the EU, USA, and a number of Asian jurisdictions, see C. Heath and A. Kamperman Sanders (eds.), *Employees, Trade Secrets and Restrictive Covenants* (Kluwer Law International, 2017).

personalised services to farmers, but also to leverage market power across entire sectoral fields.

The *EU Code of Conduct on Agricultural Data Sharing by Contractual Agreement*[29] by Copa-Cogeca[30] is the farmers branch organisation's own response to the issue of trust. The Copa-Cogeca Code seeks to facilitate a smooth transition into digital agriculture by clarifying the contractual arrangements on so-called 'ag-data' sharing in the context of a landscape dominated by the EU legislation on the legal protection of databases,[31] the General Data Protection Regulation (GDPR),[32] and the Regulation on the Framework for the Free Flow of Non-Personal Data.[33] Accordingly, the Copa-Cogeca Code provides definitions for roles and processes in data sharing in agriculture and articulates five principles dealing with: (1) data ownership, (2) data access, control and portability, (3) data protection and transparency, (4) privacy and security, and (5) liability and intellectual property rights. The Copa-Cogeca Code also contains a contract checklist for ag-data which facilitates an assessment of a contract following a practical set of questions:

- Is there an agreement/contract in place?
- What obligations are there? What warranties and indemnities are there for each party?
- What data is collected?
- Who owns/controls access to the data?
- What services are delivered?
- Will my data be used for purposes other than providing me, the data originator (e.g. farmer), a service? Is it clear what these are? Can I agree/disagree? What are/is the benefits/value for me (as a data originator)?
- Is the data shared with other parties? What rules do the external parties adhere to? Can I agree/disagree with sharing data with other parties?
- Can the service provider change the agreements unilaterally?
- What happens when the service provider changes ownership?
- Can I retrieve my dataset from the system in a usable format?

[29] Copa-Cogeca – *EU Code of Conduct on Agricultural Data Sharing by Contractual Agreement* (23 April 2018), available at https://cema-agri.org/images/publications/brochures/EU_Code_of_conduct_on_agricultural_data_sharing_by_contractual_agreement_2020_ENGLISH.pdf.

[30] Copa-Cogeca stands for: Comité des organisations professionnelles agricoles-Comité général de la coopération agricole de l'Union européenne / Committee of Professional Agricultural Organisations-General Confederation of Agricultural Cooperatives.

[31] Directive 96/9/EC Of The European Parliament And Of The Council of 11 March 1996 on the Legal Protection of Databases (1996) OJ L 77/20, available at https://eur-lex.europa.eu/LexUriServ/LexUriServ.do?uri=CELEX:31996L0009:EN:HTML.

[32] Regulation (EU) 2016/679 of the European Parliament and of the Council of 27 April 2016 on General Data Protection Regulation, available at https://gdpr-info.eu/.

[33] Regulation (EU) 2018/1807 of the European Parliament and of the Council of 14 November 2018 on A Framework for the Free Flow of Non-Personal Data in the European Union (2018) OJ L 303/59, available at https://eur-lex.europa.eu/legal-content/EN/TXT/PDF/?uri=CELEX:32018R1807&from=EN.

- Will I be updated on security breaches?
- Can I opt out of the service and have my data deleted from the system?
- Is there a contact point to assist me with any questions that I may have?
- Do I need insurance?
- What are the confidentiality terms?[34]

As the questions demonstrate, the key concerns expressed in the checklist are heavily farmer-oriented and seek the safeguarding of a balance of interests by providing the data originator (e.g. the farmers, input suppliers, nurseries, slaughterhouses, storage facilities, etc.) with control over ag-data, its subsequent use, access and/or distribution: 'when data is produced by an agri-chain operator due to their activity or is commissioned by this operator, the operator is considered the data originator. The right to determine who can access and use the data is attributed to this operator';[35] and 'The collection, access, storage and usage of the collected agricultural data can only occur once the data originator has granted their explicit, express and informed permission via contractual arrangement.'[36]

Whether the Copa-Cogeca Code can serve its purpose has, however, been questioned.[37] This is because the parties' parity is not always ensured,[38] and because the role of data originator[39] and data provider[40] may vary from relationship to relationship in the logistical chain.[41] With the entire purpose of the collection of data being the creation of a database[42] that can be analyzed or processed, we also have to consider who is legally entitled to claim rights in relation to the legal protection thereof. According to EU law, the rightholder of the database is the person who has made a substantial

[34](n 29), at p. 19.

[35]Copa-Cogeca Code, (n 29), page 8.

[36]Copa-Cogeca Code, (n 29), page 9.

[37]See S. van der Burg, L. Wiseman, and J. Krkeljas, 'Trust in Farm Data Sharing: Reflections on the EU Code of Conduct for Agricultural Data Sharing', (n 27).

[38]E. Jakku, B. Taylor, A. Fleming, C. Mason, S. Fielke, C. Sounness, and P. Thorburn, '"If they don't tell us what they do with it, why would we trust them?" Trust, transparency and benefit-sharing in Smart Farming', 90–91 (2019) *NJAS - Wageningen Journal of Life Sciences* 100285. And L. Wiseman, J. Sanderson, A. Zhang, E. Jakku, 'Farmers and their data: An examination of farmers' reluctance to share their data through the lens of the laws impacting smart farming', 90–91 (2019) *NJAS - Wageningen Journal of Life Sciences* 100301.

[39]Defined in the Copa-Cogeca Code, (n 29), page 6 as: '"the person or entity that can claim the exclusive right to license access to the data and control its downstream use or re-use", i.e. the party that the data is attributed to. The data originator of all of the data generated during the operation is the party who has created/collected this data either by technical means (eg agricultural machinery, electronic data processing programs), or who has commissioned data providers for this purpose.'

[40]Defined in the Copa-Cogeca Code, (n 29), page 6 as: 'a natural or legal person that under an agreement delivers data to the Data user and/or Data originator.'

[41]The data flow diagram included in the Copa-Cogeca Code, (n 29), page 6 appears to be extremely one-dimensional.

[42]A database being 'a collection of independent works, data or other materials arranged in a systematic or methodical way and individually accessible by electronic or other means', Art. 1(1) EU Database Directive, (n 31).

investment, qualitatively and/or quantitatively in the acquisition, verification, and presentation of the data in the database.[43] At the same time, it is likely that this is the data aggregator in control of the data platform, and the related analytical software tools, algorithms, or AI.

4. Digital agriculture and intellectual property

In other words, the intellectual property rights that are useful to the agribusiness have created positions of dominance that are only reinforced by ag-data acquisition and processing, and the subsequent ability to package the results in improved products, processes, and services by platform providers. What is also interesting, however, is that the type of relevant intellectual property rights is also supplementing traditional plant breeding, agro-chemicals, and machinery. The impact of these new innovations on the agribusiness is measured at 19% for IoT, 17% for robotics, 14% for AI, 13% for drones, 11% for precision agriculture, 6% for big data & analytics, 6% for controlled environment agriculture, 7% for agri-biotech, 4% for regenerative agriculture, and 3% for connectivity technology.[44]

The term 'digital agriculture' also yields interesting results when measured in terms of patent applications, displaying activity across the above-mentioned impact areas. Of the traditional firms, the Climate Corporation (Monsanto) and BASF are undertakings with patents in this category, most notably in the field of generation of digital cultivation maps (precision agriculture). (Figure 1).

As far as agriculture is concerned, precision agriculture functions to a large extent at the interplay with the cycle of planting seeds, growing and

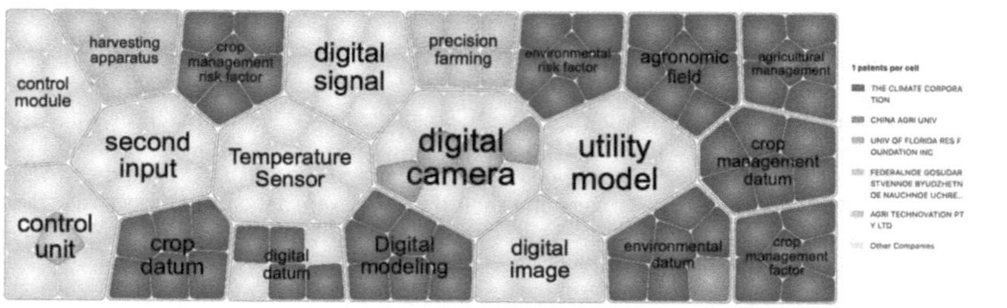

Figure 1. The cell diagram shows the keywords (Digital Agriculture) of the records owned by the top current assignees in the technology field. (Created using PatSnap on 10-01-2022).

---

[43]Art. 7(1) EU Database Directive, (n 31).

[44]For AgriTech trends see https://www.startus-insights.com/innovators-guide/agriculture-trends-innovation/

tending to crops (fertilisation and use of herbicides), all the way through to the harvest and processing of crops or fruits.

From a technical perspective, this implies that linkages between molecular or biotechnological techniques with plant varieties and seeds, and the related ag-data provide an interface between precision farming and big data analytics or biotech connectivity. In other words, this is a truly fourth industrial revolution phenomenon[45] where a variety of disciplines interface and overlap.

This move towards multi- and interdisciplinary innovation is also a global trend in the type of recent start-up activity[46] in agri-tech. In IoT, Bulgarian startup *Agrila* offers modular IoT sensory stations, Canadian *Farmer's Hive* offers remote monitoring of farm equipment, crops, and microclimates. In agricultural robotics, US startup *Advanced.Farm* offers autonomous harvesting and navigation in fields, and Canadian startup *Nexus Robotics* offers a robot that detects and removes weeds from fields. In artificial intelligence, US startup *Arwa Intelligence* offers artificial intelligence to provide customised recommendations for crop planning, and Belgian startup *Ask Attis* offers plant disease detection through an app. In drones, Omani startup *Wakan Tech* offers drone solutions for aerial pollination of date palm trees, and Indian startup *Equinox's Drones* offers drone services like crop surveillance, aerial inspection, data processing, and data analysis. In precision agriculture Australian startup *Data Farming* offers a pay-per-use cloud service providing insights through satellite images, soil mapping, auto-zoning, etc., and Italian startup *Agricolus* offers information through deployment of satellites and drones for calculating parameters relating to vigour, water stress, and the quantity of chlorophyll. In agricultural biotechnology, Canadian startup *AgGene* offers seeds and tissues with increased protein content through use of CRISPR and MAD7 gene editing platforms, and Australian startup *XytoVet* offers breeding techniques for assigning parentage information on sheep, cattle, and aquaculture enabling livestock decision-making. In big data and analytics, Indian startup *Fyllo* offers cloud services linked to sensory devices installed across the farm to analyze crop needs, irrigation requirements, pests, and diseases, as well as fertiliser schedules for crops based on the analysis of soil data, and Dutch startup *AgriData Innovations* offers greenhouse visualisation, collection, and analysis of farm data down to the specific leaf of a crop. In controlled environment agriculture, US startup *OnePointOne* builds vertical plane aeroponics farming spaces equipped with imaging and sensory devices, and Lithuanian startup *Baltic Freya* deals with irrigation and nutrients delivery by offering a new and improved fogponics technique. In regenerative agriculture, Dutch

[45] K. Schwab, *The Fourth Industrial Revolution* (World Economic Forum, 2016).
[46] See the StartUs Insights, 'Top 10 Agriculture Trends, Technologies & Innovations for 2022', (n 44).

startup *Freesoil* develops high-quality plant-based compost enriched with microorganisms that is naturally selected by plants, and Canadian startup *Acterra* specialises in fermentation technology for composting, seed, soil, and residue treatments that not only accelerates the breakdown of matter, but also captures carbon. In connectivity technologies, Australian startup *Ellenex* offers connectivity of battery-powered sensors to low-power satellite and WIFI systems, and US startup *AgriLinx* offers low-bandwidth solutions for remote locations.

These are all technical solutions that can operate in or be executed through a platform. The vertical integration of such services in a platform is well-underway. Despite the diversity in terms of the acquisition of data, the market reality shows that the corporations best placed to benefit from the advent of *digital agriculture* appear to be traditional agri-business multinationals that are already active and leading in the seed, agro-chemical, and agro-machinery industry. It is important to realises that in 2017 genetically modified seeds were already dominant in the market, with conventional breeding taking up 45.5% of the market (Figure 2).[47]

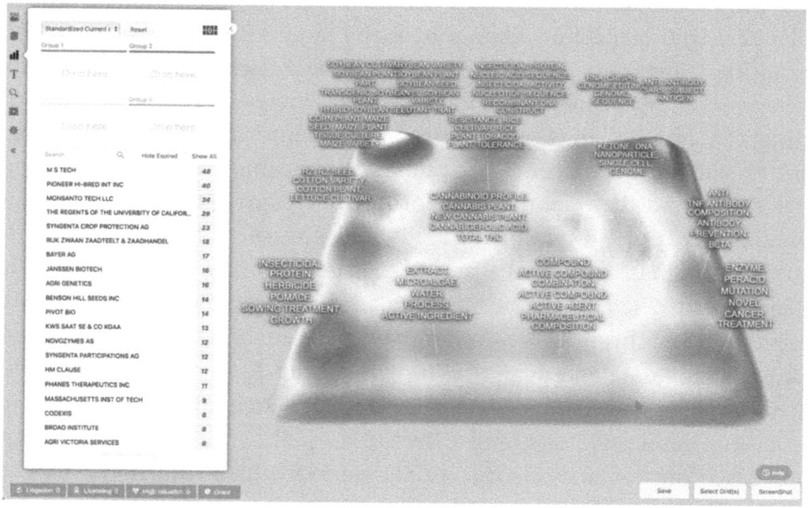

Figure 2. The patent landscape based on the keywords (Seeds and Biotechnology) shows the patents and density in the respective fields with the top patent holders in the field. (Created using PatSnap on 26-01-2022).

[47]'The global commercial seed market size was valued at USD 40.7 billion in 2017 and is projected to reach USD 61.32 billion by the end of 2025', see Fortune Business Insights, *Commercial Seed Market Size, Share and Industry Analysis by Product Type an Regional Forecast 2018-2025*,available at https://www.fortunebusinessinsights.com/industry-reports/commercial-seed-market-100078.

The leading multinationals tend to do so through acquisitions of digital agriculture startups. In the field of soil analysis services, *Solum* was acquired by Monsanto in 2014. Monsanto is one of the leading patent holders in the seeds, biotechnology and agro-chemicals market. Similarly, *YieldPop*, a startup in automated agronomic advice was acquired by Climate Corporation (the largest patent holder in the digital agriculture field, see cell-diagram above), a subdivision of Monsanto, in 2014. Similar developments are visible in terms of equipment, with Monsanto and Deere sharing data to allow the users of Deere equipment to use Monsanto Climate Corp. unit's 'Precision Planting' system. It is foreseeable that this will also allow all kinds of new services to be developed, such as pest control, automated fertilisation, seed and herbicide application.

Monsanto was in turn acquired by chemical giant Bayer in 2018. Before the acquisition, Bayer was predominantly active in health care and pharma (67% of its activities) and crop science (30% of its activities). The inclusion of Monsanto in its activity portfolio evened out the balance and allowed for a growth in sales from EUR 34.3bn to EUR 47.1bn in 2015 figures. Competition authorities compelled the new venture to transfer EUR 6 billion in operations and research facilities, mainly to the German chemical company BASF. Despite the transfer however, Bayer remains capable of leveraging an integrated business proposition through vertical integration and collaboration spanning agro-chemicals, plant breeding, biotechnology, and agronomic and soil advice. It has become a platform-provider offering multiple integrated agri-business products and data services. As one of the multisided market players it can then also integrate financial and insurance services, as well as production, marketing, and sales platforms.

It is in this light that questions on market regulation are now tabled at the OECD[48] and the European Commission in its proposed *Digital Markets Act* (DMA),[49] where merger control by gatekeepers is one of the key issues that is in dire need of new parameters for the monitoring of acquisitions of key start-ups by firms with paramount cross-market significance. The proposals seek to provide clarity in digital settings of classical exploitative issues such as self-preferencing, tying and bundling and MFN clauses, and exclusionary practices in data access, such as data portability and interoperability. What is striking, however, is that intellectual property and trade secrets are not mentioned in the context of the OECD report on *Ex ante regulation of*

[48]OECD, *Ex ante regulation of digital markets, OECD Competition Committee Discussion Paper* (2021), available at https://www.oecd.org/daf/competition/ex-ante-regulation-and-competition-in-digital-markets.htm.

[49]Proposal for a Regulation of the European Parliament and the Council on contestable and fair markets in the digital sector (Digital Markets Act), 5.12.2020 COM(2020) 842 final, available at https://ec.europa.eu/info/sites/default/files/proposal-regulation-single-market-digital-services-digital-services-act_en.pdf.

digital markets, nor in the DMA. The only mention of intellectual property to be found is in the OECD report and reads as follows:

> Generally speaking, there is evidence that intervening to promote competition will increase innovation. Firms facing competitive rivals innovate more than monopolies (although after such competition a firm may of course end up with a monopoly through a patent). The relationship is not simple: it is possible that moderately competitive markets innovate the most, with both monopoly and highly competitive markets showing weaker innovation.[50]

There is a tendency of competition regulators to shy away from intellectual property related market power. Possibly, this is because abuse assessment is common,[51] and the exercise of intellectual property rights by a dominant undertaking will only be abusive in exceptional circumstances. This may explain why the 'essential facility' doctrine has been developed in the context of a database case.[52] The complexity and converging composition of patent portfolios in the fourth industrial revolution, however, suggest that the generation and acquisition of intellectual property rights, trade secrets and data will in fact play a decisive role in establishing market dominance in digital markets and that defining what are essential facilities in terms of interconnected intellectual property portfolios may be of crucial importance.[53]

For digital agriculture, this is evidently the case, as many of the digital agriculture solutions rely heavily on the use of patented technologies in the fields of machinery, chemistry, and biotechnology as well as the growing of crops subject to plant breeders' rights. Since this has already created a relationship between farmers and the agro-chemical and plant breeding firms, it is not surprising that these firms are better-placed than agri-tech startup companies to also become the trusted parties for ancillary digital agricultural services. The incumbent industry after all knows the sector, is tuned into the needs of farmers, and knows exactly what ag-data it needs to acquire and process in order to improve its existing products. Ag-data collected in-situ allows for the creation of ever-more versioned and personalised products, especially with marker-assisted breeding and use of CRISPR-Cas yielding ever more precise results. In this sense digital agriculture is a field that interconnects hand in glove with the already existing agricultural industries where intellectual property rights portfolios are of crucial importance to maintain market access.

---

[50] OECD, *Ex ante regulation of digital markets, OECD Competition Committee Discussion Paper*, (n 48) p. 21.

[51] See V. Korah, *Intellectual Property Rights and the EC Competition Rules* (Hart Publishing, 2006).

[52] CJEU 29 April 2004, Case C-418/01, *IMS Health v. NDC Health*, ECLI:EU:C:2004:257.

[53] See B. Lundquist, 'The Proposed Digital Markets Act and Access to Data: A Revolution, or Not?' (2021) 52 *International Review of Intellectual Property and Competition Law* 239–41, https://doi.org/10.1007/s40319-021-01026-0, who is also bewildered by the lack of inclusion of intellectual property and trade secrets in the DMA proposal.

5. Other regulatory options: the law of unfair competition

Intellectual property law itself has its own dynamics of assessing acquisition and entitlement to exclusive rights. These are generally based on concepts of novelty and making contributions to science or useful arts, or through obtaining market recognition through use of trade identifiers. The nature of ag-data, apart from the database right approach described above, does not lend itself to categorisation in traditional intellectual property rights categories, nor in their related limitations and exceptions.[54] Where the vertical clustering and exercise of intellectual property in the digital economy is concerned, however, competition law may not be the only corrective instrument.

In this regard, it has been suggested that the law against unfair competition may also play a role.[55] Safeguarding fairness and ethical conduct in trade is rooted in the fundamental understanding that the competitive market 'as a whole' needs to be protected and preserved, so that certain acts of competition are unfair.[56] The advantage of the concepts underpinning the law against unfair competition is that they are uniformly applicable for the entire market, but equally allow for sector-specific or relation-specific regulation. Due to the rather flexible notion of 'unfairness' regulatory intervention can rapidly be provided with a legal foundation for *ex ante* market regulation. This is what has, for example, happened with the unfair practices directive for Business-to-Consumer commerce (B2C),[57] which has been amended[58] to ensure a 'new deal for consumers' in the guise of rules on digital markets, such as data-driven personalisation, dark patterns, influencer marketing, consumer reviews, as well as obligations of online platforms and marketplaces.[59] This also should raise the game of Business-to-Business (B2B) relations, where the promotion of innovation and competition is

---

[54]See in this context D. Gervais, 'Exploring the Interfaces Between Big Data and Intellectual Property Law' (2019) 10 *Journal of Intellectual Property, Information Technology and Electronic Commerce Law* 3–19, at 3, para 1, available at https://www.jipitec.eu/issues/jipitec-10-1-2019/4875: 'Beyond the protection of software used to collect and process Big Data corpora, copyright's traditional role is challenged by the relatively unstructured nature of the non-relational (noSQL) databases typical of Big Data corpora.'

[55]S. Scheuerer, 'Artificial Intelligence and Unfair Competition – Unveiling an Underestimated Building Block of the AI Regulation Landscape', (2021) 70 *GRUR International* 834–845, https://doi.org/10.1093/grurint/ikab021 , who argues that the law against unfair competition can serve as an underpinning for the regulation of artificial intelligence.

[56]R. Callmann, *Der Unlautere Wettbewerb* (Bansheimer, 1932); G. Bodenhausen, *Guide to the Application of the Paris Convention for the Protection of Industrial Property* (BIRPI, 1968) pp.142–6; S. Ladas, *Patents, Trademarks and Related Rights* (Harvard, 1975), pp. 1675–1742; R. Hilty and F. Henning-Bodewig (eds.), *Law Against Unfair Competition – Towards a New Paradigm in Europe?* (Springer, 2007).

[57]Directive 2005/29/EC of the European Parliament and of the Council of 11 May 2005 concerning unfair business-to-consumer commercial practices in the internal market, OJ (2005), L 149/22.

[58]Directive (EU) 2019/2161 of the European Parliament and of the Council of 27 November 2019 amending Council Directive 93/13/EEC and Directives 98/6/EC, 2005/29/EC and 2011/83/EU of the European Parliament and of the Council as regards the better enforcement and modernisation of Union consumer protection rules.

[59]B. Duinvoorde, 'The Upcoming Changes in the Unfair Commercial Practices Directive: A Better Deal for Consumers?' (2019) 8 *Journal of European Consumer and Market Law* 219–28.

concerned. In this context, and much like the social contract of enabling disclosure underlying the patent bargain, transparency in relation to (ag-)data acquisition and processing can be demanded from platform providers. Transparency, accountability, data access, data portability, FRAND licensing and/or benefit sharing should thus become part and parcel of the discussion on the regulation of multisided markets, including B2B transactions involving digital agriculture. The law against unfair competition can serve as a basis for *ex ante* regulation of the way in which intellectual property is acquired and exploited in various sectors, including that of digital agriculture.

6. Conclusion

The agricultural sector has become increasingly dependent on agro-chemical biotech firms that are also capable of establishing dominance in digital agriculture. This is in due to their established relationships with farmers, to their merger and acquisition activity, to their ability to process ag-data to improve their existing products, and to their ability to expand their services far beyond their currently existing market. Whereas competition law can provide the means to address multilateral and unilateral abuse of a dominant market position, the nature of vertical integration in multisided markets has already led to a discussion on new ways to define dominance. The law against unfair competition has meanwhile led to B2C *ex ante* regulation. It is submitted that the law against unfair competition can further be relied upon to regulate *ex ante* B2B relationships involving intellectual property and ag-data management, while supplementing *ex ante* and *ex post* competition authority intervention.

Disclosure statement

No potential conflict of interest was reported by the author(s).

OPEN ACCESS

Good advice is expensive – bad advice even more: the regulation of online reviews

Mateja Đurović and Tim Kniepkamp

ABSTRACT
Consumer decisions have always been influenced by others' opinions. The era of digital platforms, however, introduced a significant change: While in the past, consumers were likely to consult their social environment and credible literature, they nowadays rely on the views of other consumers they do not personally know via online review. Consequently, reliability of the reviews is no longer safeguarded by social coercion. This paper will explore how EU law has responded to this challenge. It will argue that while EU law prohibits a wide range of actions that harm reliability of online reviews, it is evidently failing to enforce consumer law judging from the scale of persistent violations. In response, the paper will suggest measures to minimise manipulation and scarcity of online reviews by primarily reducing the accountability deficit of online platforms. These tools could serve as an impulse during the ongoing legislative process of the Digital Services Act.

1. Introduction

If you had booked a trip to Rome in the 1990s, you probably would have consulted your friends who had visited the Italian capital before. They would have told you the hotel at which to stay, the museums to pay a visit to and the restaurants to dine at. Perhaps, you would also have read the praised Marco Polo travel guide based on the advice of travel experts. Today, you may still consult these sources, but would you follow them if the suggested hotel, for example, has less than three stars on Tripadvisor or little to no reviews? Probably not.

Online reviews play an increasing role in our life. They influence our decisions as consumers on a variety of transactions ranging from everyday purchases on Amazon to the planning of our annual leave on Booking.com or AirBnB. The more financially important the transaction, the more we want to ensure we receive exactly what has been displayed.[1] This holds particularly true in case of online trade since the consumer cannot fully scrutinise the product and has probably increased during the pandemic.[2]

Online reviews, however, are a double-edged sword. They enable consumers to consult the views of a larger peer group: Due to the translation services available, consumers can practically rely on reviews originally submitted in any language. It also allows them to have a better understanding of the overall performance of a trader in a short period of time due to accumulated ratings. Yet, it is practically impossible for a consumer to determine whether the published online reviews provide an authentic picture of past experiences. Perhaps, they have been submitted by a chatbot. Perhaps, their content has been manipulated for the better or the worse of the trader. Perhaps, authentic reviews remain unpublished due to their negative content. Perhaps, an average rating consists of online reviews that do not reflect the current state of the product.

These shortcomings render online reviews unreliable. The price will be paid by the consumers. Those aware of the unreliability will shy away from online reviews and, thus, lose a valuable source for an informed consumer decision. Those unaware of the unreliability will be guided by online reviews and might arrive at a decision they would not have taken otherwise.[3]

The purpose of this paper is to reflect on the question whether the regulation of online reviews must be reformed. Whilst this question touches upon several legal fields, such as protection of data privacy,[4] freedom of speech and expression[5] as well as the prohibition of discrimination[6], this paper focuses exclusively on the question what consumer law should do to regulate online reviews. At the start, the paper will outline the concept, the reliability, and the impact of online reviews, followed by a critical scrutiny as to whether the present EU consumer law adequately tackles the challenges online reviews pose to consumer protection. Eventually, various instruments will be proposed that boost reliability of online reviews.

---

[1]E Maslowska, E Malthouse, and V Viswanathan, 'Do Customer Reviews Drive Purchase Decisions? The Moderating Roles of Review Exposure and Price' [2017] *Decision Support Systems* 1.

[2]M Durovic, 'Adaptation of Consumer Law to the Digital Age: EU Directive 2019/2161 on Modernisation and Better Enforcement of Consumer Law' [2020] *Anali Pravnog Fakulteta u Beogradu* 66.

[3]OECD, 'Good Practice Guide on Online Consumer Ratings and Reviews – Protecting Consumers in E-Commerce' (9 September 2019) www.oecd-ilibrary.org/docserver/0f9362cf-en.pdf? (accessed 26 July 2021).

[4]Bundesgerichtshof MMR 2018, 456.

[5]M Petruzelli, 'Bewertungsplattformen – Überdehnung der Meinungsfreiheit zulasten der Betroffenen vs. gerechtfertigte Einschränkung zulasten der Bewertenden' [2017] *Multimedia und Recht* 800.

[6]V Katz, 'Regulating the Sharing Economy' (2015) 30 *Berkeley Technology Law Journal* 1067, 1118.

2. Online reviews

2.1. Concept

For the purpose of this paper, an *online review* is defined as an assessment of a physical or digital product, or a market participant submitted on an online (intermediary) platform. Typically, online reviews are made through a rating on a particular scale (e.g. from 1 to 10 on Booking.com) and may be supplemented with written comments where positive and negative impressions of the product are explained. The spectrum of rating systems ranges from thumbs up or thumbs down to stars or emoji scales to a like or a plus. Very common is the star system, where the reviewer assigns a certain number of stars to a product. These reviews without a written statement will be referred to as *online ratings* hereafter. In the ideal scenario, online reviews are solely made by people who have previously experienced the product or who have interacted with the market participant (*customer reviews*). These customers usually are consumers but could also be traders.

Online reviews are hosted by a digital platform. This term refers to Internet-based applications that bring users of the web into contact with each other and enable them to exchange goods, services, and information.[7] At this point, one should distinguish between two types. If the digital provider demands the reviewer to verify the transaction in question, the platform will be considered a *closed system*. Closed system are usually online marketplaces where the review facilitates a purchase decision. On these platforms, the verification process is simple since the transaction and the review take place within the same forum (e.g. AirBnB). If the digital provider does not continuously require verification to submit a review, the platform will be considered an *open system*. Open systems are usually pure review portals where no transaction takes place which makes it difficult for them to verify the reviewer has experienced what will be rated or commented (e.g. Tripadvisor).

Online reviews serve two main functions. First, they are customer feedback to the trader flagging up positive aspects of the products as well as potential for improvement. Second, they inform future customers how past customers perceived the product (electronic word-to-mouth). Thereby, they either supplement or even replace recommendations from the social environment or the advice in the shop.[8] As a by-product, online reviews also determine the trader's (online) reputation. Average ratings play a particularly important role in this process. On Booking.com, for

[7]G Wagner, 'Haftung von Plattformen für Rechtsverletzungen (Teil 1)' [2020] *Gewerblicher Rechtsschutz und Urheberrecht* 329, 329.

[8]Bundeskartellamt, 'Sektoruntersuchung Nutzerbewertungen' (October 2020) www.bundeskartellamt.de/SharedDocs/Publikation/DE/Sektoruntersuchungen/Sektoruntersuchung_Nutzerbewertungen_Bericht.pdf?__blob=publicationFile&v=3 (accessed 24 July 2021).

instance, customers can filter accommodations not only geographically or by price but also by the overall rating. Uber is another illustrating example. The platform reserves the right to remove drivers performing poorly according to their average rating.[9] Conversely, and more importantly for the consumer, the passenger will also be rated and (following an initial warning) may be kicked off the platform.[10]

In comparison to offline word-to-mouth, individual customers have a bigger reach. With minimal effort, they can inform a larger, global audience thanks to sophisticated translation tools. Also, online reviews are available for a longer period of time: These ratings do not lapse as soon as they are expressed. Interestingly, online and offline reviews alike suffer from the same Achilles heel: reviews only reflect previous customers' perceptions which are based on different preferences. Statistically, they follow a bimodal distribution at the top and the bottom rating range ('brag or moan').[11] To add insult to injury, herding effects apply because reviewers are influenced by previously posted reviews.[12] Thus, regardless of the medium reviews will never provide an objective assessment or replace an expert opinion on a product or a market participant. This observation is significant in two respects: First, one should not apply higher standards to digital tools than their analogous predecessors. Second, the aim from a policy standpoint is the same online as offline: safeguarding the consumers' access to authentic reviews creating trust and ultimately leading towards reliability.

2.2. Reliability

For the present purpose, reliability means that consumers have access to a sufficiently large pool of authentic online reviews. If consumers can rely on the collective experience of others, knowledge asymmetries between the consumer and the trader will be reduced.[13] In other words, online reviews

[9] G Donaker, H Kim and M Luca, 'Designing Better Online Review Systems' (November 2019) *Harvard Business Review* www.hbr.org/2019/11/designing-better-online-review-systems (accessed 5 August 2021).

[10] H Shaban, 'Uber Will Ban Passenger with Low Ratings' *The Washington Post* (Washington, 29 May 2019) www.washingtonpost.com/technology/2019/05/29/uber-will-ban-passengers-with-low-ratings/ (accessed 31 August 2021).

[11] B De Langhe, P Fernbach, and D Lichtenstein, 'Navigating by the Stars: Investigating the Actual and Perceived Validity of Online User Ratings' [2016] *Journal of Consumer Research* 817.

[12] G Jacobsen, 'Consumers, Experts, and Online Product Evaluations: Evidence from the Brewing Industry' [2015] *Journal of Public Economics* 114.

[13] M Narciso, 'The Regulation of Online Reviews in European Consumer Law' (2019) 27 *European Review of Private Law* 557, 560; for the regulatory potential of online reviews see C Koopman, M Mitchell and A Thierer, 'The Sharing Economy and Consumer Protection Regulation: The Case for Policy Change' [2015] *Journal of Business, Entrepreneurship and the Law* 529; for a rather critical view see S Ranchordás, 'Online Reputation and the Regulation of Information Asymmetries in the Platform Economy' (2018) 5 *Critical Analysis of Law* 127, 138.

can contribute to an informed consumer decision as pre-contractual information..[14] At present, however, we are miles away from this ideal because two conditions are not met.

First, published online reviews are not consistently an *authentic* reflection of how past customers perceived an experience. In other words, these reviews are not a credible source of information. The cause lies in the possibility of manipulation during three stages: the collection of online reviews, their processing and their publication.[15] The online reviews under these subheadings are classified as *manipulated reviews.* Second, reliability requires sufficient *review volume* which refers to the overall number of published online reviews. If the consumer has little but no reviews available on a product, the information available is too scarce to contribute to an informed decision.

Right at the start it is also paramount to understand the intersections of both elements.[16] If we apply too rigorous processes to create authenticity of online reviews, we risk discouraging past customers to share their impressions and, thus, shrink the data available to future consumers. If we solely want to quantify online reviews to create a sufficiently large data set, we will be unable to safeguard authenticity. This interplay will be of relevance in the later stages of this paper; in particular, concerning the adequate legal framework.

2.2.1. Authenticity of reviews

2.2.1.1. Collection. Online reviews themselves should be authentic, i.e. they should genuinely describe the perceived experience of previous customers. This is far from being the case.

At the first stage, online reviews do not necessarily originate from humans. A recent survey, for instance, suggests bots are employed to submit automatically online reviews in large quantities.[17]

Even if the reviewer is a human, he or she might not have experienced the product or have interacted with the market participant. In France, for instance, the Directorate General for Competition, Consumer Affairs and Repression of Fraud traced back traders faking consumer reviews to promote their commercial activities.[18] This behaviour is called *astroturfing* and it is not an isolated incident.[19] Statistically, traders often help themselves

[14] Narciso (n 13) 560.
[15] This division draws inspiration from Art L 111-7-2 Code de la consummation.
[16] Ranchordás (n 13) 135.
[17] Bundeskartellamt (n 8).
[18] OECD (n 3).
[19] Canada's largest telecommunications company, for example, encouraged its employees to post positive online reviews. See Canadian Competition Bureau, 'Bell Canada reaches agreement with Competition Bureau over online reviews' (14 October 2015) www.competitionbureau.gc.ca/eic/site/cb-bc.nsf/eng/03992.html (accessed 6 August 2021).

in this manner when their reputation is weak.[20] This problem particularly occurs on open platforms that do not require a verified account and/or a verification of the transaction. A survey conducted by the German Cartel Office indicates that on 21% of the review portals all visitors can submit a review without any requirement; a prior registration is required on less than half of the digital platforms. Merely one in four digital platforms requires a verification of the transaction in question. Thereby, digital platforms pave the way for the rise of manipulated online reviews.[21]

Even if the reviewers have experienced the product, they might intentionally submit an undeservingly positive opinion or a maliciously negative opinion (*opinion spam*).[22] A statement like 'I WILL post awesome review on your Amazon product'[23] is anything but uncommon. One reason might be the price: Between 15 and 30 EUR can be charged for an Amazon review.[24] The intermediation takes place through various channels. Some reviewers offer their service independently via Fiverr,[25] others gather in WhatsApp or Telegram groups, and some carry out their tricks in cooperation with e-reputation agencies.[26] In some cases, the reviewers have to purchase the product themselves and will be rewarded once the review has been submitted. In other cases, they receive the product for free. These practices are particularly insidious because they can be disguised as verified transactions, thereby masking the reviewer's underlying motivation.[27] Overall, these reviewers contribute to the distortion of authentic customer impressions.

Asymmetrical invitations to review are a worrying business practice. In general, an invitation to submit feedback after a transaction is an important tool to collect more reviews. Follow-up by email, for instance, accounts for 80% of submitted reviews online.[28] Hence, from a consumer law perspective it is a welcome step to prevent review. Some platforms, however, have developed a differentiated system. The German Cartel Office reports about a provider inviting everyone to leave a star rating but only those reviewers rating the products positively will receive an additional notification asking them for a detailed online review. Another provider required only one click for a positive rating, but a detailed explanatory note attached to every negative

[20] M Luca and G Zervas, 'Fake It Till You Make It: Reputation, Competition, and Yelp Review Fraud' [2016] *Management Science* 3412.

[21] Bundeskartellamt (n 8).

[22] For the definition of 'opinion spam' see B Liu, 'Sentiment Analysis and Subjectivity' in N Indurkhya and F Damerau (eds), *Handbook of Natural Language Processing* (Taylor & Francis 2010).

[23] 'Five-star fakes – The evolving fight against sham reviews' *The Economist* (New York, 22 October 2015) www.economist.com/business/2015/10/22/five-star-fakes (accessed 5 September 2021).

[24] Bundeskartellamt (n 8).

[25] Fiverr is a website where individuals sell freelance services for at least $5.

[26] Bundeskartellamt (n 8).

[27] OLG Frankfurt am Main openJur 2019, 29597.

[28] Spiegel Research Center, 'How Online Reviews Influence Sales' www.irp-cdn.multiscreensite.com/00a8b24b/files/uploaded/Spiegel_Online%20Review_eBook_Jun2017_Pv2.pdf (accessed 28 July 2021).

rating.[29] Notably, some traders developed similar strategies to influence the content of reviews applying rigorous T&Cs. A digital consultancy firm, for instance, restrained customers from submitting reviews and required them to delete (presumably unfavourable) reviews upon first request.[30] Thus, in these ways, the distribution of different ratings can be influenced, and an inauthentic picture of the overall performance can be created.

The growing phenomenon of incentives to submit online reviews also raises delicate questions. Some platforms, for example, apply non-material incentives such as the award of specific user rank/badge. These approaches make use of gamification.[31] Others offer a 5€ Amazon voucher or apply a 5% discount for an online review containing at least 50 words; the participation in lotteries in return for a review also enjoys increasing popularity.[32] Incentives are a borderline phenomenon: depending on their counter value they can influence online reviews for the better. Asking consumers to submit reviews in exchange for discounts of 10–25% on purchased printer supplies is a relatively clear-cut case of ill-suited influence.[33] The other aforementioned stimuli are less straightforward. These incentives are small relative to the transaction costs. Furthermore, they encourage customers to take the time and review a product/market participant which could minimise the second reliability concern, namely the limited review volume.

It is difficult to quantify the magnitude of these manipulation practices accurately; they differing significantly between open and closed review systems as well as different legal regimes. With respect to Amazon US, for instance, independent monitoring platforms estimate 42% of the reviews are fake.[34] Yelp itself estimated 25% of the reviews on its website are fake;[35] an independent study conducted in 2011 came to similar results.[36] Comparable figures emerged from a study on TripAdvisor in 2016.[37]

2.2.1.2. Processing. The processing by the digital platform is the next step in the chain. It forms the nexus between the writing and the publication of

---

[29] Bundeskartellamt (n 8).
[30] LG Koblenz MMR 2021, 656.
[31] Verbraucherzentrale, 'Fälschungen bei Bewertungen – Bekämpfen Online-Portale Sie Wirksam?' (April 2018) www.verbraucherzentrale.de/sites/default/files/2018-12/Bewertungen_Untersuchung_Marktwaechter.pdf (accessed 26 July 2021).
[32] Bundeskartellamt (n 8).
[33] OLG Hamm openJur 2011, 75961.
[34] Isabelle Lee, 'Can you trust that Amazon review? 42% may be fake, independent monitor says' *Chicago Tribune* (Chicago, 20 October 2020) www.chicagotribune.com/business/ct-biz-amazon-fake-reviews-unreliable-20201020-lfbjdq25azfdpa3iz6hn6zvtwq-story.html (accessed 24 July 2021).
[35] R Conrady, 'Customer Reviews: kaufentscheidend, glaubwürdig, strategierelevant? Eine empirische Studie der ITB und der Fachhochschule Worms' (2014) www.v-i-r.de/wp-content/uploads/2016/02/Studie-Hotelbewertungen-FHWorms.pdf (accessed 26 July 2021).
[36] W Dai, G Jin, J Lee, and M Luca, 'Aggregation of Consumer Ratings: An Application to Yelp.com' [2012] National Bureau of Economic Research Working Paper 18567.
[37] M Schuckert, X Liu, and R Law, 'Insights Into Suspicious Online Ratings: Direct Evidence from TripAdvisor' [2016] *Asia Pacific Journal of Tourism Research* 259.

online reviews. Like a virtual bouncer, providers decide which reviews make it into the public. From their perspective, processing is a fine line: They have to filter reviews which are manipulated content-wise or legally inadmissible (e.g. sexually explicit comments, threats, personal insults). As for the latter, Tripadvisor's Content Policy is rather illustrative.[38] At the same time, they have to avoid applying a too rigorous process that would discourage reviewers or would even lead to the deletion of unobjectionable reviews. If they fail at either end, the published reviews will no longer (singularly and collectively) provide an authentic picture of past customer experiences. At the moment, only a few providers manage this balancing act.

At one end, it is questionable whether digital platforms take sufficient steps to filter misplaced reviews. Word filter algorithms, for instance, can be deployed to delete reviews including discrimination or hate speech.[39] The majority of platforms have these algorithms embedded into their processing.[40] Most providers, however, fall short to implement more sophisticated algorithms that trace manipulated reviews based on meta data analysis (e.g. IP address, device ID). Only 41% of the digital providers use these filters. Stated differently, the remaining platforms fail to exploit the full potential of automatic filtration: The virtual bouncers (to stay in the picture) are too lax in some respects. Fortunately, national authorities appear to take note of the problem. The UK Competition and Markets Authority, for instance, recently opened a formal probe on Amazon and Google to determine whether the companies have breached UK consumer law by taking insufficient steps to protect consumers from fake reviews.[41] Likewise, the German Federal Cartel Office calls for tougher action against fake reviews.[42]

Another concern is called *overblocking*, i.e. different filtration standards for positive and negative reviews leading to a disproportionate deletion of negative submissions. Some platforms, for example, automatically initiate a manual inspection for reviews with less than two or three out of five stars.[43] In the meantime, these reviews will remain unpublished. One platform even went so far as to require a verified transaction for negative reviews but not for positive ones.[44] In other words, the virtual bouncer is

[38] Tripadvisor, 'Content Policy' www.tripadvisorsupport.com/hc/en-us/articles/360008133913-TripAdvisor-s-Content-Policy (accessed 21 August 2021).

[39] Note these cases are a classic example of why authenticity is not the only relevant factor to decide which reviews should be published. Authentic reviews contrary to the law should be deleted before publication.

[40] Bundeskartellamt (n 8).

[41] UK Competition and Markets Authority, 'CMA to Investigate Amazon and Google over Fake Reviews' (25 June 2021) www.gov.uk/government/news/cma-to-investigate-amazon-and-google-over-fake-reviews (accessed 25 July 2021).

[42] M Kläsgen, 'Kartellamt fordert härteres Vorgehen gegen Fake-Bewertungen' *Süddeutsche Zeitung* (Munich, 6 October 2020).

[43] Bundeskartellamt (n 8).

[44] Verbraucherzentrale (n 31).

blind in one eye. From the perspective of the consumer, however, the belated publication of negative reviews and the ensuing (temporary) distortion of average ratings is not recognisable.

Another tool worth discussing is the notice-and-take-down process.[45] If the reviewee contests an online review already published, the provider will temporarily hide it during inspection. It will notice the reviewer asking for additional information (e.g. verification of the transaction). Unless the reviewer will respond within a predefined time frame, the review will be deleted. This procedure places an additional burden on the reviewer. In the absence of clear incentives, reviewers shy away from the additional effort: 60% of these reviews will be deleted only because the reviewer does not respond within the given time period.[46] As a result, the notice-and-take-down process leads to the deletion of disagreeable reviews which disproportionately affects negative ones.

Consumers consulting online reviews benefit from negative and positive reviews alike as long as they are authentic. At present, however, the processing on some digital platforms insufficiently filters misplaced reviews or is overly cautious concerning negative reviews.

2.2.1.3. Publication. Online reviews only unfold their full potential once they are published. It is only then that they feed into the decision-making process of the consumer. Here, too, distortions can arise that create an image that deviates from the authentic, collective experience of past customers.

Average ratings are the most obvious impediment. They are usually positioned below the price or the name of the product. Due to their one-dimensional nature, their prominent position, and no need for further action (e.g. clicks) by the consumer these figures are particularly heuristic, i.e. they tempt consumers to form a final opinion on the basis of a single figure.[47] Since host platforms are surprisingly discreet when it comes to the algorithm behind their average ratings, the consumer cannot arrive at an informed decision. Some digital platforms, for example, applied different weight to positive and negative reviews.[48] Others prefer the Bayesian average[49] over the classic arithmetic mean: if a company has only one review, the platform will factor the average rating of comparable companies on their website into the average rating.[50] The aim of this practice is honourable, namely, to limit the distortion of single outlier in case of a limited review volume. The consumer, however, will confidently expect that the average rating is based on an arithmetic mean.

[45]Bundeskartellamt (n 8).
[46]Bundeskartellamt (n 8).
[47]Maslowska, Malthouse, and Viswanathan (n 1).
[48]OLG Düsseldorf openJur 2013, 28596.
[49]A Bayesian average is a method to estimate the mean using outside information that is factored into the calculation.
[50]Bundeskartellamt (n 8).

Another concern is the absence of a maximum age for reviews to be displayed. The hotel industry serves as a good example. In this business sector, the service plays an important role for online reviews. In light of the high fluctuations, however, reviews older than two years may not reflect the present state of the product. This problem is exacerbated when old reviews flow into the calculation of average ratings.

The final aspect of concern is the functionality of digital platforms. Not every provider offers a response function leaving the reviewee with no option to present his or her perspective. The alternative is only the appeal to the platform demanding the deletion of the review thereby shrinking the review volume. It is also not mandatory for host platforms to provide a reporting function for users to flag suspicious reviews which affects the scope of subsequent filtration.

2.2.2. Review volume

The review volume or, rather, the lack thereof appears to be largely overlooked in the literature.[51] In the absence of a sufficient data set, the consumer cannot confidently rely on online reviews in the process of making an informed decision. The scarcity of reviews can be traced back to two causes. First, only a fraction of customers is willing to submit a review after a transaction which in turn leads to a selection bias since overly positive and negative reviews dominate the fora. Second, the portability of online reviews is practically non-existent. Therefore, consumers can only benefit from the online reviews submitted via the platform they visit rather than the accumulation of all reviews submitted on the identical product on various platforms.

2.2.3. Summary overview

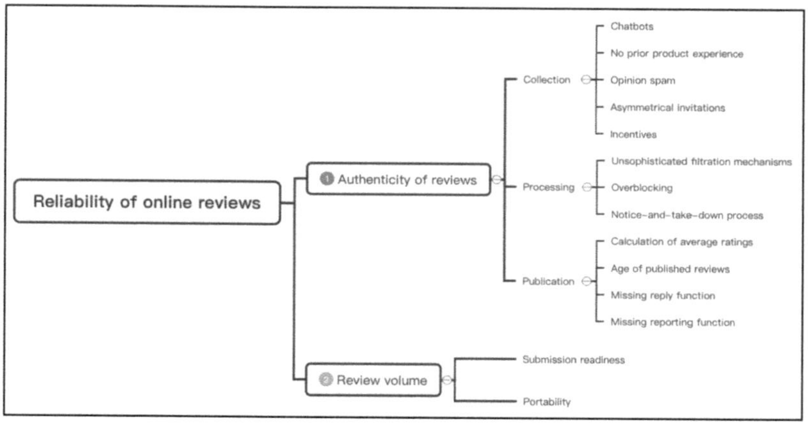

[51]Narciso (n 13).

2.3. Impact

Online reviews are not static. They impact future consumer decisions. To understand the magnitude of the impact in light of the aforementioned manipulations, is to understand the extent of the present problem.

From the consumer perspective, every commercial transaction has an attached risk due to knowledge asymmetries in relation to the trader. Therefore, consumers consult different sources to make an informed decision. Online reviews play an increasing role in this process. In the hotel sector, for instance, more than eight out of ten consumers read reviews prior to a transaction.[52] When we turn towards online shoppers, surveys indicate up to 95% read reviews before making a purchase.[53] Note at this point that only 50% still consult their friends, family, or colleagues.[54] More specifically, consumers place enormous weight on average ratings compared to the number of ratings.[55] Paradoxically, however, they seem to be aware of their shortcomings, yet value them as an important determinant for transaction decisions.[56]

From the perspective of the trader, online reviews have a substantial effect on sales. One factor is the volume of online reviews. Products with five reviews can increase conversion rate by 270% over products without any review; for high-priced items even by 380%.[57] Verifying reviews is also in the interest of the trader since it increases the conversion rate by 15%.[58] Average ratings are particularly decisive:[59] A one-star increase can elevate restaurants' revenue by 5–9%.[60] For later sections it is also worth highlighting negative reviews can in fact drive sales: businesses with 15–20% negative reviews actually average 13% more revenue than competitors with a 5–10%

---

[52]Commission, 'Study on Online Consumer Reviews in the Hotel Sector – Final Report' (2014) www.op.europa.eu/en/publication-detail/-/publication/7d0b5993-7a88-43ef-bfb5-7997101db6d5 (accessed 24 July 2021).

[53]Spiegel Research Center (n 28); Bitkom, 'Kundenbewertungen sind wichtigste Kaufhilfe' (11 January 2017) www.bitkom.org/Presse/Presseinformation/Kundenbewertungen-sind-wichtigste-Kaufhilfe.html (accessed 24 July 2021); Bizrate Insights, 'The Impact of Consumer Reviews on Purchase Decisions' (2021) www.bizrateinsights.com/resources/shopper-survey-report-the-impact-reviews-have-on-consumers-purchase-decisions/ (accessed 28 July 2021).

[54]Bitkom (n 53).

[55]De Langhe, Fernbach, Lichtenstein (n 11) 817.

[56]A Flanagin, M Metzger, R Pure, A Markov, and E Hartsell, 'Mitigating risk in ecommerce transactions: perceptions of information credibility and the role of user-generated ratings in product quality and purchase intention' [2014] *Electronic Commerce Research* 1.

[57]G Askalidis and E Malthouse, 'The Value of Online Customer Reviews' in S Sen and W Geyer (eds), *RecSys '16: Proceedings of the 10th ACM Conference on Recommender Systems* (Association for Computing Machinery 2016). See also Maslowska, Malthouse, and Viswanathan (n 1).

[58]S Kim, E Malthouse, and E Maslowska, 'Understanding the Role of Different Review Features in Purchase Probability' [2017] *International Journal of Advertising* 29.

[59]Flanagin, Metzger, Pure, Markov, Hartsell (n 56).

[60]M Luca, 'Reviews, Reputation, and Revenue: The Case of Yelp.com' [2016] *Harvard Business School Working Paper* 12-016 www.hbs.edu/ris/Publication%20Files/12-016_a7e4a5a2-03f9-490d-b093-8f951238dba2.pdf (accessed 28 July 2021).

quota respectively.[61] The reason is plainly simple: too positive reviews lead to consumer suspicion.[62]

From the macroeconomic perspective, these figures can be translated into consumer spending. In 2015, the UK Competition and Markets Authority estimated that transactions in the United Kingdom worth £23bn have potentially been influenced by online reviews.[63]

2.4. Interim summary

Online reviews have a significant influence on consumer decisions. As a result, they were loaded with a monetary value which led to increasing manipulation and declining reliability. This development poses the central question for the remainder of the paper: what regulatory framework is adequate to safeguard reliability of online reviews for consumers?

3. EU consumer law – a blunt sword?

The European Commission has been aware of manipulated online reviews as a threat for consumer protection.[64] Its efforts cumulated in the New Deal for Consumers[65] in 2018, most notably the Omnibus Directive.[66] Along with the Unfair Commercial Practices Directive,[67] Consumer Rights Directive,[68] the Unfair Contract Terms Directive[69] and the E-Commerce Directive[70] it forms the relevant EU legal framework for consumer protection. Each of these directives will be scrutinised as to its contribution to online review reliability.

---

[61] Womply, 'Impact of Online Reviews on small business revenue' www.womply.com/impact-of-online-reviews-on-small-business-revenue/ (accessed 28 July 2021).

[62] D Bosman, C Boshoff, and G Van Rooyen, 'The Review Credibility of Electronic Word-of-Mouth Communication on E-Commerce Platforms' [2013] *Management Dynamics* 29.

[63] UK Competition and Markets Authority, 'Online Reviews and Endorsements – Report on the CMA's call for information' (19 June 2015) www.assets.publishing.service.gov.uk/government/uploads/system/uploads/attachment_data/file/436238/Online_reviews_and_endorsements.pdf (accessed 24 July 2021).

[64] Commission, 'Comparison Tools – Report from the Multi-Stakeholder Dialogue' (2013) www.ec.europa.eu/info/sites/default/files/consumer-summit-2013-msdct-report_en_0.pdf (accessed 24 July 2021); Commission, 'Study on Online Consumer Reviews in the Hotel Sector – Final Report' (n 52); Commission, 'Study on Coverage, Functioning and Consumer Use of Comparison Tools and Third-Party Verification Schemes for Such Tools' (2014) www.ec.europa.eu/info/sites/default/files/final_report_study_on_comparison_tools_2013_en.pdf (accessed 24 July 2021).

[65] Commission, 'Communication from the Commission to the European Parliament, the Council and the European Economic and Social Committee – A New Deal for Consumers' COM (2018) 183 final.

[66] Directive (EU) 2019/2161 on better enforcement and modernisation of Union consumer protection rules [2019] OJ L328/7.

[67] Directive 2005/29/EC on unfair business-to-consumer commercial practices [2005] OJ L149/22.

[68] Directive 2011/83/EU on consumer rights [2011] OJ L304/64.

[69] Directive 93/13/EEC on unfair terms in consumer contracts [1993] OJ L95/29.

[70] Directive 2000/31/EC on e-commerce [2000] OJ L178/1.

3.1. Unfair commercial practices directive

In neglect of chronologicity, the UCPD shall be addressed first due to its central role in regulating online reviews at present. The directive prohibits certain commercial practices that might distort an informed consumer decision by rendering them as *unfair*.[71] The scope of application is limited to traders in a business-to-consumer transaction (B2C). 'Trader' under Art 2(b) UCPD includes businesses, e-reputation agencies but also intermediaries like digital platforms if they act for the purpose relating to its business (e.g. charge commission fee, offer additional paid services, draw revenue from advertising).[72] The Italian Tribunale Amministrativo Regionale per il Lazio, for instance, confirmed that Tripadvisor is a trader within the meaning of the UCPD due to its classification and systematization of information; including online reviews.[73] Conversely, it does not apply to the consumer as the reviewer. Notably, the UCPD scrutinises commercial practices before (e.g. calculation of average ratings) and after (e.g. asymmetrical invitations) the B2C transaction from the consumer's standpoint.[74] For the present purpose, three forms of unfairness under the UCPD are relevant.

Under Art 5(2) UCPD, a commercial practice is unfair 'if it is contrary to the requirements of professional diligence' as defined in Art 2(h) UCPD and materially distorts the consumer's economic behaviours or is likely to do so under Art 2(e) UCPD. Asymmetrical invitations to submit and asymmetrical processes to filter reviews are likely to be covered by this provision. The former exerts influence on the group of customers submitting a review which can hardly be reconciled with the general principle of good faith and evidently distorts the consumers ability to make an informed decision. The latter is in line with honest market practice as long as the differentiated filtration criteria are prominently displayed for the consumer. Otherwise, the consumer is entitled to assume that all online reviews were subject to equal filtration standards regardless of their content.[75] Moreover, it is equally questionable whether automatic processing solely based on word filters (i.e. unable to detect most manipulations) as well as the unlimited age of published reviews satisfy the standard of special skill.

Under the UCPD, a commercial practice will be considered unfair if its action or omission is misleading. A consumer will be considered actively misled if the commercial practice contains wrong information. Conversely, a consumer will be considered passively misled if the trader fails to disclose

---

[71] See: M. Durovic, *European Law on Unfair Commercial Practices and Contract Law* (Hart Publishing 2016).

[72] Commission, 'Guidance on the Implementation/Application of Directive 2005/29/EC on Unfair Commercial Practices' COM (2016) 320 final.

[73] Tribunale Amministrativo Regionale per il Lazio (13 July 2015), Sezione I, Sentenza n. 09355.

[74] Case C-453/10 *Pereničová and Perenič* [2012] ECLI:EU:C:2012:144, para 39.

[75] Commission, 'Guidance on the Implementation/Application of Directive 2005/29/EC on Unfair Commercial Practices' (n 72).

all information material for an informed decision. In both instances, the commercial practice must also have caused a transactional decision the consumer would not have otherwise taken. The term 'transactional decision' will be interpreted broadly:[76] the provider will fall within the ambit even if the consumer will not make a purchase on a digital platform but, for example, only reads reviews to decide whether he or she will make a transaction. This broad scope is particularly relevant for host platforms that almost exclusively provide reviews (e.g. Tripadvisor). The broad interpretation also bars arguments that quantity of manipulated reviews or visitor frequency on the relevant platform impact the misleading character of business practice:[77] One positive fake review is capable of persuading the average consumer to make a transactional decision.[78]

Through the years, national courts identified various commercial practices which fall within the ambit of the UCPD. The Higher Regional Court of Frankfurt am Main in particular has contributed to the existing case law. One case concerned e-reputation agencies that omit to indicate reviewers have received an incentive in return for their submissions. One agency, for instance, has offered traders to provide them with reviews on a third-party online marketplace in exchange for a commission fee.[79] The reviewer received the product in question for free or for a small sum. The court concluded the agency can be classified as an accessory under Art 7 (2) UCPD failing to identify the commercial nature of the review. Another misleading and deceiving business practice recognised by said court is the transfer of likes and online reviews after a restaurant had changed the franchise system.[80] It also concluded that paid customer reviews are inadmissible due to the improperly created appearance of objectivity.[81]

Asymmetrical procedures for positive and negative reviews have also been recognised as a misleading business practice. The German Federal Supreme Court was faced with a host platform that published positive reviews automatically while neutral and negative reviews were subject to conciliation procedures – a classic notice-and-take-down process.[82] At the same time, the provider advertised 'genuine customer reviews guaranteed'. The court ruled that said filtration process is contrary to Art 6(1)(b) UCPD due to the slogan's impression that positive and negative reviews alike would be published without filtration. The ruling, however, is limited to definite

[76]Narciso (n 13) 575.
[77]For the opposite opinion see A Ahrens, H Richter, 'Fingierte Belobigungen im Internet' [2011] *Wettbewerb in Recht und Praxis* 814, 817.
[78]P Heermann, 'UWG §5a Irreführung durch Unterlassen' in P Heermann and J Schlingloff (eds), *Münchener Kommentar zum Lauterkeitsrecht* (Beck C.H. 2019).
[79]OLG Frankfurt openJur 2019, 29597.
[80]OLG Frankfurt WRP 2018, 1107.
[81]OLG Frankfurt WRP 2019, 1041.
[82]Bundesgerichtshof openJur 2016, 7145.

statements by the provider.[83] In the context of active statements alleging authenticity of online reviews, the European Commission advises providers to take 'reasonable and proportionate steps which (...) increase the likelihood for such reviews to reflect real users' experiences'[84] to satisfy Art 6 (1)(b) UCPD. Admittedly, however, to take reasonable steps to solely increase the *likelihood* of authenticity is rather unambitious to say the least. Nevertheless, this question rarely arises in practice because many platforms opt for *e contrario* approach: they avoid making too pretentious statements as to the authenticity of the reviews and, thus, are under no obligation to prominently inform the consumer about their filtration process. To this end, one might question whether host platforms generally provide sufficient information in an easily accessible manner. For example, in the course of writing this paper, an unsuccessful attempt was made to find clear information as to Tripadvisor's processing algorithms, filtrations mechanisms and publication standards. It stands to reason that a consumer might arrive at a differing decision regarding a future transaction if he or she would be aware how the average rating has been generated:[85] you would probably also think differently about a restaurant after you've seen the kitchen. The UCPD, however, seems to be unapproachable to such subtle questions given advanced age.

Finally, under Art 5(5) UCPD, a commercial practice listed in Annex I will consistently be classified as unfair. The only relevant business practice of the UCPD's original version is number 22.[86] It prohibits traders from 'falsely representing oneself as a consumer'. Hence, if a trader or an e-reputation agency post online reviews purporting to reflect the genuine opinion of a consumer, it is considered unfair in all circumstances.[87] The Omnibus Directive widened the legal regime blacklisting two particularly relevant business practices which will be addressed below.[88]

At this point, one is tempted to assume the UCPD keeps pace with technological advancements. Thanks to the broad understanding of a 'transactional decision' most intermediary platforms fall within the ambit of the UCPD. The present legal regime prohibits a wide range from manipulations including asymmetrical invitations as well as incentivised reviews. Some forms of overblocking are likely to be caught by two different provisions of the directive. The UCPD also has the potential to address unsophisticated filtration processes and time-wise unlimited review publications, although

[83]See also OLG Düsseldorf openJur 2013, 28596.
[84]Commission, 'Guidance on the Implementation/Application of Directive 2005/29/EC on Unfair Commercial Practices' (n 72).
[85]See for a similar conclusion Narciso (n 13) 576.
[86]Commission, 'Guidance on the Implementation/Application of Directive 2005/29/EC on Unfair Commercial Practices' (n 72).
[87]Commission, 'Study on Consumer Online Reviews in the Hotel Sector – Final Report' (n 52) 52.
[88]See section 3.4.

no court decisions in this respect are known so far. Unfortunately, however, the UCPD lags behind a number of harmful business practices, particularly those by online providers during processing and publication of reviews. Furthermore, its enforcement runs sluggishly – and the European Commission is aware of it since 2014.[89] Finally, the tailoring on traders prevents the directive to regulate private opinion spam (e.g. writing a negative review for the restaurant of your ex's new boyfriend).

3.2. Unfair contract terms directive

The UCTD comes into play during the consumer transaction regulating terms in B2C contracts that have not been individually negotiated.[90] Like the UCPD, this directive circulates around unfairness. Yet, the contract terms instead of business practices are under scrutiny. This structural difference affects the consequence of a breach which is contractual rather than competitional: unfair contract terms must not be binding for the consumer, Art 6(1) UCTD. Unfairness is defined autonomously in Art 3(1) UCTD and supplemented by a list of explicitly unfair terms in the Annex. Notably, unfair commercial practices under the UCPD can influence whether contract terms are considered unfair under the UCPD.[91] The platform economy poses difficulties for this legal regime.

Some concerns arise from the contract between the consumer and the trader. Clauses that, for example, restrict or even prevent the right of consumers to submit reviews have evidently not been considered by the EU legislator in 1993. Therefore, they are not mentioned in the Annex and the umbrella clause in Art. 3(1) UCTD does not provide a clear answer either. The Regional Court of Koblenz took the trouble and solved the problem by considering the above-mentioned clauses as interfering with the consumer's freedom of expression.[92]

Concurrently, contract terms between the digital provider and the consumer can be harmful for the reliability of online reviews. Amazon, for instance, only allows incentivized reviews submitted via their own Amazon Vine[93] programme. Other platforms like Tripadvisor prohibit incentivized reviews in their contract terms altogether.[94] As pointed out above, however, incentives are harmless as long as they are proportionate to the transaction value. More importantly, they can stimulate review volume. Yet, it is unlikely these clauses will be intercepted by the UCTD.

[89] Commission, 'Study on Consumer Online Reviews in the Hotel Sector – Final Report' (n 52) 105.
[90] Commission, 'Guidance on the Implementation/Application of Directive 2005/29/EC on Unfair Commercial Practices' (n 72).
[91] *Pereničová and Perenič* (n 74), paras 43–44, 47.
[92] LG Koblenz MMR 2021, 656.
[93] See Amazon, 'What is Amazon Vine?' www.amazon.de/gp/vine/help (accessed 13 August 2021).
[94] Tripadvisor, 'Content Policy' (n 38).

Although these clauses may work to the detriment of the consumer, they pose no *significant* imbalance under Art 3(1) UCTD.

For the moment, one should note the UCTD's umbrella clause can be bent to address some harmful contract terms in the context of online reviews. Yet, the directive's Annex would benefit from some additions that clarify the unfairness of contract terms common in the platform industry.

3.3. E-Commerce Directive

In contrast to the UCDP and the UCTD, the E-Commerce Directive draws the attention away from traders. Instead, it provides valuable insights on liability of review platforms as the provider of information society services. The gateway for the application of the directive is the term 'information society service' in Art 2(a) ECD. According to the definition in Art 1(2) Directive 98/34/EC and respectively Art 1(b) Directive 2015/1535, it refers to 'a service normally provided for remuneration, at a distance, by electronic means and at the individual request of a recipient of services'. Recital 18 adds it extends to services 'not remunerated by those who receive them, such as offering online information'. This element is particularly relevant for review platforms where the business model is based on advertisements paid by companies instead of the user. In recent years, the CJEU refined the term 'information society service' for intermediation services.[95] In *Uber Spain*, the Grand Chamber established two criteria whereupon a service will be excluded from the ambit of the ECD.[96] First, the intermediation service must form an integral part of an overall service whose main element allows another legal qualification. Second, the platform operator must exercise decisive influence over the conditions for the provision of said service. Subsequently, the court provided further guidance on the interpretation of these conditions in *AirBnB Ireland*[97] and *Star Taxi App*.[98] The significance of said classification for service providers emerges from the advantages of the ECD. Art 14 ECD exempts service providers from liability for illegal, third-party information stored on the platform. Art 15 ECD prohibits the creation of a general monitoring obligation for stored and transmitted information. For Uber Spain, for instance, excluding its service from the ambit of 'information society service' meant that national legislators can impose far-reaching monitoring obligations which would seriously affect the business model.

[95] E Murati, 'AirBnB and Uber: two sides of the same coin' [2020] *Rivista di Diretto dei Media* www.medialaws.eu/rivista/airbnb-and-uber-two-sides-of-the-same-coin/ (accessed 6 September 2021).
[96] Case C-434/15 *Asociación Profesional Elite Taxi* [2017] ECLI:EU:C:2017:981, para 40.
[97] Case C-390/18 *AirBnB Ireland* [2019] ECLI:EU:C:2019:1112.
[98] Case C-62/19 *Star Taxi App* [2020] ECLI:EU:C:2020:980.

Provided that the provider can invoke Art 14 ECD, the liability privilege does not apply without restriction. Instead, it is carried out on the basic assumption that it is foreign content. Art 14(1)(a) ECD makes clear a service provider will not benefit from the exemption if it possesses actual knowledge of illegal information while Art 14(1)(b) ECD excludes service providers who fail to act promptly upon (at least) awareness by removing or disabling said illegal information. These categories are particularly relevant for the internal filtration process conducted by employees of the review platform. Yet, in the context of online reviews it remains nebulous which information the EU legislator considers illegal. Narciso argues fake and defamatory reviews fall within the ambit.[99] This statement cannot be endorsed universally. Who, for instance, renders it illegal for an individual to submit opinion spam? Is it illegal or merely contractually infringing to submit opinion spam contrary to the T&C of the platform? To this end, it is difficult to determine when the platform liability will resurface.

Alternatively, the liability privilege may be withdrawn in light of Recital 42. The CJEU clarified that Art 14(1) ECD only applies if the provider 'has not played an active role allowing it to have knowledge or control of the data stored'.[100] So far, however, the court has been reluctant to develop standards when a service provider plays an active or a passive role. It is to be hoped the court seizes the opportunity presented by a currently pending Austrian preliminary ruling procedure.[101] The German Federal Supreme Court, for instance, argued the liability privilege will prevail even if the provider processes user statements statistically or applies word filters and examines the filtered reviews manually to ensure the adherence of its T&Cs.[102] Even if this interpretation would be sound, it must be admitted – without prejudice to the various different processing and publication procedures – that most digital platforms exceeds these activities. They develop asymmetrical invitation and processing standards. They apply complex procedures like the notice-and-take-down process. They generate average ratings based upon complex calculations. And they present reviews as user-friendly as possible. It is visibly difficult to argue this 'activity is of a mere technical, automatic and passive nature' as demanded by Recital 42. Moreover, the purpose of the liability privilege – namely protection against liability for illegal third-party content – no longer applies in the present case since platforms appropriate the content through comprehensive processing and presentation procedures. After all, no privilege applies to one's own conduct.[103]

---

[99] Narciso (n 13) 569.
[100] C-324/09 *L'Oréal SA* [2011] ECR I-06011, paras 123–124.
[101] C-500/19 *Plus 4 TV*.
[102] Bundesgerichtshof openJur 2015, 13104.
[103] For the abstract recalibration of platform liability for one's own conduct under the E-Commerce Directive see G Wagner, 'Haftung von Plattformen für Rechtsverletzungen (Teil 2)' [2020] 447, 448.

Concurrently, service providers benefit from Art 15 ECD. The provision prevents the imposition of a general obligation to monitor platform content.[104] For example, national legislators are prevented from imposing a compulsory audit of every review submitted by an employee of the review platform. Conversely, however, specific monitoring duties can be invoked, e.g. taking care a notorious user known for the submission of fake reviews will be barred from the platform.[105] These specific obligations correlate with the duty to apply professional diligence under the Art 5(2) UCPD.[106] Yet, one gropes in the dark to determine professional diligence and the admissible, specific monitoring standard. In this respect, future EU legislation should determine a professional diligence standard for the industry.

Overall, the E-Commerce Directive leaves one wondering. It is unclear whether the liability privilege still applies to the publication of online reviews and to which degree specific monitoring obligations can be invoked. More importantly, the directive sets the wrong incentives rewarding platforms for their ignorance.[107] The fewer filtration processes they apply, the fewer illegal reviews they will actually know, Art 14(1)(a) ECD. The fewer illegal reviews they are aware of, the fewer they have to remove or disable promptly, Art 14(1)(b) ECD.

3.4. Omnibus Directive

The Omnibus Directive emerged from the Regulatory Fitness and Performance Programme (REFIT).[108] Although the directive marks the first time that EU consumer law directly addresses online reviews,[109] its changes are limited.

The most notable modification are two additions to the Annex II ('blacklist') of the UCPD.[110] This classification renders both business practices unfair *per se*. First, traders are prohibited to state the reviews on their platform are authentic 'without taking reasonable and proportionate steps to check' (Nr. 23b). What exactly is meant by these steps remains largely open. Recital 47 names the verification of the transaction as one option.

[104] C Busch, 'Crowdsourcing Consumer Confidence – How to Regulate Online Ratings and Review Systems in the Collaborative Economy' in A De Franceschi (ed), *European Contract Law and the Digital Single Market: The Implications of the Digital Revolution* (Intersentia 2016).

[105] OLG Frankfurt openJur 2021, 22593.

[106] Commission, 'Guidance on the Implementation/Application of Directive 2005/29/EC on Unfair Commercial Practices' (n 72).

[107] Narciso (n 13) 580.

[108] Commission, 'Report on the Fitness Check' SWD (2017) 209 final; MH Austgulen, 'Understanding National Preferences in EU Consumer Policy: A Regime Approach' [2020] *Journal of Consumer Policy* 767, 773.

[109] Durovic (n 2).

[110] Art 3(7)(b) Directive 2019/2161.

No information can be retrieved about what obligations arise during the processing and the publication of reviews. In the end, companies are also able to avoid the application of this provision by making vague statements as to reviews' authenticity. Second, 'submitting or commissioning another legal or natural person to submit false consumer reviews or endorsements, or misrepresenting consumer reviews or social endorsements, in order to promote products' will fall under the UCPD (Nr. 23c). Although submitting fake reviews oneself already falls under Nr. 22, the first half is a useful addendum. It attributes responsibility to the trader for inauthentic reviews commissioned from individuals or via e-reputation agencies. The second half leaves more questions open than it answers. What does 'misrepresenting' mean in this context? Do certain processing procedures like the notice-and-take-down process fall within the ambit? How about a ranking that places the most positive reviews at the top? The only guidance available can be derived from Recital 49 that names 'publishing only positive reviews and deleting the negatives ones' as an example. Evidently, the subtleties of the problem are overlooked here.

Another change of the UCPD concerns Art 7 where a sixth paragraph has been added.[111] Thereupon, 'information about whether and how the trader ensures that the published reviews originate from consumers who have actually used or purchased the product shall be regarded as material'.[112] In other words, it will be misleading under Art 7(1) UCPD if the trader omits to inform the consumer on safeguards concerning review authenticity and this omission is at least likely to have caused the consumer to make a transactional decision he would otherwise not have taken. This new information obligation should be read in conjunction with Recital 47. It states platforms are advised to provide information on their processing (e.g. handling of negative and positive reviews). Moreover, they are obliged to inform the consumer whether reviews have been 'sponsored or influenced by a contractual relationship with a trader'. Although disclosure obligations will not lead to measures that increase reliability of online review, they are generally appreciated. They allow the consumer to put the published reviews into context. Yet, the mechanisms behind processing, for instance, are technical and one must fear they are a burden rather than a blessing for the consumer. Also, the obligation only applies if the platform provides reviews itself rather than embedding third-party content.[113]

Finally, the Omnibus Directive created individual remedies for the victims of unfair commercial practices responding to what has previously been

---

[111] Art 3(4)(c) Directive 2019/2161.

[112] C Cauffman, 'New EU rules on business-to-consumer and platform-to-business relationships' (2019) 26 *Maastricht Journal of European and Comparative Law* 469, 476.

[113] R Albrecht, 'Herausforderung für Unternehmer – Neue Rechte für Verbraucher und Bußgeldmöglichkeiten aus dem UWG ab Mai 2022' [2021] Gesellschafts- und Wirtschaftsrecht 273, 274.

considered a big shortcoming.[114] This will be added as Art 11a UCPD.[115] If a transaction was influenced by an unfair commercial practice, the consumer will be entitled to claim compensation for damages, a price reduction and/or contract termination.[116] The burden of proof will fall on the consumer since neither Recital 16 nor Art 11a UCPD establish a reversal. Practice will show whether remedies play an active role in case of online reviews for two reasons. First, the Omnibus Directive failed to address central aspects like the *ex tunc* or *ex nunc* effect of termination but also the potential deterrence effect of the burden upon the consumer to prove the contract was concluded under the influence of an unfair commercial practice.[117] Second, it is questionable whether remedies play a role in the specific context of online reviews. Would it make sense, for instance, to allow a consumer to terminate the contract if 5 out of 50 reviews have been written by the trader?

Overall, the Omnibus Directive missed the opportunity to realise its potential in the context of online reviews. The approach is rather conservative creating mostly information obligations.[118] The legislative content consists of minor changes during the collection stage. The introduction of remedies provides relief to the consumer but it just distracts the legislative attention from the root cause, namely the manipulation of reviews.

3.5. Interim conclusion

The aforementioned directives can cover various forms of review manipulation. At the same time, EU consumer law is porous. Many harmful commercial practices are not covered by the UCPD, the UCTD does not reduce knowledge asymmetries, and it is unclear whether online platforms can still rely on the liability privileges of the ECD. Lastly, the Omnibus Directive has failed both to provide the necessary remedy and develop measures against review scarcity. Therefore, while EU consumer law is not a blunt sword in the fight for the review reliability, it should be re-sharpened.

4. Sharpening EU consumer law

If the application of EU consumer law does not function adequately, the question arises as to where adjustments can be made in order to adapt the European legal framework to the particularities of the digital age and

[114] Durovic (n 2) 75.
[115] Art 5 Directive 2019/2161.
[116] Albrecht (n 113) 275.
[117] C Pavillon, 'Private Enforcement as a Deterrence Tool: A Blind Spot in the Omnibus Directive' (2019) 27 *European Review of Private Law* 1297, 1313; Albrecht (n 113) 276.
[118] M Grochowski, 'European Consumer Law after the New Deal: A Tryptich' [2020] *Yearbook of European Law* 387, 393.

challenges brought by the new technologies.[119] The EU legislator should primarily sharpen accountability of digital platforms due to their gatekeeping function. At this point, one might be tempted to make a case for self-regulation by the host platforms. This approach loses its attraction, however, when one consults Amazon for example: its guidelines clearly prohibit incentivized online reviews. Did it help? A market price between 15 and 30 EUR speaks for itself. Others might argue in favour of private sector correctives to the manipulation of reviews. In fact, legal and technical providers have positioned themselves on the market. Specialised law firms offer to handle the deletion of disagreeable reviews if needed with legal action for around 200 EUR per review.[120] ReviewMeta and Fakespot offer their own analysis tools to determine reliability of product reviews on third-party platforms like Amazon. However, the European legislator would not do justice to its own ambitions if it outsourced the reliability of online reviews. Instead, it should seriously consider incorporating the following ideas into the ongoing legislative process of the Digital Services Act and the anticipated revision of the E-Commerce Directive.[121]

Therefore, this paper will take a different path suggesting a co-regulatory approach.[122] A directive could embed the new rules in the EU legal framework while an EU norm would set the technical standards for online platforms. This flexible approach would keep pace with rapid technical advancements: The European Committee for Standardization could respond even at short notice and adjust the EU standard whenever it is out of touch with the platform economy. The ISO Norm 20488:2018 on online reputation systems could serve as an inspiration.[123] Furthermore, this approach prevents the consumer being overburdened with additional information which would lead to rational apathy and would also demand platforms to disclose sensitive information (e.g. algorithms).

4.1. Authenticity of online reviews

4.1.1. Reviewer identification

On most platforms, reviewers can submit their impressions anonymously. Certainly, this approach is appealing in the sense that reviewers are more willing to reveal their true impressions since they fear no retaliation. It might even increase review volume due to an increase in willingness. Conversely, however, demanding that reviewers stand up by their name prevents

[119] R. Brownsword, *Law 3.0: Rules, Regulation, and Technology* (Routledge 2020) 5.

[120] See for example ADWUS Reputation in Austria and Germany.

[121] Commission, 'Proposal for a Regulation of the European Parliament and the Council on a Single Market for Digital Services (Digital Services Act) and amending Directive 2000/31/EC' COM (2020) 825 final

[122] This approach draws inspiration from Busch (n 104).

[123] Commission, 'Study on Consumer Online Reviews in the Hotel Sector' (n 52) 84.

frivolous online reviews. More importantly, anonymity grants protection to opinion spam and encourages traders to submit reviews themselves since such conduct can neither be traced back by the host platform or the consumer.[124]

In response, the ISO Norm 20488:2018 excludes anonymous reviews, and the Danish Consumer Ombudsman indicates they would be contrary to domestic law.[125] Yet, a more conceivable approach to resolving said dilemma could be to require users to solely reveal their identity to the host platform. To create as few hurdles as possible, the identification process could be simplified using an existent social media account (e.g. Facebook). Thereby, the review platform would benefit from the spam filters of the social media provider and could also team up with external online reputation assessment tools like Traity which measures people's reputation based on their social media footprint. Other official documents (e.g. ID or passport) would be available as a fallback. As an additional safeguard, multi-factor authentication should be in place. Jameda, for instance, generally requires users to submit their email. If the impression arises that the same person is submitting reviews via different accounts (with different email addresses), the platform will require identification via SMS. Then, the number can no longer be linked to another account. The combination of both factors poses a much higher hurdle, because a second mobile number is much more difficult to obtain than just another email address.

This approach would allow users to remain unknown to the public and foremost to the trader in question. Thus, it would safeguard honesty and benefit review volume. At the same time, it would help the provider to trace back users breaking the rules and ban them from their platform.

4.1.2. Disclosure obligations

The most straightforward approach to support an *informed* decision is to provide the consumer with additional information. Amazon Vine serves as a good example. Instead of the one-dimensional idea to supply additional text information, the company created a small icon next to the review signalling to the consumer that the review in question is the result of product testing. An explanatory note should open if the consumer hovers over the icon with the mouse. This approach could be particularly useful in two instances.

First, an icon aside the review could indicate to the consumer that the reviews has been submitted without a verification. For example, in the form of a small exclamation mark that would act as a warning sign as to

[124] Busch (n 104) 10.

[125] Danish Consumer Ombudsman, 'Guidelines on Publication of User Reviews' (1 May 2015) www.consumerombudsman.dk/media/49717/guidelines.pdf (accessed 24 July 2021).

the risk of a manipulated review. This balanced approach would be particularly instructive for open systems. The alternative – compulsory verification[126] – would lead to the undesirable outcome that the business model collapses: since no transaction takes place via their portal, it would be particularly difficult to receive solely verified reviews. The attentive reader might ask why this paper rejects the opposite approach, namely the labelling of verified reviews. After all, this approach is applied on Amazon Marketplace. The intended warning function, however, would go astray. A clear response concerning this issue would be particularly useful given that the lower instance courts in Germany came to different conclusions as to the legality of a red exclamation mark next to an average rating where some underlying reviews might have been manipulated.[127]

Second, incentivized reviews could be flagged for the consumer with an icon, for example, a small dollar sign. This would recognise incentives as an important tool for increasing the review volume, while allaying concerns consumers may gain a distorted impression being unaware of the underlying incentives. Finally, it could pave the way to legality for e-reputation agencies if host platforms generally allow incentivized reviews.

This approach, however, also bears an inherent risk: information overflow. If the host platform overburdens the consumer with information, it will lead to the opposite effect that the consumer either disregards the abundance of data before a transaction or abstains from using the platform. Therefore, disclosure obligations should be supplemented with EU processing and presentation standards allowing the consumer to trust that reviews adhere to minimum quality standards regardless of the forum.

4.1.3. EU processing standards

The current EU regulation on processing is only partially able to banish harmful business practices by review portals. It might be tempting to respond with additional disclosure obligation to inform the consumer about the procedures. Yet, and this leads back to the information overflow, one must admit processing is a rather technical subject. Therefore, the average consumer can hardly be expected to enquire about the details. Instead, universal standards for review providers should apply in form of EU norms. Breaching these norms could be considered contrary to professional diligence under the Art 5(2)(a) UCPD.[128] Thus, it would be considered unfair if the breach materially distorts economic behaviour. Also, it would trigger a specific monitoring duty under Art 15 ECD.

---

[126] Commission, 'Key principles for comparison tools' www.ec.europa.eu/info/sites/default/files/key_principles_for_comparison_tools_en.pdf (accessed 4 September 2021).

[127] LG Frankfurt am Main openJur 2021, 5950; LG Kassel openJur 2021, 4825.

[128] See also Art 5(3)(a) Model Rules on Online Platforms, in European Law Institute, 'Model Rules on Online Platforms' (2019).

In terms of content, the cornerstones of the EU standard should aim to prevent (temporary) asymmetries. All reviews – regardless of their content – must be processed in an equal manner.[129] The same applies for the invitation to submit a review. If a suspicious review is under inspection, it must remain published rather than being suspended; perhaps accompanied by a small icon. Every digital platform should have an alert button that allows users to inform the platform about suspicious reviews.[130]

In terms of method, platforms should marry two approaches: automatic and manual verification procedures. The former consists of sophisticated filters that apply metadata analysis of account data (e.g. IP address, email address, device ID, account age) and user behaviour (e.g. submission frequency, time to submit a review, similar text patterns). Together with user alerts these automatically filtered reviews should feed into the manual verification procedure. At this stage, humans should take the final decision on whether to delete or publish a posted review. If a review will be rejected or removed, it should be for legitimate reasons.[131]

Lastly, the notice-and-take-down process should be abolished in favour of a comment/reply function for the trader.[132] The extent to which reported reviews are deleted plainly because the reviewer does not want to be involved in the conciliation process exceeds the benefits of the procedure compared to the value of a public statement below the review itself.

4.1.4. EU publication standards

It should come as no surprise that EU norms can be an effective tool not only for the processing but also the publication, most notably the presentation, of online reviews. On a European level, the situation is also comparable to the extent that it is questionable whether the current directives cover all harmful business practices. However, on a national level, Member States like France have laid the foundation on which this paper will build.[133]

The prime focus of future regulation should be average ratings since they are particularly influential, heuristic, and available without additional clicking usually positioned next to the product price. First, EU standards should curtail underlying reviews in two respects – age and verification. Year-old reviews hardly reflect the present state of the product. In the hospitality sector, for instance, 'service' is a central element of online reviews while the annual staff turnover leads up to 50%.[134] Moreover, the majority of

---

129 Danish Consumer Ombudsman (n 125).

130 See also Art 6(i)(a) Model Rules on Online Platforms, in European Law Institute (n 128).

131 See Art 6(d) Model Rules on Online Platforms, in European Law Institute (n 128).

132 See section 4.1.4.

133 Art. D111-17° b Code de la consummation.

134 Commission, 'Study on Consumer Online Reviews in the Hotel Sector' (n 52) 34.

consumers consider reviews older than a few months irrelevant.[135] Accordingly, ratings should only feed into averages for a maximum of twelve months.[136] Also, it might be instructive to exclude unverified ratings from the calculation – especially on closed systems. Second, EU standards should concern the calculation process. Consumers can reasonably expect that averages are solely based on the arithmetic mean. Therefore, all other calculation methods (like the Bayesian average) should be added to the blacklist of the UCPD. At most, it would be conceivable to introduce a different weighting of ratings, e.g. between verified and unverified reviews. Third, platforms could be obliged to publish averages only if a sufficient number of reviews has been submitted to create a reliable figure. Google, for instance, used to require at least five reviews before the average rating would have been published.[137] A viable alternative could be a mandatory display of the underlying number of ratings positioned next to the average.[138] Thereby, the consumer would make a judgement as to the reliability according to the review volume.

Another relevant aspect of review presentation is the order. The exact procedure is often hidden in algorithms. Therefore, the default setup of reviews should be chronological, and it should be possible to filter verified reviews or those without incentives.

Finally, review platforms should be obliged to include a reply/comment function for the trader.[139] In this sense, the Latin phrase *auditor et altera pars* ('listen to the other side') translates into the modern words of Tripadvisor that 'there are two sides to every story'.[140] A reply function would not only allow the trader to put a review into context but can also be useful for the consumer who can learn more about the service provider.

4.2. Review volume

4.2.1. Incentivization

Few customers make the effort to submit an online review after their transaction.[141] One might sympathise from the individual standpoint. Yet, from a consumer protection standpoint the behaviour is counterproductive. It

[135] Brightlocal, 'Local Consumer Review Survey 2020' (9 December 2020) www.brightlocal.com/research/local-consumer-review-survey/ (accessed 28 August 2021).

[136] See also Art 6(h) Model Rules on Online Platforms, in European Law Institute (n 128).

[137] A Heitzman, 'Google Reduces Star Rating Threshold: Why Businesses Should Take Notice' (21 February 2017) Search Engine Journal www.searchenginejournal.com/google-reduces-star-rating-threshold-businesses-take-notice/185947/#close (accessed 28 August 2021).

[138] See also Art 6(h) Model Rules on Online Platforms, in European Law Institute (n 128).

[139] See also Art 6(i)(bb) Model Rules on Online Platforms, in European Law Institute (n 128); UNWTO, 'Recommendations on the Responsible Use of Ratings and Reviews on Digital Platforms' (2017) 7.

[140] Tripadvisor, 'Reported Reviews that Remain Published' www.tripadvisorsupport.com/hc/en-us/articles/200614347-Reported-Reviews-that-Remain-Published (accessed 28 August 2021).

[141] Commission, 'Study on Consumer Online Reviews in the Hotel Sector' (n 52) 11.

means products often lack a reliable review volume. Even if the review volume is sufficient, it will not reflect the collective customer experience. Incentives, however, have proven useful to boost customer willingness to submit online reviews. AirBnB, for example, offered a 25$ voucher in exchange for online reviews and noticed a 6.4% increase in review volume.[142] Regrettably, most platforms apply restrictive rules[143] and some organisations argue for their general inadmissibility.[144] The Higher Regional Court of Frankfurt even went so far to conclude that an average rating (partially) based upon reviews incentivized by lottery is misleading within the context of the UCPD.[145] In the absence of clear standards, this approach is relatable. This paper, however, advocates for the general admissibility of incentives subject to three conditions. First, incentives should not exceed five percent of the transaction value. Offering a larger incentive could be added to the blacklist of the UCTD. Second, incentivized reviews should fall under the aforementioned disclosure obligations;[146] the average consumer expects reviews to have been submitted without consideration.[147] This obligation already applies in the Netherlands.[148] Third, incentivized reviews should be excluded from average ratings;[149] these figures are too heuristic to sufficiently inform consumers about incentivized feeding into the calculation. The latter aspects could be regulated via the aforementioned EU norm and embedded in the blacklist of the UCPD.

4.2.2. Review portability

Online reviews are growing determinants for the reputation of companies but also individuals. Ten overwhelmingly positive reviews on AirBnB may not only impress a future host but perhaps also your future landlord or bank. Likewise, a hotel might profit from transferring their existing reviews on Tripadvisor to a newly emerging platform. Yet so far it is practically impossible to transfer reviews between different platforms which leads to lock-in effects: you are bound to the platform you are currently using. Although the European Commission described review portability (or rather the lack thereof) as 'a general issue of peer review' already in 2017,

[142] A Fradkin, E Grewal, D Holtz, and M Pearson, 'Bias and Reciprocity in Online Reviews: Evidence from Field Experiments on AirBnB' (2015) *Proceedings of the Sixteenth ACM Conference on Economics and Computation*.

[143] Tripadvisor, 'Content Policy' (n 38).

[144] Ibid; Consumer Commission Baden-Württemberg, 'Gekaufte Bewertungen im Internet verbieten' (2020).

[145] OLG Frankfurt MMR 2020, 764.

[146] See also Danish Consumer Ombudsman (n 125); Art 6(c) Model Rules on Online Platforms, in European Law Institute (n 128).

[147] OLG Frankfurt openJur 2019, 29597.

[148] Authority for Consumers & Markets, 'ACM calls for increased transparency in online reviews' (11 May 2017) www.acm.nl/en/publications/publication/17222/ACM-calls-for-increased-transparency-in-online-reviews (accessed 22 August 2021).

[149] Commission, 'Key principles for comparison tools' (n 126) 5.

it abstained from regulating the subject so far.[150] Furthermore, it is unclear whether reviews submitted by third parties would fall under Art 4(1) GDPR as prerequisite of data portability under Art 20(1) GDPR.[151] Even if this would be the case, it would only help individuals and not legal persons. In response, private providers like Deemly emerged where customers can create a reputation passport which is based upon the peer's online behaviour.[152] However, the EU legislator should not rest on others' laurels. Instead, it should create an EU norm setting out the cornerstones for the transfer of online reviews from one reputational system to another. Art 7 of the Model Rules on Online Platforms developed by the European Law Institute could serve as an inspiration.[153]

4.2.3. Platform pooling

Products are often listed on various review platforms simultaneously. The same hotel, for instance, might appear on Tripadvisor and Booking.com. In consequence, a sufficiently large pool of reviews might be available to consumers, but it is spread across several platforms. This leaves the consumer with two choices: either invest the time to browse several portals or stick to the limited information provided on the preferred platform. Conversely, it is unrealistic that customers would take the time to submit reviews on multiple portals after their transaction, in particular without incentives. Instead, a viable solution could be to pool review platforms which would break the silo effect. Platform pooling means that customers can share their impressions on various portals via one centralised submission. The reviewer would choose the platforms for publication, for instance, by clicking on checkboxes. Questions between Tripadvisor and Booking.com, for example, overlap to some degree (e.g. rating system) while other aspects differ (e.g. rating scale). Therefore, the system would merge the identical and add the platform-individual questions in one form. This procedure would take marginally longer for the reviewer and would significantly increase the review volume on the consumer's preferred online platform.

5. Conclusion

In the modern World, online reviews are playing an increasingly important role in the consumers' decision-making process, based on the recent technological development. Online reviews can help consumers make better

[150] Commission, 'Exploratory study of consumer issues in online peer-to-peer platform markets' (2015) 93.

[151] European Law Institute (n 128) 29; V Kathuria and JC Lai, 'User review portability: Why and how?' (2018) 34 *Computer Law & Security Review* 1291, 1297–1298.

[152] Commission, 'Exploratory study of consumer issues in online peer-to-peer platform markets' (n 150) 93.

[153] Art 7 Model Rules on Online Platforms, in European Law Institute (n 128).

informed decisions while acting on the market, which is a demonstration of how a modern technology can contribute to strengthening of the internal market.[154] Therefore, proper regulation of online reviews is necessary to secure adequate level of consumer protection, securing that online reviews are true, real, objective, timely, etc. as part of a wider process of adapting consumer law framework to all the challenges brought by new technologies.[155] However, as shown in this paper, the existing European legal framework does not seem to provide adequate level of consumer protection despite the recent innovations brought by the Omnibus Directive in 2019. Accordingly, this paper suggests certain actions and changes that could be taken to improve the existing online review regulation, securing the adequate level of consumer protection.

Disclosure statement

No potential conflict of interest was reported by the author(s).

[154]See: S Deakin and C Markou (eds), *Is Law Computable?* (Hart, 2020).
[155]R Brownsword (n 119) 5.

The eligibility requirements for legal protection of publicly accessible datasets

Guobin Cui

ABSTRACT
This article proceeds on the assumption that Chinese legislators are likely to choose special legislation of a property rights regime to protect publicly accessible datasets. Under such legislation, data collectors would be granted limited exclusive rights (right of public communication). It is argued that there should be three principal eligibility requirements in relation to such datasets, namely: the data entries in a dataset are made public; it contains a substantial number of data entries; and, it reflects a substantial collection cost to the collector. Through these elements, the special property rights legislation can be connected consistently with the existing trade secret protection system and copyright law. It can be distinguished from the US-style hot news doctrine and EU-style database directive to achieve different legislative purposes and effectively balance the interests of data collectors, competitors, and the public.

1. Introduction

In the era of artificial intelligence and big data, the importance of large-scale datasets as an industrial resource has been raised to a new level and the issues relating to the legal protection of datasets have also become a hot topic among the legal academia. Actually, current trade secrets law, copyright law, anti-unfair competition law (misappropriation doctrine) and contract law have already provided effective protection for most data or datasets.[1]

---

[1] According to Josef Drexl and others, 'Data Ownership and Access to Data' (Position Statement of the Max Planck Institute for Innovation and Competition of 16 August 2016 on the Current European Debate) para 7, 'even without actual exclusive rights, data is already the object of daily transactions' (www.ip.mpg.de/fileadmin/ipmpg/content/stellungnahmen/positionspaper-data-eng-2016_08_16-def.pdf) (accessed 23 February 2022). The firms usually rely on technical means, trade secrets law or contracts to protect their data. The Statement focuses on individual data rather than large-scale datasets. But the above-mentioned technical measures or contracts mechanism fit for datasets as well. For a more detailed introduction to the legal protection of datasets under the existing intellectual property

What left in the blank is limited to datasets that have no originality and are made public, such as geographic data in electronic map provided by Google or Baidu Maps,[2] consumer reviews information on catering companies collected by Dianping.com or Yelp.com,[3] user-generated contents collected by social media platform Linkedin or Weibo.com,[4] and information about sale items displayed in e-commerce platform Taobao.com or eBay.com.

There is not yet a good solution to this problem of datasets protection in the world. For small-scale datasets, like the news information in AP v. INS case, the US common law provides very limited protection under the so-called hot news doctrine.[5] Such a protection has not been extended to medium size regular datasets (databases) of no time sensitivity. In the mid-1990s, both European and the US legislators tried to create a sui generis protection for such databases, which triggered heated discussions among the European and American legal communities. At that time, many scholars held a positive attitude towards the protection for regular datasets either under a sui generis property right regime or anti-unfair competition regime.[6] The focus of the theoretic dispute is under which regime and/or to what degree of legal protection is sufficient to prevent so-called market failure.[7] This was also why we witnessed vigorous efforts to introduce sui generis legislation for database protection in Europe,[8] and similar

laws, see Cui Guobin, 'Towards a Theory of Limited Exclusive Right for Big Data' (2019) 5 *Chinese Journal of Law* 4.

[2]See Wikipedia, 'Google Maps', www.en.wikipedia.org/wiki/Google_Maps. Google Maps also provide copyrighted contents, like satellite photographs, street view pictures. Typical judicial case in China on this type of datasets in China: *Beijing NavInfo Technology Co., Ltd. v Beijing Baidu Netcom Technology Co., Ltd.*, Beijing Intellectual Property Court, (2017) Jing 73 Min Chu No. 1914.

[3]Typical judicial cases on this type of datasets in China: *Shanghai Hantao Information Consulting Co., Ltd. v Aibang Juxin (Beijing) Technology Co., Ltd.*, Beijing No. 1 Intermediate Court, (2009) Yizhong Minzhong Zi No. 5031; *Shanghai Hantao Information Consulting Co., Ltd. v Aibang Juxin (Beijing) Technology Co., Ltd.*, Beijing No. 1 Intermediate Court, (2011) Yi Zhong Min Zhong Zi No. 7512; *Dianping v Baidu Shanghai Hantao Information Consulting Co., Ltd. v Beijing Baidu Netcom Technology Co., Ltd.*, Shanghai Intellectual Property Court, (2016) Hu 73 Min Zhong No. 242.

[4]Typical judicial cases on this type of datasets in China and the US: *Beijing Weimeng Chuangke Network Technology Co., Ltd. v Beijing ByteDance Technology Co., Ltd.*, Beijing Haidian District People's Court, (2017) Jing 0108 Min Chu No. 24530; *hiQ Labs, Inc. v LinkedIn Corp.* (2019) 938 F.3d 985.

[5]*International News Service v Associated Press* 248 U.S. 215 (1918).

[6]JH Reichman and Pamela Samuelson, 'Intellectual Property Rights in Data' (1997) 50 *Vanderbilt Law Review* 51, 137.

[7]James Gibson, 'Re-Reifying Data' (2004) 80 *Notre Dame Law Review* 163, 171, 232.

[8]For an introduction to the EU legislative efforts, see Mark Schneider, 'The European Union Database Directive' (1998) 13 *Berkeley Technology Law Journal* 551. However, the only outcome of the efforts is the EU Database Directive, which provide very broad sui generis rights for databases. Comments on this legislation from academia and industry were mostly negative. The European Commission's own 2018 evaluation report on the Database Directive gave a negative review of the legislation as well: 'The Directive has been quite effective in harmonising database protection in Europe, but there is no evidence to conclude that the sui generis right has been fully effective in stimulating investment in the European database industry, nor in creating a fully functioning access regime for stakeholders.' European Commission, Evaluation of Directive 96/9/EC on the Legal Protection of Databases, 2018, at 46, www.ec.europa.eu/newsroom/dae/document.cfm?doc_id=51764 (accessed 10 February 2021).

attempts made by the United States[9] and the World Intellectual Property Organization in the past.[10] The Chinese intellectual property community has been exploring the path of legal protection for datasets for quite a long time,[11] but legislators have never enacted any specific law in this area directly. The latest development is just a vague announcement in the Civil Code (2020) that 'where any laws provide for the protection of data and network virtual property, such laws shall apply'.[12] There is no doubt that the 'data' here includes the 'dataset' described in this article.[13] The Code does not make clear whether a publicly accessible dataset is protectable under the current law.

Nowadays the size of datasets, the scale of investments, and their commercial value have increased significantly, which further strengthens the legitimacy of additional legal protections. And at the same time, China does see a great number of high-profile cases in which the contents of publicly accessible datasets were copied and made available to the public by competitors without the permission of their owners.[14] Most of the courts have stopped such data utilisation according to the Anti-Unfair Competition Law. Mainstream academic opinion, while disputing over the proper scope of the legal protection for datasets, generally does not question the need for a minimum level of such a protection.[15] Against this background, it is the right time to take the legal protection of datasets seriously. Assuming that Chinese legislators would adopt a property right regime in the future – to grant data collectors a very limited exclusive right, i.e. the right of public communication[16] – this article analyzes the eligibility requirements that the dataset as a protectable subject matter should meet under this regime.

This article believes that in order to protect the investment incentives of data collectors, balance the interests of data collectors, competitors, and the public, and ensure that the special dataset property right regime is

[9]For example, the following bills were debated by the US congress in 1990s: H R 3531, Database Investment and Intellectual Property Antiprivacy Act of 1996; H R 2652, Collection of Information Antiprivacy Act of 1997; H R 354, Collection of Information Antiprivacy Act of 1999.

[10]See the WIPO Draft Database Treaty of 1996.

[11]See Liu Jiangbin, 'Legal Issues in Digital Information Exchange: Intellectual Property Rights Protection of Data and Databases' (1999) 6 *Intellectual Property* 7; Ma Haisheng, 'Evaluation of Several Issues in Database Protection' (2001) 4 *Intellectual Property* 40; Zheng Shengli and Cui Guobin, 'The Legislative Status and Basic Theory of Database Protection' (2002) 1 *Peking University Intellectual Property Review*; Li Yang, 'The Defects in the Sui Generis Right Protection Regime for Databases and its Legislative Improvement' (2003) 4 *Studies in Law and Business* 26.

[12]The Chinese Civil Code of 2020, Article 127.

[13]See Huang Wei, *Interpretation of the Civil Code of the People's Republic of China (Part 1)* (Law Press China, 2020) 250–52.

[14]See (n 2 and 3).

[15]See Kong Xiangjun, 'Commercial Data Rights: A New Type of Industrial Property Rights in the Digital Age – The Affiliation of Industrial Property Rights and the Three Principles of the Ownership' (2022) 1 *Journal of Comparative Law*; Mei Xiaying, 'The Legal Nature of Data and Civil Law's Response' (2016) 9 *Chinese Social Scienceso*; Shen Weixing, 'On the Right to Use of Data' (2020) 11 *Chinese Social Sciences*; Long Weiqiu, 'Research on the Construction of New Data Property Rights and Its System' (2017) 4 *Tribune of Political Science and Law*.

[16]For detailed justifications of this proposal, see Cui Guobin (n 1) 9–10.

coordinated with the existing intellectual property system, the subject matter of protectable datasets should at least meet the following three requirements: (1) its data entries should be publicly accessible to the public; (2) it should include a substantial quantity of data; (3) it should contain a substantial collecting cost from the collector. This article analyzes the rationality and the determination (or criterion) of each eligibility requirement specifically. In addition, the following part will further point out that under the future property right regime of datasets protection, there should be no need to take the legality of the collector's act, the time sensitivity of data, or the adoption of technical measures as preconditions for eligibility of protection.

2. Presumptions before analyzing eligibility requirements

2.1. Presumed necessity of legal protection

Currently, intellectual property laws provide substantial protection for a dataset. Specifically, if a data item of the dataset or the dataset as a whole is confidential, the collector can seek trade secret protection for it. If the dataset is finally made public, but data entries of the dataset or the selection and compilation of data entries are original, they can be protected as regular works or compilation works under copyright law. However, for a compilation work, the copyright protection only extends to the selection and compilation of data entries, not to the content of the data itself.[17] Besides trade secrets or copyright protection, some countries provide extra protection for datasets and its contents. For instance, as mentioned above, time-sensitive factual information can obtain limited protection under the hot news doctrine in the United States.[18] The European Union provides sui generis protection for databases whose makers incur substantial investment in obtaining, verifying or presenting its contents.[19] China does not have a similar misappropriation doctrine under its Anti-Unfair Competition Law, but it does allow a court to apply the principle of business ethics to protect some public datasets, no matter whether its contents are time-sensitive or not.

Based on the above observations, it is clear that under the Chinese intellectual property law framework, there is no significant loophole in the legal protection of datasets. Some Chinese scholars not only mislead decision makers to believe that a broad legislative framework for datasets protection is needed by over-exaggerating the institutional gaps in intellectual property laws, but also confuse subsequent researchers into accepting a chaotic map of

[17]For detailed explanations of the copyright and trade secrets protection for datasets, see Cui Guobin (n 1) 5–8.
[18]See *International News Service v Associated Press* (1918) 248 U.S. 215.
[19]Article 7, the EU Directive on Databases.

thoughts in the IP field. This is very harmful. Under Chinese law, public datasets are not in a blank area in a strict sense. Although we do not have sui generis legislation on it, courts at all levels are permitted to apply the general provisions of the Anti-Unfair Competition Law to prohibit competitors from copying and exploiting datasets without permission. And the industry in China has already become used to judicial practices starting from the very early cases in 1990s[20] to the recent series of cases as mentioned previously.[21] Moreover, publicly accessible datasets actually only account for a small part of the datasets collected by the industry. So, even if we could say there is a legal gap in the protection of public datasets, it is a very narrow one. What needs to be enacted now is not a broad law to protect all type of data collections, but a narrow regime to deal with the problems in legal protection of publicly accessible datasets.

Although Chinese courts have long applied the general principles and provisions of the Anti-Unfair Competition Law to protect public datasets, this judicial practice has never been codified by a specific legislation. That is, Chinese legislators have not clarified whether legal protection for public datasets beyond the existing specific intellectual property regimes is necessary. The closest legislative effort is the ambiguous statement of Article 127 in the Civil Code, providing that 'where any laws provide for the protection of data and network virtual property, such laws shall apply'.

Among the Chinese academics, the author and many other scholars already have in-depth discussions on the justification of the special property rights for datasets in their papers. So far, the majority of opinions tend to believe that such a protection is necessary to protect the investment of data collectors, although they split over many specific issues of this legal protection.[22] To be brief and problem-focused, this article presumes that a minimum level of legal protection of datasets (that is, only granting the right of public communication) is justified, and then discusses the institutional choices in enacting such a regime.

It is worth mentioning that whether the protection of public datasets could be justified, to a large extent, depends on the feasibility or operability of such a legislation. If there is no a workable approach to reduce the inherent uncertainty and administrative costs, it is unlikely that the legislators would support a legislation on public datasets. In this sense, the justification and the feasibility of datasets protection have interplay. This means at this early stage when the society still doubts about the necessity of such a regime, the discussion of specific institutional choices is of particular significance – helping to justify the legal protection of public datasets in an indirect

[20]Such as *Beijing Sunshine Data Corp. v Shanghai Bacai Data Corp. Limited*, Beijing High People's Court, (1997) Gaozhi Zhongzi No. 66.
[21]See (n 2–4).
[22]See (n 16).

way. In other words, even if the legitimacy of the legal protection of public datasets is still in doubt, it is still of great theoretical value to discuss the eligibility requirements under such a regime in depth.

2.2. Presumed rationality in adopting a limited-exclusive-right regime

After the justification of datasets protection is presumed, the next question is what kind of regime or protection model should be adopted. There are two competing choices, namely, the property right regime and the unfair competition regime. The theoretic dispute on choosing a proper model for protecting public datasets is long-existing and worldwide. For example, in the past, the European Union chose the property right model of legislation for database protection,[23] while many of the original legislative proposals in the United States were typical anti-unfair competition models.[24] Theoretically, there are significant differences between these two models.[25] It is generally believed that the unfair competition model only focuses on specific competition behaviours among competitors and usually requires the existence of market failure,[26] thus it provides relatively narrower scope of protection than the property right regime,[27] which usually emphasise one's dominance over tangible or intangible things. Those who oppose the property right regime believe that subsequent uses of public datasets are diverse, and the property right regime may excessively restrain them,[28] resulting in excessive social costs. There are such disputes in China as well.[29]

In previous research, the author has discussed in depth the two competing choices, and concludes that in the field of datasets protection, there is no essential difference between the property right regime and the anti-unfair competition regime. The breadth and strength of protection depends on the specific institutional rules in each regime. The property right regime can be designed very narrowly, for example, having very rigid eligibility

---

[23]When Europe started enacting the database directive, it initially hoped to adopt an anti-unfair competition law model, but later moved towards a broad property rights model under the lobbying of interest groups. See JH Reichman and Pamela Samuelson (n 6) 81.

[24]Jacqueline Lipton, 'Balancing Private Rights and Public Policies: Reconceptualizing Property in Databases' (2003) 18 *Berkeley Technology Law Journal* 773, 817.

[25]See Shyamkrishna Balganesh, '"Hot News": The Enduring Myth of Property in News' (2011) 111 *Columbia Law Review.* 419.

[26]FW Grosheide, 'Database Protection – The European Way' (2002) 8 *Washington University Journal of Law & Policy* 39, 44; Pamela Samuelson, 'Mapping the Digital Public Domain: Threats and Opportunities' (2003) 66 *Law & Contemporary Problems.* 147, 159.

[27]Dennis S Karjala, 'Misappropriation as a Third Intellectual Property Paradigm' (1994) 94 *Columbia Law Review* 2594, 2605.

[28]Rui Wenbiao, Li Guoquan and Yang Fuyu, 'An Analysis of the Intellectual Property Protection Model of Data Information' (2015) 4 *Electronic Intellectual Property* 98.

[29]For opinions supporting a special property right regime, see Shen Weixing (n 15); Long Weiqiu (n 15); for opinions advocating unfair competition law model, see Liu Jianchen, 'Reflections and Solutions on Enterprise Data Entitlement and Protection' (2021) 6 *Nanjing University Law Journal.*

requirements, granting very narrow exclusive rights and offering a short term of protection; and the anti-competition regime can be designed very broadly, for example, defining competitive relationships loosely, setting up very few evaluation elements, and banning a broad scope of behaviours. Discussing the scope of protection provided by the two modes in an abstract manner has no practical meaning.[30] Take Japanese or Korean unfair competition regime as an example. It allows a collector to exclude others from reproducing, using or publicising contents of a dataset.[31] The protection under this anti-unfair competition regime is much broader than the limited exclusive right suggested in this article. The next section on 'the relevance of the eligibility analysis to the anti-unfair competition model' further verifies this point. Framing the protection of public datasets as a property right would make it easier for the society to understand the nature of this right and the practice of licensing or transfer. In other words, a property right regime is more friendly to transactions or licensing activities. For this reason, the author sticks to his position in the previous paper, preferring the limited-exclusive-regime. In the following parts, it further assumes that the Chinese legislators will adopt such property right regime in the future. To some extent, the statement in Article 127 of the Civil Code also support this presumption because if the legislators view datasets protection as an unfair competition law issue, it would not regulate it in the Civil Code.

In the future, if adopting the property right regime, legislators will have to solve a series of basic problems such as the scope of subject matter (eligibility requirements), the content of the exclusive right, the ownership of the right, the term of protection and exceptions or limitations on the right. Undoubtedly, every problem is complex,[32] and deserves a special study. The feasibility of the legislation depends on whether we can formulate specific and workable solutions for all the problems. At this stage, most research papers remain at the macro level such as clarifying the concept of 'data property right', justifying such a protection, arguing for a legislative model, and drawing up a general legislative framework. The above-mentioned basic problems have not been discussed in depth. Merely staying at the macro level, researchers tend to underestimate the challenge of enacting such a property right regime and put forward unrealistic or overbroad legislative suggestions.[33]

This article assumes that legislators will choose a narrow property right regime to protect public datasets. It will not fully reveal the complexity in

[30]Cui Guobin (n 1) 22.
[31]Article 2(1)(k), the Korean Unfair Competition Prevention and Trade Secret Protection Act (2021).
[32]See Josef Drexl (n 1) 3, para. 8.
[33]Some civil law scholars propose to create very broad property rights for data collections, without considering the protection already available under existing intellectual property laws. See, Mei Xiaying (n 15); Long Weiqiu (n 15).

creating such a brand-new regime, instead, it only focuses on one aspect, the eligibility requirements for such a protection. This is not an isolated issue. On the contrary, the eligibility requirements work in concert with the aforementioned rules on other parts of the regime, such as the contents of the exclusive right, the allocation of ownership, the exceptions or limitations on the right and the term of protection. To illustrate, if the law only grants a very limited exclusive right (right of public communication), the eligibility requirements could be set relatively loose; on the contrary, if we grant relatively broad rights, the eligibility requirements should be correspondingly stricter. It is equally true for other rules such as exceptions or limitations on the right and the term of protection. Unfortunately, the legal community is far from reaching a consensus on the basic institutional framework for the regime, not to mention the specific rules of other parts that match and correspond with eligibility requirements. This makes the research on eligibility requirements quite difficult.

Having analysed almost all the previously-mentioned datasets cases in China, this author believes that the collectors would be able to stop the accused from unfair competition either under the existing intellectual property laws or under the proposed regime that only grants a right of public communication. So, this author believes that so far there is no real need to grant more rights to the collectors.[34] That is also why this Article presumes that future special legislation will only grant the right of public communication on public datasets. In addition to this, it further presumes that its term of protection is very short, just 5–10 years,[35] and the law will recognise independent collection and fair uses as defenses in infringement suits. And, it is also presumed that competition law or consumer protection law may be applied to restrict the collectors' rights as well. Under this hypothetical

---

[34]For a more detailed explanation on this, see Cui Guobin (n 1) 9–10.

[35]The term of protection for datasets is a complicated issue. Initially, the proposed term of protection in the draft EU Database Directive was 10 years. Later on, the approved version changed it to 15 years. See Article 10 of the EU Database Directive. The term of protection in the WIPO Draft Database Treaty is 15 years (proposed by EU) or 25 years (proposed by the US). See JH Reichman and Pamela Samuelson (n 6) 109. At that time, the UK data industry thought the proposed terms were still too short, compared with the 50-year protection under the UK copyright law. Mark Schneider (n 8) 556. In contrast, some scholars believe 3 or 4-year protection is adequate. See Jacqueline Lipton, 'Balancing Private Rights and Public Policies: Reconceptualizing Property in Databases' (2003) 18 *Berkeley Technology Law Journal* 773, 839.

Actually, the term of protection needed by different industries varies. For example, it might be normal for the medical record database accumulated by a hospital to have an update cycle of five to ten years; the update cycle of transaction data in online e-commerce may be several weeks or months; and the update of news data in the real-time news service industry may be even shorter. Setting different term of protection for different types of datasets presents many challenges. For example, it can lead to complex rent-seeking problems. This Article argues that, for the convenience of legislation and law enforcement, the most feasible solution is to set a uniform term of protection.

Another important issue is how to determine the start date of the protection period. This paper tends to believe that the term of protection should be calculated from the collection date of the earliest data entry in the data set. An in-depth discussion of the term of protection rule is beyond the purpose of this Article and therefore omitted.

institutional framework, the author considers the eligibility requirements for public datasets to satisfy.

2.3. The relevance of eligibility analysis to unfair competition model

Before discussing the eligibility requirements in details, it should be emphasised that even if the legislators choose to refine the existing provisions of anti-unfair competition law in the future rather than enact a new property right regime for datasets, the discussion of the eligibility requirements is still highly relevant to the legislative and judicial practices.

Under the anti-unfair competition model, legislatures or courts also need to define the boundaries of improper use of datasets. Take the typical *NBA v. Motorola* case as an example. The US federal court clarified in this case the necessary elements for degerming a misappropriation under the hot news doctrine. That is, the use of factual data constitutes misappropriation only when the following five elements are met: (1) the collection of information requires some cost or expense; (2) the value of the information is highly time-sensitive; (3) the defendant's use of the information constitutes free-riding on the plaintiff's costly efforts to generate or collect the information; (4) the defendant's use of this information is in direct competition with a product or service offered by the plaintiff; (5) The ability of other parties to free-ride on the efforts of the plaintiff will so reduce the incentive to provide the product or service that its existence or quality would be substantially threatened.[36]

The elements defining the boundaries of an infringing behaviour under anti-unfair competition law as mentioned above can be easily translated into the eligibility requirements under the property right regime. To illustrate, the first element requires certain cost to collect information, and the second element requires the value of the information to be time-sensitive. Both elements describes the characteristics of the information itself and can be directly regarded as eligibility requirements under the property right regime.

The third and fourth elements require that there is a competitive relationship between the defendant and the collector and the defendant's behaviour constitutes free-riding. Many scholars believe that the scope of protection under an anti-unfair competition law model is much narrower than that of the property right regime because these classical elements of anti-unfair competition law only exclude competitors, but not other members of the public.[37] In fact, similar effects can also be achieved through narrowing the scope of subject matter or restricting the content of rights under the

---

[36] *National Basketball Association v Motorola, Inc.* (1997), 105 F.3d 841, 852–53.
[37] See Rui Wenbiao (n 28) 98; Dennis S Karjala (n 27) 2599.

property right regime. For example, if the law requires that the data entries used by the defendant reaches a substantial amount and entails substantial collection cost on the collector, and at the same time the law only grants the right of public communication, it would result in that only those who have communicated to the public a substantial amount of data entries would infringe the right. Naturally, the law would guarantee that there exists a competitive relationship between the defendant and the collector. And, since the collector makes substantial investment to collect the data and the defendant avoids the cost, the defendant's behaviour almost always constitutes a free-riding. The general public, who has no competitive relationship with collectors and usually does not use datasets in this manner, will not be bothered by the property regime.

Finally, the fifth element requires that the defendant's act constitutes a substantial threat to the collector's service. This requirement can also be translated into an eligibility requirement under the property right regime. As described later, the law should require that the cost of collection reaches a substantial level. The court could raise or lower the standard of this element to the extent that it poses a substantial threat to the 'existence or quality of the product or service'. Apart from that, the requirement for substantial amount of data entries in a dataset under a property right regime also implies the 'substantial threat' element under the anti-unfair competition model: if the amount of data entries used by competitors is small, it usually will not materially harm the plaintiff's investment incentives and a legal remedy would not be necessary.

The above analysis once again shows that the boundary between the so-called property right regime and the anti-unfair competition regime is not as clear-cut as some scholars might imagine.[38] In essence, the nature of property is 'the right to exclude others from some thing'.[39] What the property law supposed to regulate is not a right holder's domination of tangible or intangible objects, but the interaction or relationship between a right holder and the public. In this sense, it is very similar to the anti-unfair competition regime, which regulates the relationship between the right holder and its competitors. The only difference is that property right regime relies more on the 'physical or imagined boundary of a subject matter' to define the behaviours it regulates or the scope of people it affects. In other words, the subject matter is just a proxy that helps to reduce the cost in delineating the scope of the property right. The anti-unfair competition regime has a different approach. It directly describes the defining features of regulated behaviours and does not rely on the proxy of subject matter. In theory, the scope of protection under two regimes could be roughly the same or

[38]For opinions emphasizing the difference between the two models, see Shyamkrishna Balganesh (n 25).
[39]Thomas W Merrill and Henry E Smith, *Property* (Oxford University Press, 2010) 4.

sharply different. The size of the difference depends on the legislator's choices of specific eligibility requirements, the content of rights, the term of protection or infringement defenses, and has no direct relationship with the legislator's choice of the property right regime or the anti-unfair competition one at the macro level. This is probably the same reason why the protection of trade secrets could constitute either a property right or an interest under the anti-unfair competition law in the eyes of different scholars.[40]

Since many contents of the eligibility requirements under a property right regime can be translated into the constitutional elements under the unfair competition regime with slight changes, then even if the legislators adopt the anti-unfair competition regime to protect public datasets in the future, this Article, although focusing on the eligibility requirements of datasets protection, could still guide judicial courts to demarcate the boundaries of specific unfair competition behaviours. Moreover, the future anti-unfair competition regime might even rely on the 'eligibility requirements' to define the boundaries of improper conducts just as the current trade secrets regime under the anti-unfair competition framework.

3. Public availability of data entries

3.1. Justifications for public availablity requirement

In according to the trade secrets law, the contents of datasets usually can be protected as trade secrets before it is made public.[41] Such protection extends to not only any data entry that is kept secret, but also the dataset as a whole even if the data entries are made public.[42] If additional special property rights protection is provided thereon, it overlaps with the trade secret protection. So far, the EU Database Directive, which is very close to a property rights regime for large-scale datasets, has not avoided the overlap protection of sui generis rights and trade secrets. In contrast, the latest Korean law avoids the overlap by requiring a dataset is not managed as secret.[43]

A research report sponsored by the European Commission states that the overlap of the two regimes is not problematic since it neither poses any significant challenge nor changes the actual value of the sui generis protection.

[40]For example, the US Supreme Court treats the protection of trade secrets as a property right. See *Ruckelshaus v Monsanto Co.* (1983), 467 U.S. 986, 1004. For a better understanding to relevant theoretic disputes, see Mark A Lemley, 'The Surprising Virtues of Treating Trade Secrets as IP Rights' (2008) 61 *Stanford Law Review* 311.

[41]see Cui Guobin (n 1) 5–7.

[42]When a dataset as a whole is claimed as a trade secret, the law does not require each data entry of the dataset to be in secret. Instead, it only requires the dataset 'as a body or in precise configuration and assembly of its components' is not generally known among or readily accessible to persons within the circles that normally deal with the kind of information in question. See Article 39(2) of the Agreement on Trade-Related Aspects of Intellectual Property Rights ('TRIPs Agreement').

[43]Article 2 (7), the Japanese Unfair Competition Prevention Act (2018); Article 2(1)(k), the Korean Unfair Competition Prevention and Trade Secret Protection Act (2021).

According to the report, 'cumulative protection for intellectual property is widely accepted and practiced'.[44] For example, trade secrets and copyright protection for unpublished works may overlap, and so do copyright and patent protection for industrial designs or works of applied art. Under certain circumstances, these regimes can all be used to prevent unauthorised reproduction, publication or distribution (sale) of protected works or designs.

Indeed, some cumulative protections in the fields of intellectual property may not necessarily cause serious problems. Nevertheless, considering some special factors of datasets protection, this Article disagrees with the EU research report and believes that the prerequisite for a large dataset to receive special property rights protection should be that data entries in the dataset is already made public. The main reasons are as follows.

First, before the data entries of the dataset are disclosed, the trade secrets regime can provide effective protection. Collectors can prohibit others from illegally acquiring, disclosing and using the secret data entries.[45] This protection actually is much broader than the protection of special property rights regime. For example, the EU Database Directive provides sui generis rights for databases, and collectors can prohibit others from obtaining or using substantial parts of the contents of the database.[46] Although this legislation is generally considered to grant a broad protection to the database, it is still narrower than the protection of the trade secrets law, which covers every secret data entries. Since overlap protection does not generate additional benefits and it is not difficult to avoid it, there is naturally no need to deliberately maintain it. More importantly, the proposed special property right regime only grants the right of public communication. Without right to reproduce and right to use, such protection is much narrower than that offered by trade secrets law. Thus, it is almost meaningless to insist that the data entries in secret should also be protected by the special property right regime.

Second, requiring the disclosure of data entries makes the calculation of the term of protection easier. The special property rights protection in most cases only makes sense for collectors who disclose data to the public because of the need of their business models. The date of disclosure is relatively easier to verify than the date of creation of a secret data entry, which has no effective way to publicise. Therefore, it would be better to calculate the term of protection from the date of disclosure rather than the date of creation. In addition, the proposed term of protection is relatively short. If the preparatory work prior to the commercialisation of a dataset takes a long time, data collectors may be caught in an embarrassing situation

[44] European Commission, Evaluation of Directive 96/9/EC on the Legal Protection of Databases, 2018, at 43–44, www.ec.europa.eu/newsroom/dae/document.cfm?doc_id=51764 (accessed 10 February 2021).
[45] Article 9, the Chinese Anti-Unfair Competition Law (2019).
[46] Article 7, Directive 96/9/EC on the Legal Protection of Databases.

where the term of special property rights protection expires before the data entries are made public. Then, the special property rights protection cannot achieve its intended purpose.

Third, the scope of subject matters under the special property rights regime has a great deal of uncertainty. Refusing to offer cumulative protection, the law can urge data collectors to rely on trade secrets regime as effectively as possible, and thus limit their dependence on the special property rights regime. The trade secrets regime requires a collector to take effective confidentiality measures to reduce the negative impact on freedom of action in the public domain. The public know they are safe if they don't cross the line secured by confidentiality measures. In contrast, the special property rights regime relies on relatively vague elements such as the 'substantial amount of data entries' and 'substantial investment' as mentioned later to delineate the boundaries of subject matter. There line between protected datasets and those in the public domain is inevitably ambiguous, and thus it poses a certain threat to the freedom in the public domain. Therefore, if there is no necessity, we should try to avoid extending this protection to datasets that are kept in secret.

3.2. Connection between trade secrets and datasets protection

In the past, many studies on datasets did not seriously consider the connection between trade secrets and the special property rights protection, and there has been some confusion in understanding the relationship between the two regimes. In some judicial cases, the collectors of datasets could have claimed the protection of trade secrets, but they failed to do so. Instead, they sought the protection of 'data property rights' in the name of Article 2 of the Anti-Unfair Competition Law. *Taobao Corp. v. Anhui Meijing Corp.*, and *Beijing Weimeng Corp. v. Beijing Taoyou Tianxia Corp.*, are representative examples. In *Taobao* case, Taobao is the leading e-commerce platform in China. It granted to the defendant a license of online access to its data product 'Business Advisor'. At request of the its users, the product generates reports on market conditions of various commodities, including market trend charts, sub-category commodity trade ranking index, hot-selling products list, popular brands list, users' search term analysis, and so on. The reports are based on the trace information of Taobao users' browsing, searching, purchasing and other behaviours. Taobao desensitised the behavioural trace information, thus no personal information issues are involved here. All the behavioural trace information and the automatically-generated reports are backend data secured with technical measures and not publicly accessible. The defendant granted sublicenses of online access to third parties without the permission of the plaintiff. Then, the dispute arose.[47] In *Beijing Weimeng* case, Weibo.com, the leading Twitter-alike social medica platform in China, collected the registration information of hundreds and millions of users, and granted to the defendant a license of API access to the users' information. Later, the defendant exceeded the scope of license to download extra users' information from the database. Then, the plaintiff sued to the court.[48] Here the database of users' registration information is kept in secret as well. According to the author, it is pretty clear that the data collectors in both cases should have claimed trade secret protection for their datasets, rather than a general 'data property right' under Article 2 of the Chinese Anti-unfair Competition Law. Surprisingly, both courts upheld the plaintiffs' claims and many scholars in China applaud them as exemplary judicial decisions on data property rights.[49]

In addition to the above cases, the academic community's response to the famous dispute on data sharing between SF Express and Cainiao Company also illustrate the problem. In this case, established under the leadership of Alibaba Group, Cainiao platform obtained massive e-commerce transaction information from Taobao Company and provided logistics platform services for many logistics companies. Cainiao handed over transaction information of both sellers and buyers to a specific follow-up logistics platform based on the sellers or buyers' choice to facilitate subsequent logistics services. SF Express was a main logistics company that Taobao sellers often chose. According to its contract with Cainiao, SF Express obtained users' transaction information from Cainiao, and then, having added information about the users' follow-up cargo delivery and receipt confirmation, fed it back to Cainiao. Later, Cainiao accused SF Express of improperly using Taobao users' phone numbers and other information beyond a reasonable need, therefore threatening data security. During the dispute between the two parties, they stopped providing data to each other, which concerned the public widely in China, and finally they settled the dispute.[50] This controversy is generally labelled as a data property right dispute by the press and academia to illustrate the importance of a new data property rights legislation. In fact, this case should also have been treated as a typical trade secrets licensing dispute, which is nothing new in law. Whether SF Express accessed and used the secret data provided by Cainiao beyond permission depends entirely on the trade secret license agreement between the two and the relevant provisions on trade secrets in the Anti-Unfair Competition Law.

[47] *Taobao (China) Software Co., Ltd. v Anhui Meijing Information Technology Co., Ltd.*, Hangzhou Intermediate People's Court of Zhejiang Province, (2018) Zhe 01 Min Zhong No. 7312.

[48] *Beijing Weimeng Chuangke Network Technology Co., Ltd. v Beijing Taoyou Tianxia Technology Co., Ltd.*, Beijing Intellectual Property Court, (2016) Jing 73 Min Zhong No. 588.

[49] See Mei Xiaying (n 15) 1206.

[50] Zhang Xiaoxiang, 'The Battle between Cainiao and SF Express Ends: Logistics Data Control, Security and Business Competition Continue' *The Paper* (6 June 2017) www.thepaper.cn/newsDetail_forward_1700457 (accessed 17 February 2022).

Under this analytical framework, we do not need to introduce any new special data property rights.

In order to seamlessly connect the regimes, the special property rights legislation should use a criterion of public availability contrary to the secrecy requirement of trade secrets law to define the disclosure requirement for the data entries in a dataset. The protection of special property rights starts at the place where the protection of trade secrets ceases. For a dataset to be protected under the new regime, data entries in the dataset should be readily accessible by the relevant public. For example, in the famous *Dianping* case, Dianping.com discloses all user reviews information on catering companies on its web pages.[51] Another one is the *Baidu v. Dianping* case, in which Baidu Maps presents map information to all users through its navigation application.[52] In both cases, the public can freely obtain any piece of data entries in the datasets through client applications. Therefore, the data entries of the datasets should be regarded as being publicly accessible and should no longer receive trade secrets protection. However, when the content of the data entries is presented only to users under a duty of confidentiality, even if the number of users is very large, the data entries are still legally in secret.[53]

It should be noted that the law should require data entries in the dataset, but not the file that contains the dataset as a whole, to be publicly accessible. In fact, it is quite possible that the content of each data entry in a dataset is accessible online but the complete file that contains the dataset itself is still not readily available to the public. Take the services in *Dianping* or *Baidu* cases as an example. In theory, the public can download all user-review information or map information one by one through the Internet, and then piece them together into a dataset. If this process is time-consuming and laborious, for example, the download process being interrupted by technical measures of the targeted website from time to time and thereby unsustainable,[54] it means that the file stored on the server side that contains the entire

[51]See *Shanghai Hantao Information Consulting Co., Ltd. v Aibang Juxin (Beijing) Technology Co., Ltd.*, Beijing No. 1 Intermediate Court, (2009) Yizhong Minzhong Zi No. 5031; *Shanghai Hantao Information Consulting Co., Ltd. v Aibang Juxin (Beijing)) Technology Co., Ltd.*, Beijing No. 1 Intermediate Court, (2011) Yi Zhong Min Zhong Zi No. 7512.

[52]*Beijing NavInfo Technology Co., Ltd. v Beijing Baidu Netcom Technology Co., Ltd.*, Beijing Intellectual Property Court, (2017) Jing 73 Min Chu No. 1914.

[53]The US Supreme Court makes it clear in the *Board of Trade v Christie Grain & Stock Co.* (1905) 198 U. S. 236, 251–52: 'The plaintiff does not lose its rights by communicating the result to persons, even if many, in confidential relations to itself, under a contract not to make it public, and strangers to the trust will be restrained from getting at the knowledge by inducing a breach of trust, and using knowledge obtained by such a breach.' Here the information in dispute is quotations of prices offered and accepted for wheat, corn and provisions in Chicago Stock Exchange. The plaintiff distributes them under contract to persons approved by it and under certain conditions. The defendants are sued for using the quotations obtained without authority of the plaintiff.

[54]For a brief introduction to anti-crawling technology, see Chen Liting, 'Anti-Crawling Technology in the Era of Big Data' (2016) 6 *Computer and Information Technology* 60.

dataset is not easy to download. Thus, the file stored on the server that contains the dataset as a whole may still be treated as a trade secret, although the data entries within it has been published through the website. If someone breaks the effective confidentiality measures on the server and directly downloads the file containing the entire dataset, he may still infringe the collector's trade secrets. In other words, the protection of trade secrets prohibits others from taking shortcuts to download the file that records the overall content of the dataset after directly undermining the protective measures taken by the collector.

The *Kumike* case is a typical one in this regard. The plaintiff Gumi Company stored on its server the information about the real-time status of public transportation and authorised its users to search through it from client-side applications. The users could not directly obtain the backend data. The defendant cracked the plaintiff's client-side applications and disguised its program as an authorised one to obtain back-end data. Then, the defendant relied on the back-end data to serve its own users. The court pointed out:

> The real-time bus information stored in the server of the Kumike APP can bring out real or potential, current or future economic benefits to the right holder, thus it already possesses the attributes of an intangible property. Gumi Company is the copyright owner of the Kumike software, and accordingly it has legitimate interests in possessing, using, processing and disposing the data contained in the software. Without the permission of Gumi Company, no one may illegally obtain this backend data and use it for business purposes.[55]

Unfortunately, the court did not consider the possibility that back-end data might constitute trade secrets, but directly regarded the dataset as a kind of intangible property and applied the general clause, Article 2 of the Anti-Unfair Competition Law to resolve the dispute.

The data acquisition behaviour of the defendant in *Kumike* case is different from other typical authorised users who extract data entries bit by bit through the client-side applications and then might reintegrate them into a dataset. The latter does not infringe the collector's trade secrets. If a collector wants to prevent the users from communicating the lawfully-reintegrated dataset to the public, he needs the help of special property rights legislation. Of course, if the process of downloading and piecing together data from the collector's website was not time or resource-consuming, namely that the public could easily reconstruct the entire dataset with contents obtained through public channels, then the file that contains the whole dataset and is stored on the server-end would probably not be

[55] *Shenzhen Gumi Technology Co., Ltd. v Wuhan Yuanguang Technology Co., Ltd.*, Shenzhen Intermediate People's Court of Guangdong Province, (2017) Yue 03 Min Chu No. 822.

viewed as confidential and could not be protected as a trade secret. Even so, it does not mean that those who circumvent the technical measures taken by the collector to access to the files would not bear any legal liabilities. In fact, if the technical measures are taken to restrict visitors' manner or frequency of accessing the server and limit the download of backend files, they may be protected by computer security law. Visitors' circumvention of technical measures and download of data without the authority may constitute the crime of 'illegal acquisition of data from computer information system' under Chinese Criminal Law.[56]

3.3. Voluntary and involuntary disclosure

There are two ways for the contents of datasets to become public. One is voluntary disclosure done by collectors during the business process. For example, in the aforementioned Dianping or Baidu Maps cases, the collectors voluntarily provides consumer reviews or electronic map information to the public. The second is involuntary or passive disclosure done by a third party without permission of data collectors.

According to the logic of trade secrets law, the liability for infringement can effectively deter third parties from disclosing the secret dataset. Refusal of additional data property rights protection for these passively disclosed datasets usually will not result in a market failure. However, effective protection of trade secrets does not mean that the law should completely eradicate any cases that may be scattered across the society. On the contrary, trade secrets infringements happen frequently. As long as the law can control the overall infringing activities at a reasonable level, the trade secrets protection may still be viewed effective. Otherwise, the law may cause excessive deterrence, increase preventive costs, and thus result in too much inefficiency. Since existing trade secrets law does not provide extra protection for passively disclosed trade secrets, should special legislation on datasets also refuse to protect passively disclosed datasets?

In theory, if special property rights legislation refuses to protect involuntarily disclosed datasets, some data collectors will be encouraged to voluntarily disclose their data earlier to avoid the consequences of being disclosed by a third party after the failure of confidentiality. To assess the effect of policy

[56]See Shanghai Shengpin Network Technology Co., Ltd. and Hou Mingqiang, 'Illegal acquisition of data from computer information system', Beijing Haidian District People's Court, (2017) Jing 0108 Xing Chu No. 2384. In this case, the defendant used technical means to capture the video data stored in the server of the victim, Beijing ByteDance Network Technology Co., Ltd. The defendant cracked the anti-crawling measures of the victim and used the 'tt_spider' file to implement video data scraping. In the process of data scraping, fake device id is used to bypass the server's identity verification, and fake UA and IP are used to bypass the server's access frequency limit. A similar case is Shao Moumou and Chen Mou, 'Illegal acquisition of data from computer information system', Shenzhen Nanshan District People's Court, (2017) 0305 Xingchu No. 153.

in encouraging disclosure, we can refer to the strategy in the US patent law that discriminates against inventors who intend to keep the invention in secret from the beginning of its commercialisation. If an inventor chooses to commercialise the invention in secret rather than applying for a patent, the court will interpret this commercial use as a 'public use' in the sense of patent law.[57] According to the so-called statutory bar doctrine, the inventor will be prevented from seeking patent protection afterwards, even if the invention has not been in fact disclosed to the public by the inventor or a third party.[58] Nevertheless, the opportunity for a third party to seek patent protection for the invention is not affected by the secret commercial use of the prior inventor. In other words, the commercialisation of the undisclosed invention is not viewed as a 'public use' against the third party's patent application. Through this interpretation, the US court forces the inventor to make a choice between two alternatives when commercialising his invention: either immediately apply for a patent or forever adhere to trade secrets protection. The inventor can only go one way to the end and cannot switch between them. He cannot first choose trade secrets, and wait until the situation becomes unfavourable before turning to patent protection. The US courts do not allow inventors to make a profit on both sides, and thus show a bias in favour of timely patenting and disclosing an invention.[59] In theory, this system encourages inventors to early disclose and patent the inventions that by nature cannot be kept in secret in commercial use for a long time; if the inventors can hide them for a period longer than the term of patent protection, they probably will commercialise their inventions secretly and will not patent them.

Given the practice of the US patent law, should the new legislation discriminate against datasets that are initially kept confidential but are later disclosed by a third party, therefore to encourage earlier disclosure of datasets? After weighing various pros and cons, this article believes that there is no need for legislators to do so.

First of all, there are an important difference between large datasets and technological inventions, which make it is difficult to encourage earlier disclosure of datasets by discriminating against the data collectors who initially keep them in secret. In the technical field, if an inventor chooses to secretly commercialise an invention, others may come out with the same or similar inventions very soon. This threat of competition from independent inventors is the key factor that urges the original inventor to patent and disclose the

[57]Mark A Lemley, 'Does "Public Use" Mean the Same Thing It Did Last Year?' www.law.berkeley.edu/files/Lemley_Mark_IPSC_paper_2014.pdf (accessed 5 February 2021) 4–6.

[58]The leading case in US is *Metallizing Eng'g Co. v Kenyon Bearing & Auto Parts Co.*, 153 F.2d 516 (2d Cir.1946). In 2019, the US Supreme Court stated its support for the above case in *Helsinn Healthcare S.A. v Teva Pharmaceuticals USA, Inc.* (2019) 139 S. Ct. 628.

[59]Mark A Lemley (n 57) 16–18.

invention rather than keep it in secret. In this sense, restricting an inventor's secret commercial use can promote social welfare.

However, the same strategy hardly works in the field of large datasets. When a collector's business model allows it to keep the contents of a dataset in secret, it would be difficult for competitors to independently collect the same contents and disclose to the public. Once the dataset is disclosed to the public, the protection under the new regime (a limited exclusive right) is much shorter and narrower than trade secret protection. Obviously, if a collector can commercialise the dataset secretly and feel no real threat of competition from independent collectors, it would rarely have incentive to voluntarily disclose the dataset in exchange for a much weaker protection. This means that, as for the special property rights legislation, the effect of encouraging earlier voluntary disclosure of datasets by discriminating against involuntary disclosure would be minimal compared to the US patent law's possible effect in encouraging earlier disclosure of inventions.

Second, the protection of involuntarily-disclosed datasets has very limited impact on the freedom of action in the public domain. The copyright law, which is very close to the special property rights regime of datasets, does not distinguish between voluntary and involuntary disclosure of copyrightable works. As long as a work is completed, no matter whether it is published voluntarily by the author or involuntarily by a third party, it will automatically be protected.[60] In some cases, while whether a work is published will affect the calculation of the term of copyright protection,[61] copyright law does not distinguish between voluntarily and involuntary publication to achieve a public policy goal. Similarly, neither do special property rights legislation. As mentioned earlier, it only prevents others from communicating the contents of a dataset to the public. Its impact on the freedom of action in the public domain is much less than copyright protection of ordinary works, therefore almost negligible: Apparently, discriminating against an involuntarily disclosed dataset and allowing others to freely communicate the dataset to the public simply invites competitors to free ride without achieving any meaningful policy goal.

Third, failing to protect involuntarily disclosed datasets will also harm the interests of data collectors who originally plan to use the datasets publicly and increase social costs. From the completion of a dataset to its first public commercial use, there may be a considerable time interval or many steps of commercial transactions.[62] If an accidental passive disclosure of the dataset in this process causes the loss of special property rights

[60] Article 2, Chinese Copyright Law (2020).

[61] For example, the term of protection for a legal person's work depends on whether the work is published. See Article 23, the Chinese Copyright Act (2020).

[62] 'In a sense, without the circulation of data, there is no realization of data value ... The need for circulation is the natural attribute of data.' Gao Fuping, 'A Theory of Data Circulation: The Allocation of Data Resource Rights' (2019) 6 *Peking University Law Journal* 1410.

protection, it is equivalent to punishing the collector and his partners just because they have not taken effective confidentiality measures before making a public use. In response, the collector will adopt more rigid technical or management measures before disclosing the dataset, and thus incur a higher operating cost. On the contrary, if passively disclosed datasets are equally protected, this kind of cost could be reduced or avoided.

Lastly, if the special property rights legislation does not deliberately distinguish between voluntary or involuntary disclosure, the administrative costs of this system will be reduced. In specific cases, the parties need not to provide evidences on the disclosure process of the datasets, and neither do the court need to review the evidences to identify active or passive disclosure. Thus, the social resources will be saved.

4. Substantial number of data entries

4.1. *Justifications for the 'substantial number' requirement*

Under the existing copyright system, once ordinary data information is disclosed, its communication and use will no longer be restricted unless it falls within the scope of protectable subject matters. This rule applies to technical information, scientific experiment data, and business management information (such as stock indexes, customer lists, etc.). Even if the production or collection of the data information is very expensive, there is no exception.[63] There may be several reasons for this. First, as mentioned earlier, in most cases, the trade secrets law has provided effective protection before such data information is disclosed.[64] If the collector does not want to lose its control over the data information, it can keep it in secret. Therefore, the law usually need not to provide supplementary property rights protection after the data is disclosed. Second, protecting data information in public domain will greatly increase the overall cost to society.[65] The general public rely on the data information in the public domain in many ways. For them, the cost for identifying the owner of data information and negotiating licenses might be much higher than the value of using the data. To avoid such market failure, the law chooses to ensure the free dissemination of such public information. Lastly, the administrative cost of property rights protection for such public data is too high. The data information usually lacks distinctive and personalised characteristics when it is of small

---

[63]Actually, besides intellectual property law, there are other laws that restrict the use of publicly available information or data. For example, the right to name, right to portrait, and personal information right under the Chinese Civil Code may also impose certain restrictions on the subsequent use of data information. However, these rights are not directly related to the protection of datasets and will not be discussed in details here.

[64]See Section 3.2.

[65]See Cui Guobin (n 1) 10–11.

amount, therefore it is difficult to trace its association with a specific collector when widely circulated and used. Then, it is relatively difficult to determine its ownership of rights and the scope of protection. To protect such data information, the system will have a high administrative cost.

In order to reduce its negative impact on the public domain, future special property rights legislation should stipulate that datasets must have a substantial number of data entries to be eligible for special property rights protection. First of all, as the number of data entries increases, the commercial nature of the dataset will become more obvious. So does its commercial value. From the perspective of freedom of speech, commercial speech receives a limited form of protection[66]; the stronger the commercial character, the smaller the chilling effect caused by the protection of property rights,[67] and more justifiable the property rights regime. Legal protection of the property rights will not easily lead to the disappearance of an infringing commercial speech, since subsequent speakers, out of their own commercial interests, are willing to overcome this cost barrier and seek for collectors' permission to deliver the speech to the public.

Second, by ensuring that the size of a protected dataset far exceeds the number of data entries contained in an ordinary work, the negative impact on the public's freedom of creation and expression will be minimised. The special datasets regime is essentially to provide protection for unoriginal collections of data or facts. If the threshold for the number of data entries is too low, it will greatly hinder the general public from using public data and information to communicate with each other or create regular works, resulting in huge negative externalities.[68] As the number of data entries increases, these negative externalities gradually decrease because the need for the public to use the massive data intactly to recreate or express would be very rare. Especially, when a dataset achieves a scale that only can only be processed by a computer, it is more like a machine-readable-only industrial product rather than a speech for natural persons. If it is stipulated that the number of data entries in the protected datasets far exceeds that in ordinary works, the protection of datasets will not interfere with the public's freedom in creating regular works. So there is no need to worry that the protection of special property rights would affect their freedom of action.

Lastly, with the increase of the size of datasets, the legitimacy of special property rights regime is strengthened. According to Demsetz's theory of property rights, in the social context of resource value appreciation, the public's tolerance for the institutional cost of property rights will increase.[69]

[66] *Posadas de Puerto Rico Assoc. v Tourism Company of Puerto Rico* (1986) 478 U.S. 328, 341.
[67] *Virginia State Pharmacy Board v Virginia Citizens Consumer Council* (1976) 425 U. S. 748, 771.
[68] *Feist Publications, Inc. v Rural Telephone Service Company, Inc.* (1991) 499 U. S. 340, 347–48.
[69] See Harold Demsetz, 'Toward a Theory of Property Rights' (1967) 57 *Am. Econ. Rev. Papers & Proc.* 347, 352.

The protection of datasets actually follows a similar logic. On one hand, the value of datasets and the willingness of the society to tolerate the possible negative effects of the protection will increased; on the other hand, the administrative cost of the regime will decrease, since the increase in the size of datasets also makes it relatively easier to demarcate the boundaries of subject matter, identify ownership of rights, and determine infringements.

Different from the proposals in this article, some of the existing legal systems for protecting public data or small-scale datasets (databases) in other jurisdictions – such as the hot news doctrine in the United States and the EU Database Directive – did not clearly set requirements on the number of data entries.[70] If these practices are reasonable, how to justify the obvious differences between the proposals in this article and these previous practices?

In fact, the hot news doctrine in the United States is not a property right rule that specifically addresses the protection of large-scale datasets, but is only an exception for protecting purely factual news or small-scale datasets outside the copyright law.[71] As mentioned earlier, under the framework of the copyright law, purely factual news or datasets, if not original, are not protected,[72] otherwise it will damage the freedom of creation and expression in the public domain. Nevertheless, the hot news doctrine creates an exception to this principle and directly protects purely factual news, such as real-time news in the INS case[73] or the Dow Jones index of thirty industrial stocks in the Board of Trade v. Dow Jones & Co. case.[74] The negative impact of this exception is self-evident. Therefore, the US courts have set extremely strict requirements. Take the famous NBA case as an example. As mentioned earlier, the court pointed out that the information is protected merely when the collection requires a certain cost, the information is time-sensitive, the defendant's behaviour constitutes free-riding, the two parties have a direct competitive relationship, and the plaintiff's incentive is substantially impaired.[75] Obviously, the time sensitivity requirement here greatly limits the scope of protectable information and the term of protection. It

---

[70]In its opinion of 23 June 1993 on the Commission proposal for a Council directive on the legal protection of databases, the European Parliament had suggested defining a database as a collection of a 'large number' of data, works or other materials, that condition no longer appears in the definition in Article 1(2) of the directive. *Fixtures Marketing Ltd v Organismos prognostikon podosfairou AE (OPAP)(2004)*, Case C-444/02.

[71]That is why the US Congress Bill of H.R. 1858 of 1999 proposes to treat 'hot news' and databases separately. As to database, the Bill requires it should be a collection of a large number of discrete items of information. See H.R. 1858 §§ 101, 102, 201, 106th Congress (1999–2000).

[72]*Feist Publications, Inc. v Rural Telephone Service Company, Inc.* (1991), 499 U.S. 340.

[73]See *International News Service v Associated Press* (1918) 248 U.S. 215.

[74]See *Board of Trade v Dow Jones & Co.* (1983), 456 N. E. 2d 84. In this case, the Chicago Board of Trade created a futures contract based on the Dow Jones index of thirty industrial stocks. The Supreme Court of Illinois held that the Board of Trade had misappropriated Dow Jones's investment in its index.

[75]See *National Basketball Association v Motorola, Inc.* (1997) 105 F.3d 841, 852–53.

institutionally ensures that the damage of this exception to the freedom in the public domain under the copyright law is reduced to a minimum level.

Most of the ordinary datasets that this article focuses on are not time-sensitive as typical hot news, and they need to be protected for a relatively long period of time. The dataset of consumer reviews in *Dianping* case is a good example.[76] Without the limitation of time sensitivity, the legislator's alternative choice is to set a certain standard on the number of data entries for the dataset to meet. In the above case, the dataset has millions of data entries, therefore the disputed subject matter is far from small-scale collections of data that the general public would use for creating regular works. So, it would avoid the special property rights system from unduly undermining the freedom of the general public.

Different from the hot news doctrine in the United States, the sui generis rights protection of the EU Database Directive are closer to the special property rights legislation proposed by this article. The EU Directive provides protection for a collection of 'independent works, data or other materials arranged in a systematic or methodical way' that consumes substantial resources.[77] It also requires database producers to make 'a substantial investment' in the obtaining, verification or presentation of the contents, but does not directly require the amount of data in the database itself.[78] In the past, some scholars even believe that a single web page content may constitute a database because it involves a combination of copyrightable or noncopyrightable content such as written works, pictures, videos, audio information, and even computer programs.[79] Article 8 of the Directive stipulates from the perspective of limitations on rights that the maker of the database shall not prevent others from extracting and/or re-utilizing insubstantial parts of its contents, evaluated qualitatively and/or quantitatively. This more likely indicates that the insubstantial part of the protected database can be used freely but not that the database itself must meet an absolute quantitative requirement.

Failure to specify the quantity standard of data entries in a database is one of the obvious shortcomings of the EU Database Directive. This leads to the low threshold and wide scope of protection for databases. For example, in the *Kidnet* case, the plaintiff verified and collected 251 website links information about parental organisations and self-help groups. The German court held that the investment made by the plaintiff met the requirement for substantial

[76]See (n 3).

[77]Article 1, Directive 96/9/EC on the Legal Protection of Databases.

[78]Article 7, Directive 96/9/EC on the Legal Protection of Databases. Interestingly, Recital 19 of the Directive points out: 'A compilation of several musical performances on CD does not qualify as a database.' Similarly, the directive does not protect computer programs 'used in the making or operation of databases.'

[79]See L Kaye, 'The Proposed EU Directive for the Legal Protection of Databases: A Cornerstone of the Information Society?' (1995) 17 *Egyptian Initiative for Personal Rights* 215, 584.

investment.[80] A collection of only 251 website links information is almost equal to the size of ordinary works. It is quite common for an ordinary work to contain hundreds or thousands of data entries. The number of data entries in the *Kidnet* case does not significantly exceed the scale of the data in an ordinary work. If protected, it will threaten the freedom in the public domain.

The EU Database Directive has the requirement of so-called 'substantial investment', but it cannot be a substitute for the 'substantial number of data entries' requirement to eliminate the threat of property rights protection to the public domain. For example, the number of data entries in a dataset of technical information may be relatively limited, but the investment required to obtain the dataset may be huge. The social consensus on this type of technical information is that once it is disclosed, it should not receive additional protection beyond trade secret law or patent law, otherwise the public will always worry about whether the technical information they learn from the public domain can be used or further disseminated. To eliminate the insufficiency of a separate 'substantial investment' element, the Court of Justice of the European Union (CJEU) later explained the 'substantial investment' element in individual cases and held that it only included collectors' investment in obtaining, verifying or presenting existing data.[81] In many cases, this is equivalent to a disguised requirement that the number of data entries must reach a certain level, otherwise the collection or arrangement may not consume substantial investment. However, this cannot completely replace the quantitative requirement for data entries. In some cases, the collection of a limited number of data entries may also consume substantial investment from the collector, if each data entry requires considerable search costs to be collected. The dataset may have met the threshold of substantial investment, but it has not met the requirement for 'substantial number of data entries'.

Conversely, a dataset that satisfies the requirement for 'substantial number' of data entries may not necessarily meet the 'substantial investment' requirement. For example, using a common Web crawler to download a massive number of data entries from a single undefended website may not cost the collector substantial resources. Therefore, this article believes that the quantitative requirement on the number of data entries in a dataset is not a disguised requirement of 'substantial investment', but one with independent value. Accepting the guiding principle that 'the number of data entries should far exceed an ordinary work, a court would have a clear direction of discretion when determining the scope of protectable datasets.

[80] Datenbankeigenschaft von Hyperlinksammlungen, www.jurpc.de/rechtspr/20020082.htm; Kidnet.de *v Babynet.de* (1999) Cologne District Court, www.netlaw.de/urteile/lgk_14.htm, quoted from Estelle Derclaye, 'Database Sui Generis Right: What Is a Substantial Investment? A Tentative Definition' (2005) 36 IIC 2, 19–20.

[81] See *British Horseracing Board v William Hill* (2004) Case C-203/02.

4.2. Quantitative standard for data entries

A certain degree of ambiguity in the 'substantial number of data entries' standard is an inevitable defect of the property rights system. Professor Yoshiyuki Tamura, an leading IP professor in Japan, believes that it is difficult for the property rights regime to deal with the problem of the unclear scope of protectable datasets. Therefore, he proposed to use an unfair competition law model to protect datasets, which requires the data collector to take technical measures before a third party infringes its rights.[82] Professor Tamura's proposal can help to avoid the problem of ambiguity in the standard of 'substantial number' if the dataset is kept in secret. Then, as long as a third party destroys or circumvents the technical measures and accesses the content of the datasets, it voliates the boundary of protection. In other words, whether the number of data entries in the dataset is substantial is not that important. However, if the dataset consists of data entries in public, it will be difficult to determine infringement by simply relying on whether a competitor has disrupted the technical measures. Moreover, even if technical measures can effectively control the access to a dataset, allowing its collector to unilaterally prohibit the public from using any piece of data entries in the dataset would excessively restrict the freedom of action in the public domain. Apparently, only focusing on technical measures, it is not a reasonable solution. Therefore, it is not surprising that, athough Japan eventually did adopt the so-called unfair competition law model, and in addition to the requirement of technical measures, the law still requires that the datasets contain a considerable number of data entries.[83]

Interestingly, it is believed that the legislative purpose behind the 'considerable amount of data' requirement under the Japanese law is to ensure that the data is 'stored to the amount that can generate value'. Therefore, whether the amount of data is 'considerable' depends on 'the nature of data entries, such as the added value generated by the electromagnetic method, the possibility of use, the transaction price, the labour, time, and cost invested in the collection and analysis of the data'.[84] In essence, the above requirement actually makes sure that the protected dataset has substantial commercial value or entails a substantial collection cost, the

[82]See the Speech of Professor Yoshiyuki Tamura at the Intellectual Property and Big Data Conference at Waseda University Law School on April 16, 2018. At that time, this author was also one of the invited participants. For another explanation on why Japan prefers the unfair competition law model, see Liu Ying and Sui Jigang, 'The "Restricted Provision of Data" Clause in Japan's Big Data Legislation and Its Implications to China' (2019) 4 *Intellectual Property* 88.

[83]Article 2 (7), the Japanese Unfair Competition Prevention Act (2018).

[84]See Liu Ying and Sui Jigang (n 82) 88–96. For the legislative reasons for the quantitative requirement of data entries under the Japanese law, please refer to the Intellectual Property Policy Office of the Ministry of Economy, Trade and Industry of Japan, '*The Article-by-Article Explanations of the Unfair Competition Prevention Act*', 48–49, www.meti.go.jp/policy/economy/chizai/chiteki/pdf/20190701Chikujyou.pdf (accessed 7 Febrary 2021).

purpose of which is obviously different from that of the quantitative standard advocated in this article. As mentioned earlier, the drawback of the Japanese or the EU approach is that in the case individual data entry entails a high cost of collection, the threshold of the number of data entries to be protected may be lowered. So it cannot effectively guarantee the freedom of action in the public domain. Nevertheless, this article agrees that, when considering the 'substantial investment' requirements, a court can consider the above-mentioned factors to evaluate the substantiality of the investment.

It is not easy to further quantify the 'substantial number of data entries' standard. The content of datasets in different fields varies significantly and the degree of threats posed by the protection of these content to the freedom in the public domain are different. Accordingly, the possibility that competitors' free-riding leads to market failure is also different. It is unlikely for legislators to set a uniform quantitactive standard of 'substantial number' for all industries. The rationale is the same with the copyright law that it cannot set more specific and uniform quantitative standard of originality for all types of works.[85] In addition, advances in science and technology will also change the custom of using data in public domain, which may require adjustments to the quantitative standard from time to time.

In the absence of specific legislative guidelines, we inevitably have to rely on judicial discretion to determine if a dataset has a substantial number of data entries. In individual cases, the criteria temporarily selected by courts may result in either over-protection or under-protection.[86] However, the courts will gradually adjust and establish guiding standards based on the response of the society, thereby forming a stable expectation in society. This is very similar to the way of determining originality of works under copyright law. Neither does copyright law have a quantitative standard for originality, but generally we do not think that its originality rules are unworkable. For example, we don't know exactly how many Chinese characters in a text or how many lines and colours in a painting constitute an original work. However, we still believe that judges can decide whether texts with a certain length or paintings with some complexity are original based on the consensus of the general public in relevant fields, even though judges' holdings in marginal cases may cause controversy – for example, for phrases composed of only several Chinese characters and a simple geometric pattern, we may not be sure whether they are original or not, but this uncertainty has not fundamentally shaken our confidence in the copyright system.

The emphasis here is on the number of data entries, rather than the amount of information within a single entry. In theory, the latter in some

[85]For example, under the US Copyright Law, the uniform originality standard is just an ambiguous statement like 'originality requires independent creation plus a modicum of creativity'. See *Feist Publications, Inc. v Rural Telephone Service Company, Inc. (1991)* 499 U.S. 340, 346.

[86]Dennis S Karjala (n 27) 2603.

datasets may be very large. For example, in a dataset consisting of video entries, the data volume of a single video entry may be very large, which can easily exceed one Gigabytes. However, in this type of dataset, the video is just one data entry, which is not essentially different from a data entry of only a few hundred bytes in a regular user information dataset. What counts is the number of data entries, not the size of any individual data entry.

In future judicial practice, as a principle, the court should ensure that the number of data entries in a protectable dataset far exceeds that in ordinary works (including works of compilations), so as to avoid harming the policy goal of copyright law. Taking the legal database as an example, the data volume of the CD-ROM version of the leading legal database in China, PKULAW.COM, is roughly 'more than 200,000 files, totaling more than 500 million Chinese characters'.[87] From the perspective of datasets protection, the element of 'substantial number of data entries' does not require that all datasets of this type should reach such a commercial scale. Instead, the minimum quantity requirement could be much lower. One or two thousand data items might be well enough because it would far exceed the number of data entries in ordinary works. The number of entriess in other types of datasets may have to reach tens of thousands or hundreds of thousands to be distinguished from traditional works, like dictionaries, cyclopedias books, or yellow books of phone numbers.

Under the above quantitative standards, some common collections of limited number of data entries may not meet the quantity requirement advocated in this article. This might so, for example, in the cases of TV program schedules, small-scale telephone directories of ordinary entities, NBA or CBA game schedules for a certain season, compilations of limited number of works, and datasets containing experimental data generated from a single research project. In the past, the weekly TV schedule information involved in the famous *Guangxi Radio and TV Newspaper* case, which has no originality in the sense of copyright law, but is still treated as a protectable fruit of labour by the court,[88] obviously cannot meet the 'substantial number of data entries' requirement here (in fact, there is also a doubt whether it could meet the 'substantial collection cost' requirement as described later). The number of data entries in the TV program schedules is even less than that in an ordinary work, not to mention to approximate a typical dataset in the era of big data. Therefore, that case should have only been handled in accordance with the traditional rules of intellectual property law, and

[87] See PKULaw.com, 'Products Introduction Page', www.chinalawinfo.com/bdfb/ChanPinLieBiao.asp#3 (accessed 1 December 2020).
[88] *Guangxi Radio and Television Newspaper v Guangxi Coal Miners Newspaper*, Guangxi Liuzhou Intermediate Peoples Court, (1994) Liudi Famin Zhong Zi No. 127.

the conclusion is that the TV program schedule should not be protected because it does not satisfy the 'substantial number' requirement.

Finally, it is noteworthy that in practical cases, when determining if a dataset in dispute can be protected by the new property rights regime, a court should look at the number of data entries copied by the defendant to see if it is protectable or not, rather than the number of data entries collected by the plaintiff. In copyright cases, a court follows the same the principle to determining the originality of a disputed work. The court focuses on the originality of the content copied by the defendant rather than the complete work of the plaintiff.[89]

4.3. Data entries accumulated within a time period

When determining the number of data entries, it is also necessary to consider the time dimension. Some collectors continuously produce data entries and gradually disclose them to the public as a data stream. Their competitors keep copying and disseminating the latest data entries but not using historical ones. For example, in the case of *Beijing Sunshine Data Company v. Shanghai Bacai Data Information Co., Ltd.*, the defendant forwarded to its clients the real-time financial data information provided by the plaintiff every day[90]; in *INS v. AP* in the United States, INS plagiarised factual news every day.[91] Assume that the number of data entries used by competitors within a time period per unit (such as a day) does not meet the minimum quantitative requirement for datasets. In these cases, shall the law allow the collectors to total up the number of data entries copied by the competitors within a certain period of time to claim datasets property rights?

This article is of the opinion that the data entries used by others at different points in time cannot be accumulated to claim datasets property rights as long as the number of data entries used within a time period per unit does not meet the minimum quantitative threshold In this situation, the number of data entries that users within a time period per unit only stays within the range of the number of data entries that traditional works may contain. According to the copyright law, these data entries should stay in the public domain, if the content of data entries itself is not copyrighted. That means the users should not be subject to restrictions of special property rights of datasets. If the special property rights legislation permits the accumulation of data volume throughout a longitudinal dimension of time, the freedom in public domain will be restricted by the special

[89]See Cui Guobin, 'Copyright Law: Cases and Materials' (Peking University Press, 2014) 678.
[90]See *Beijing Sunshine Data Corp. Limited v Shanghai Bacai Data Corp. Limited*, Beijing High People's Court, (1997) Gaozhi Zhongzi No. 66.
[91]See *International News Service v Associated Press (1918)*248 U.S. 215.

legislation. In extreme cases, if policymakers believe that there is an urgent need to restrict such use of small-scale data, they may consider to adopt a rule similar to the hot news doctrine in US law and restrict such protection to a very narrow scope and a very short time.

In addition, if the accumulation of data entries used in the longitudinal time period is permitted, the uncertainty of the boundaries of property rights will be a big challenge. At a specific point in time, the general public will not be clear when the data they use begins to accumulate and when it ends. So it is difficult to predict whether their use of a small amount of data will infringe on the special rights of the datasets.

Finally, it needs to be emphasised that the data accumulation within a period of time mentioned here is an issue considered from the perspective of the data user (defendant), not the collector. It is a common practice for collectors to collect data entries over a certain period of time. The collector can certainly combine these data entries collected during a certain period of time as one claim basis.[92] In specific cases, the dispute is whether the part used by the defendant rather than the dataset as a whole collected by the plaintiff meet the eligibility requirements. As mentioned earlier, this is the same as it is in the determination of copyright infringement, where the court only cares about whether the part copied by the defendant constitutes a work.

5. Substantial investment in collecting data

5.1. Reasons for additional investment requirement

There is another requirement that needs to be met for a dataset to be protectable. That is, the data collector should make a substantial investment in collecting data. Only after this, the society needs to offer a certain degree of protection to maintain the collector's investment incentives. And, also only after this, competitors can gain a certain competitive advantage by copying the data. In many cases, there is no direct correspondence between the number of data entries and the cost of collection, so these two elements need to be treated as independent eligibility requirements. The example of web crawler mentioned previously can help to illustrate this. A collector may use crawlers to automatically download publicly available data from a third-party server, and then simply piece them together to form a new dataset. Even if the dataset meets the quantitative requirement of data entries, its collection cost may not reach a substantial level, and therefore should not obtain special protection.

---

[92]It should be noted that the rules on term of protection might restrict the collector from doing so. For example, if the term of protection is calculated from the collection date of the earliest data entry, then data entries spanning the term of protection cannot be held together to claim datasets right.

Data property rights legislation's requirement of substantial costs is in sharp contrast with the low threshold of investment under the copyright law. The copyright law only requires a work to be original. It is irrelevant whether a work consumes a substantial cost.[93] Why is it that copyright law can ignore the cost, but data protection legislation can't? Why not accept that, after the number of data entries reaches a substantial number, the dataset will be protected no matter whether there is a substantial cost?

This article believes that the key factor that determines the level of substantial cost should be the negative impact of the protection on the public domain and the administrative cost of the property rights system. The main reason for defending lower investment standard is that lowering the threshold will not restrict freedom in the public domain since the public's freedom to collect the same data on their own is not affected. This line of thinking clearly traces back to the copyright law, which protect works with originality but low cost of creation. For example, paintings created casually by children or common pictures taken by a lay person with a digital camera can still be protected, even the average cost in creating this kind of works is negligible. Such copyright protection is not problematic because the originality of the works ensures that the general public usually has sufficient alternative choices and does not need to rely on a specific work to achieve self-expression. At the same time, the fair use doctrine exempts certain use of works to avoid market failures in some circumstances.[94] Therefore, protecting those works that do not consume substantial creation costs will have minimal impact on latecomers.

The dataset is inherently different from ordinary works in this respect. Many datasets at the market contain sole-source data,[95] which is difficult to obtain through alternative channels. At the same time, the items in many datasets are often mere factual, transactional or scientific information. In this sense, datasets are closer to functional or utility products. The possibility of the public relying on those data items for subsequent uses is far beyond the original or personal expression in ordinary works. Thus, the public's access to the content of such datasets should be much more important than that to specific original works.[96] For many sole-source data and information, society has even fewer alternative choices. Restricting the dissemination of these datasets by latecomers will restrict the public's access to them and thus negatively affect subsequent uses. It is inefficient for the law

[93] Article 3, Chinese Copyright Law (2020).

[94] Article 24, Chinese Copyright Law (2020).

[95] Amar A Hasan, 'Sweating in Europe: The European Database Directive' (2005) 9 *Computer Law Review and Technology Journal* 479, 483.

[96] For more detailed discussion on the importance of public access to scientific data, see JH Reichman and Paul F Uhlir, 'Database Protection at the Crossroads: Recent Development and Their Impact on Science and Technology' (1999) 14 *Berkeley Technology Law Journal* 793; Samuel E Trosow, 'Sui Generis Database Legislation: A Critical Analysis' (2004) 7 *Yale Journal of Law & Technology* 534, 538.

to force the public to re-collect the same datasets on their own or to overcome transaction cost barriers to obtain a license when the cost of collection is quite low and the original collectors do not need incentives. Under this situation, externalities caused by datasets protection can easily exceed that caused by the copyright protection for original expressions of works.

The aforementioned 'substantial number' requirement reduces the threat of special property right protection of datasets to freedom in the public domain to a certain extent, but it is not sufficient. The 'substantial number of data entries' requirement mainly focuses on the need for the freedom of expression of the general public. It does not fully consider the needs of data collection and utilisation in different fields. In the Internet age, the scale of datasets automatically collected and utilised by Internet platforms far exceed those of traditional industries. The limitation on the number of data entries usually does not constitute a meaningful screening proxy for the Internet industry. Some datasets that pass the threshold of 'substantial number of data entries' might only entail a negligible cost for data collectors; and the collectors does not really need to be incentivized. If the threshold for actual input is too low, the special property right protection will force the public to bear the transaction costs and obtain the permission of the collectors, or simply restrain from using the datasets, or make repeated investment to collect similar data. As a result, this type of protection will significantly increase social costs. To avoid the negative consequences, in addition to the 'substantial number of data entries' requirement, legislators should set another requirement of 'substantial investment in collecting data', so as to provide double insurance for the realisation of the legislative goals.

Those who adhere to a lower standard of investment may also believe that there is an alternative to reduce the negative impact of the property rights protection without relying on substantial investment requirement. That is, the law might exempt some infringing uses through fair use exceptions, thereby reducing the social cost of the property rights protection. For example, if the collection cost is relatively low, while the subsequent spread of the dataset certainly has a high social value and the transaction cost is high, the law may declare such use as fair use to avoid a possible market failure. This is similar to what copyright law has done: protect low-cost works, and then rely on broad fair use or statutory licenses to eliminate market failure. However, as mentioned earlier, personal expressions embodied in datasets are limited, and the public's reliance on datasets can easily exceed their reliance on ordinary personalised works. Relying on vague fair use doctrines to eliminate more-likely-to-happen market failures in the field of datasets would be more harmful than doing so in the field of copyright law. Thus, it should be more efficient to increase the predictability of the law by directly increasing the input threshold for datasets so as to avoid protecting these low-cost datasets.

5.2. Distinguishing costs in producing and collecting data

When considering the input of a collector, we need to distinguish between the production cost of data entries and the collection cost of the dataset. The production cost of data entries refers to the cost incurred in the process of creating data entries from scratch; the collection cost of a dataset refers to the cost incurred in the process of gathering and compiling existing data entries into a dataset. In many cases, the production of a single data entry itself is very expensive. For example, the producing of trade secret that reflects a core business strategy may cost thousands of dollars; the shooting of a movie as an item in the video database may also require millions; the developing of drug formulations with a good market prospect may cost ten millions or even more. No matter how much production cost a collector or third party consumes to produce a data entry from scratch, the data entry will automatically enter the public domain as long as it is made public and not protectable under the existing intellectual property laws. The scale of the production cost of the data entry does not affect this result.

When determining whether the collector has made a substantial investment, a court should not consider the production cost of the data entry itself, but only the cost of collection. To understand the rationality of doing so, we can look for inspiration from the cases on database protection ruled by the European courts. The important early case was *Fixtures Marketing*, in which the Court of Justice of the European Union (CJEU) pointed out that the substantial investment required by the EU Database Directive refers to 'investment in the creation of that database as such' or 'the resources used to seek out existing independent materials and collect them in the database'. It does not include 'the resources used for the creation as such of independent materials'.[97] To be more specifically, the resources paid by the plaintiff to establish the dates, times and team pairings for various matches in the football league schedule are not part of the protected investment stated in the directive; on this basis, the cost paid by the plaintiff in acquiring, verifying or presenting the contents of the database did not meet the substantial investment standard. In subsequent cases, the European Court of Justice continued to rely on the so-called spin-off doctrine, holding that the 'investments' in the Database Directive refers to resources used for obtaining and verification of the contents of the database but does not cover the resources used for the creating data materials. Accordingly, the protection of the database does not extend to the data entry itself in the database, even if the data item itself is brand new.[98] For example, in the Ryanair case, the ECJ held that the airline's flight information database (generally considered to be sole-

[97]See *Fixtures Marketing Ltd v Organismos prognostikon podosfairou AE (OPAP)*(2004), Case C-444/02.

[98]'The purpose of the protection by the sui generis right provided for by the directive is to promote the establishment of storage and processing systems for existing information and not the creation of

source information) was a by-product of the airline's normal operations. The airline did not make any substantial investment in this regard.[99] In the famous British horse racing case, the ECJ held that the horse racing organisers' collection and verification of information on millions of horses and competitions was not a substantial investment covered by the Database Directive.[100] Many other courts in European countries have also made similar judgments. For example, in the Dutch *NMA TV program schedule* case, the court of first instance held that the investment in compiling the TV program schedule was not an investment protected by the Database Directive. The Hague Court of Appeal affirmed that this is only a by-product of the regular activities of the TV station, and there is no substantial cost protected by the Database Directive.[101]

The conclusions of the European courts are not problematic in individual cases, but the courts' argument for distinguishing between the production cost of data entries and the collection cost of the datasets is not very satisfying. The courts did not further clarify why the fact that the sui generis rights do not protect a data entry in a database prevent them from considering the production cost of the data entry when determining if the investment is substantial. Some scholars in China believe that the ECJ emphasises the cost of creation and collection in order to avoid data collectors' monopolisation of the sole-source data. Collectors of sole-source data usually can prove they incur a substantial cost for producing data entries. Denying the relevance of this cost would weaken the protection they receive to a certain extent, thereby making it easier for the public to use the data. From the perspective of this article, a more straightforward explanation may be that, in most cases, the cost of producing data entries is recovered through the protection offered by existing trade secret law, copyright law, or patent law, and no special data property rights regime is needed to provide incentives. For example, data entries such as business information, drug formulas, or movies that entail substantial costs as mentioned above fall into this situation. If the existing intellectual property laws provide insufficient incentives to the producers of these data entries, legislators can directly modify them to increase the incentives without the need to provide additional protection through a new property rights regime. Therefore, as a complement to the existing intellectual property laws, the dataset property rights regime only needs to pay attention to the collection cost of the dataset and the corresponding

materials capable of being collected subsequently in a database.' *British Horseracing Board v William Hill (2004)*, Case C-203/02.

[99] *Ryanair Ltd v PR Aviation BV(2015)*, Case C30/14, para.31.

[100] 'The resources used to draw up a list of horses in a race and to carry out checks in that connection do not constitute investment in the obtaining and verification of the contents of the database in which that list appears.' *British Horseracing Board v William Hill (2004)*, Case C-203/02.

[101] *Telegraaf v NOS c.s.*, Hof.Den Haag Jan. 30, 2001, cited in Ranjit Kumar. G. 'Database Protection – The European Way and Its Impact on India' (2005) 45 IDEA 97.

reward mechanism, rather than the production cost of a single data entry. In other words, it is required that substantial investment must be used for the value-added part of a dataset, which is in line with the legislative purpose of the special property rights regime – namely, to promote the incentives of data collectors.[102]

If no additional property rights protection is provided for public data entries or small-scale collections of data, there may indeed be situations where the production cost of the data entries itself is very high. Although the informaiton can be protected as a trade secret, it may be difficult to obtain a reasonable return through a licensing or transfer mechanism. Moreover, keeping it in secret may also greatly limit the public interest. For example, this might be so in relation to daily weather forecast information, city traffic information, hot news, etc. In these situations, to maximise the public interests, the information may need to be treated as public goods funded by the government rather than a subject matter protected by the property rights regime. Another option is to adopt the aforementioned hot news doctrine under the US law to provide limited protection for highly time-sensitive information. In theory, if necessary, policymakers can make alternative solutions work in concert with the datasets property rights regime to protect data collections of different scale without contradicting or negating each other.

5.3. The scope of collection cost

After explaining the necessity of distinguishing between the production cost and collection cost of data entries, this article next focuses on an operational issue: how to distinguish the production cost of the data entries from the collection cost of the dataset.

When the producer of data entries and the collector of a dataset are independent of each other, and no direct contact exits between them before the data entries are generated, it is easy to distinguish the two types of costs. For example, in the case of legal database, the collector collects the existing statutes and regulations, and the boundary between the collection cost and the production cost of legal documents as data entries is very clear. Another example is video-sharing website. The users independently make and upload videos, and the website provides content storage and sharing services. There is a clear line between the users' investment in making videos and the website's cost in collecting the video files. Similarly, at Weibo or WeChat-like social platforms, the production cost of data entries generated by users is completely borne by the users.

[102] Jane C Ginsburg, 'Copyright, Common Law, and Sui Generis Protection of Databases in the United States and Abroad' (1997) 66 *University of Cincinnati Law Review* 151, 174.

However,when an Internet service provider provides certain material incentives to its users who create the data entries, or participates in the users' creation process of the data entries in some way, the investment of the service provider may become part of the production cost of the data entries. For example, video-sharing websites may share the creation costs of some users by means of cash rewards or advertising fee rebates; e-commerce platforms may provide subsidies or other material assistance to attract users to do transactions through their platforms, thereby promoting the generation of user transaction information. Although this type of cost is borne by the data collector, it still has to be regarded as the production cost of the data entries. If the collector wants to recoup this cost, it can contract with the users on the ownership of the intellectual property rights of the data entries. The contract may stipulate that the collector enjoys some kind of exclusive right to the funded data entries or will be compensated by other arrangements. In short, the collector does not need to rely on the property rights protection of the datasets to recover the above costs.

When producers and collectors of the data entries are independent of each other, data collectors often spend resources on purchasing equipment, renting office space, and paying staff salaries in order to maintain the normal operation of the network platforms and promote their market competitiveness. These resource inputs are not used to directly subsidise specific users' creation process, nor do they directly constitute collection costs of data entries. Under these circumstances, it would be very difficult, even if possible, to specifically identify the part of inputs that are directly related to the collection of data. Nevertheless, maintaining a competitive online platform is naturally a prerequisite for attracting users and collecting their data. The inputs in this respect are both the need of the collector's own business model and necessary material preparations for collecting users' data. There is no clear boundary between the two needs. In individual cases, the courts can recognise part of the inputs as the reasonable collection cost based on factors such as the proportion of data collection work in the network platform business, the relevance of related inputs to data collection work, and the average reasonable collection cost of the society. If the data-collecting work accounts for a large proportion of the platform business and the resource inputs are closely related to the data-collecting work, then the operating costs are more likely to be regarded as collection costs. The courts can refer to the average reasonable cost of the society to avoid under or over-estimation of investments in cases that the collector's efficiency is too high or too low.

When the producers of data entries and the collector of datasets are the same person, the boundary between the production cost and the collection cost is very blurred.[103] The flight schedule case and horse racing schedule case mentioned earlier fall into this category.[104] For an airline or horse racing organisation to operate normally, it must determine its own flight or horse racing schedule, and then provide it in a timely manner to the public. The ECJ believes that the resources invested by the organisations are not specifically used for collecting data, and therefore not the investments protected by the EU Database Directive.[105] In other words, the datasets that are almost automatically generated as a by-product when the operators engages in other business activities are not protected.[106]

In theory, if courts are permitted to examine whether the collector gathers data entries for normal business purposes, and then treats different datasets accordingly, they can avoid protecting certain datasets that do not need the protection. Where data collectors are at one of the two extremes, it may be relatively easy to make a judgment. For example, airlines or horse racing organisations may be the typical representatives that do not need special protection because they have sufficient incentives to collect and share data in order to expand existing businesses. Online platforms such as Dianping or Baidu Maps may be the typical representatives at the opposite end that need additional property rights to protect their investment.[107] However, there is a large number of data collectors sitting between these two extremes. It is not easy to determine whether their normal businesses provide sufficient motivation for collecting and disclosing data. For example, a hospital that collects a large number of patient medical records; a social network service provider that collects a huge amount of user information; an e-commerce platform that collects a large amount of information on products on sale, and so on. If a court is permitted to determine whether the data collection effort is only a collateral business of the collector that does not need additional property rights incentives in individual cases, it is tantamount to permitting a court to determine whether the mechanism for incentivizing data collection in individual cases is in the optimal state. It will greatly increase the information cost of the special property rights regime, and will introduce new uncertainties. A more reasonable choice is to allow a court is to assess the collection cost from the society's perspective, that is, whether a reasonable man would incur substantial cost to collect the data. The court does not need to further determine on a case by case basis

[103] Miriam Bitton, 'Exploring European Union Copyright Policy through the Lens of the Database Directive' (2008) 23 *Berkeley Technology Law Journal* 1411, 1461.

[104] Case C-203/02 *The British Horseracing Board Limited v William Hill Organisation Ltd* [2005] ECDR 1.

[105] See *Ryanair Ltd v PR Aviation BV*, Case C30/14, 15 January 2015; Case C-203/02 *The British Horseracing Board Limited v William Hill Organisation Ltd* [2005] ECDR 1.

[106] See Mark J Davidson and P Bernt Hugenholtz, 'Football Fixtures, Horse Races and Spin-offs: the ECJ Domesticates the Database Right' (2005) EIPR 114.

[107] See (n 2–4).

whether the collector has recovered the collection costs from its own main business.

Providing additional property rights protection for those collectors who have sufficient motivation to collect and share data for purpose of promoting their main business will limit the subsequent dissemination of datasets to some extent. However, since the protection proposed in this article is conditioned on the dataset's public availability and only limited to the right of public communication, the negative impact of this additional protection on subsequent derivative uses is limited. At the same time, the additional protection makes licensing the datasets a new revenue channel for the collectors. This will encourage collectors to provide data in a more timely and comprehensive manner and reduce the collectors' impulse to prevent non-client users from accessing their data with technical measures. This would be beneficial to the whole society.

Based on the above analysis, this article believes that the European Court of Justice does not thoroughly implement the dichotomy of production costs and collection costs of data entries. There is a room to improve. Taking the flight schedule case as an example. If a piece of flight information can be roughly regarded as a so-called data entry, and multiple flight information compilations or lists constitute a dataset, then the cost paid by airlines to arrange flight time, aircraft types, take-off and landing airports, ticket gates and other aaffairs constitute the cost of production, and the cost paid for garthering all flight schedule information constitutes the collection cost mentioned above. This conclusion should not be affected even if the airline collects those flight schedule information for normal business needs. It should be noted that this article does not conclude that the datasets of airlines or horse racing organisations in the above EU cases will always be able to meet the double requirements under the new property rights regime. To draw a conclusion, more specific analysis is needed. Actually, the volume of such data collections is likely to be small, and the collection costs are not substantial. The above assumptions are made only for the convenience of discussion.

5.4. Quantitative standard for collection costs

How to determine the 'substantial' degree of collection costs is a difficult problem.[108] The EU database directive also has the requirement for

[108]Judicial practices in Europe suggest that there is great uncertainty in the judgment of courts on what constitutes a qualifying substantial investment. See Indranath Gupta, *Footprints of Feist in European Database Directive: A Legal Analysis of IP Law-making in Europe* (Springer Nature Singapore Pte Ltd., 2017) 155–56. A study commissioned by the European Commission noted that 64% of experts surveyed believe that substantial investment determinations lead to uncertainty and become a barrier to data acquisition and utilisation. See JIIP & Technopolis Group, Study in Support of the Evaluation

'substantial investment', which is supposed to be evaluated from two dimensions: quality and quantity. It is generally believed that the investment can be financial, material or human.[109] The so-called quantitative dimension is easier to understand. It means that the investment of quantifiable resources (human or material) must reach a certain amount; while the qualitative dimension usually means that human investment that does not meet the quantitative requirements should have a high quality. However, the EU directive does not have more specific provisions on the substantial investment requirement, neither has the European Court of Justice has not proposed a clear quantitative standard.[110] Basing on the recitals of the directive, some believe that a low threshold of investment is sufficient. However, the meaning expressed in the recitals is not clear,[111] it is hard to know the original legislative intent.

There are huge disagreements among the European academics as to whether the Directive adheres to a higher investment standard or a lower one. The opinions in favour of a lower one believe that this allows smaller-scale databases to be protected and is conducive to incentivizing small and medium-sized investors and promoting the prosperity of the database market. In their view, a higher threshold is beneficial to large companies, which would easily lead to monopoly and delayed data disclosure (because the collectors will wait until the higher threshold is met)[112] At the same time, how high the higher threshold is has greater uncertainty, and so on. On the contrary, those who advocate a higher threshold believe that only a large investment is worthy of the protection because it could avoid excessive encroachment of the public domain.

As some scholars have pointed out the courts of European member states generally prefer a lower threshold. The most extreme case in this regard may be the above mentioned *Kidnet* case, in which the court held that the investment made by the plaintiff in verifying and collecting 251 website links met the requirement of substantial investment.[113] Obviously, the collection cost was actually very close to the creation cost of regular works. At a lower threshold, an investment of a few hours may be sufficient to meet the

of Directive 96/9/EC on the Legal Protection of Databases: Final Report, at 20, www.ec.europa.eu/newsroom/dae/document.cfm?doc_id=51599.

[109]Estelle Derclaye (n 80) 5.

[110]Indranath Gupta (n 108), 152.

[111]EU Database Directive, Recitals 19, 40.

[112]In fact, this article inclines to the view that the level of this standard is not directly related to the problem of data monopoly. Monopoly is usually established on the basis of legal property rights. With a lower standard, large corporations can also monopolize data. And, because of the lower standard, the monopolist can prohibit others from using smaller datasets, which is obviously more beneficial to the monopolist. Conversely, if a higher standard is adopted, more small-scale datasets can be used freely, which will not be good for the monopolist.

[113]Datenbankeigenschaft von Hyperlinksammlungen, www.jurpc.de/rechtspr/20020082.htm; Kidnet.de *v Babynet.de*, Cologne District Court, 25 August 1999, www.netlaw.de/urteile/lgk_14.htm, quoted by Estelle Derclaye (n 80) 19–20.

minimum requirement. Probably, only those small-scale personal address information lists or bon mots cannot meet the minimum requirement.[114]

Although this article believes that the threshold of substantial collection costs should be relatively high, this does not mean that legislators can set a uniform quantitative threshold for 'collection costs'. On the contrary, we can only rely on the court to consider the actual needs of different industries in individual cases, and then gradually build a consensus. In general, the collection cost of a dataset should reach a substantial proportion of a typical collector's investment in the same industry; correspondingly, by copying and communicating to the public the dataset without permission, the competitors will gain a substantial competitive advantage. There is no doubt that the scale of collection costs and the sensitivity to free-riding of competitors varies in different industries. Therefore, the absolute threshold of 'substantial collection cost' also varies in different industries.[115]

On the above basis, this article believes that the following factors should be considered when the court applies the above guidelines in individual cases to determine the threshold of 'substantial collection cost': the investment scale of the industry in which the operator is engaged; the scale of the dataset in the relevant industry; the importance of the dataset in business operations; the proportion of the disputed data in the entire datasets of the operator; the actual human or financial investment spent by the operator in collecting the disputed data; the possibility of the subsequent use of the dataset by the public; the customs of data utilisation in relevant industries, and so on. After weighing up these factors, the court in individual cases should be able to grasp a general understanding of the standard of 'substantial collection cost' for a specific industry, which in all cases should be much higher than the creation cost of ordinary works. For example, for the legal database industry in China, the investment threshold may be millions of dollars, and a typical dataset with commercial value may have about 200,000 data entries. Assuming that avoiding 1% of the collection cost of the initial collector will bring a competitive advantage to a competitor. What corresponds to a substantial collection cost is about ten thousand dollars. For the social media industry, it is necessary to collect activity information generated by millions or even ten millions of users, and the investment threshold may be ten million dollars or even more. In this situation, the threshold of substantial collection costs should be much higher than that of the legal database industry, reaching the level of one hundred

---

[114]Estelle Derclaye (n 80) 21.

[115]The opposite view is that the substantial investment standard should be a uniform lower standard and should not vary based on the size of the data collector's business, which would be fairer and more logical. See Estelle Derclaye (n 80) 8.

thousand dollars or even higher.[116] It is noteworthy that the assumption of the proportion (1%) and the estimation of investment scale here are just an arbitrary choice made for the convenience of discussing the legal standards. In practical cases, a court can make more accurate judgments and more refined choices.

6. Other possible considerations

6.1. The legality of data-collecting behaviours

Collectors may infringe on the prior rights of others in the process of collecting data, such as exceeding the scope of its users' permission to collect their personal information, downloading images from the Internet without the consent of the copyright owners, or misappropriating others' trade secrets. Then come outs a question: should the law prevent the collector from obtaining the property rights for its dataset?

One leading Chinese scholar advocates that the legality of data-collecting behaviour is a prerequisite for the protection of datasets, but did not explain the reasons.[117] Probably it is viewed as a common sense. The article disagrees with the scholar and argues from a two perspectives: the inherent logic of the property rights regime and the public policy. In theory, allowing collectors to claim property rights protection for datasets that contains the above-mentioned infringing contents, will not result in inherent logical contradictions in the property rights regime. If infringing the prior rights of others, the collectors shall bear legal responsibility according to the laws that protect those rights. Legislators do not need to further deter the collectors by denying their property rights to the datasets. And, the collectors only enjoy a negative exclusive right to prevent others from disseminating the datasets. In this sense, the datasets right is similar to a copyright, which is also only a negative right by nature. The legal protection does not guarantee the collectors a right to disseminate the datasets to the public. Whether they can do so depends on other laws. So, recognising the collectors' property rights to the dataset is not equal to legalise the collectors infringing uses of the dataset, therefore it will result in no legal conflicts between the special property rights legislation and other laws.

---

[116]There are rough estimates that the licence value of a dataset of ordinary personal information (such as age, gender and address, etc.) is very low, about $0.50 per thousand persons. See Emily Steel, Callum Locke, Emily Cadman & Ben Freese, 'How Much is Your Personal Data Worth?' www.ig.ft.com/how-much-is-your-personal-data-worth/ (accessed 20 February 2021). Of course, more granular data on more valuable users may be more valuable. Based on the above estimates, a licence would be worth about $500 when the number of data entries in such a dataset reaches millions. Competitors who use the dataset of this size without permission would gain very limited competitive advantage. This suggests that it is reasonable to require that the collection cost threshold of such data collections is much higher than that of ordinary works.

[117]See Kong Xiangjun (n 15) 14.

From the perspective of public policy, there is no easy answer to the question whether the law should deny protection of the above datasets. In the field of copyright law, there are indeed precedents that deny copyright protection for unlicensed derivative works. For example, the US copyright law refuses to protect derivative works created without the permission of the original author.[118] It is pointed out that, as a matter of policy, denying copyright protection to unlicensed derivative works can prevent the licensee of original author to be harassed by the author of unlicensed derivative works. Thus, it better protect the author of the original work.[119] In this author's opinion, the US law also reduces the willingness of the public in making illegal derivative works at the beginning, thereby reducing the threat of infringement. However, China's copyright law does not explicitly accept this principle. Academia generally believes that derivative works created without permission can still enjoy copyright protection as long as they satisfy the originality requirement.[120] However, the author of derivative works cannot freely disseminates the derivative work, otherwise he should bear the liability for copyright infringement.[121]

On the issue of datasets protection, both the US and Chinese approaches under the copyright law has some validity. Nevertheless, this article tends to accept the Chinese one and believes that the illegality of data-collecting behaviours should not affect the collectors' property rights to the datasets. Since Chinese copyright law permits the protection for unlicensed derivative works, it should be more able to accept the protection of illegally collected datasets. The reason is that datasets usually contains millions of data entries, the collectors' risk of infringing prior rights such as copyright, trade secret, or personal information right, is much higher than the authors of derivative works. If the property rights to datasets are denied because some of the data entries are illegally collected, it will be easy for an infringer to rely on this defense to escape the infringement liability. This rule may violate the principle of proportionality and over-punish dataset collectors in cases that only a small portion of data is infringing others' prior rights. At the same time, there is no stronger moral or public policy justification for allowing the infringer to have a freeride. Even if the law required that the collector's illegal activities reach a substantial level before depriving the collector of the datasets property rights, it would still not be a reasonable institutional choice. Doing so would force the courts

[118] 'In any case where a copyrighted work is used without the permission of the copyright owner, copyright protection will not extend to any part of the work in which such material has been used unlawfully.' The United States Copyright Office, Copyright in Derivative Works and Compilations, www.copyright.gov/circs/circ14.pdf (accessed 20 February 2022).

[119] see *Pickett v Prince* (1999) 52 F. Supp. 2d 893, 908–09.

[120] See Yang Yanchao, 'Research on the Copyright of Illegal Works and the Amendment of Article 4 of the Chinese Copyright Law' (2010) 3 *Legal Forum* 140.

[121] Article 52, Chinese Copyright Law (2020).

to review the degree of illegality of the collector in individual cases. It would increase administrative costs and uncertainty of property rights.

It is worth mentioning that this article does not deny the importance of protecting the public's prior rights. It is the mission of other specific laws. There is no need to provide additional deterrence outside those laws by denying the collector's property rights to datasets. The social cost of doing so outweighs the gains.

6.2. Time sensitivity of data

In the proposed special property rights regime, whether the value of datasets is time-sensitive is not an element to consider, although some scholars argue for it.[122] The reasons for this have already been discussed in the previous sections and further explained here.

The time-sensitive element is derived from the hot news doctrine of the US law. This doctrine extends anti-unfair competition protection to factual news at the same quantitative scale of copyrightable works, provided that the value of the factual news is highly time-sensitive. As mentioned earlier, from the perspective of copyright law, this protection threatens the freedom in the public domain. Some critics argue that such doctrine actually protects outdated business models and hinders the application of new technologies and new business models.[123] Although this doctrine is no longer effective under the US federal law since the Supreme Court of the United States denied the existence of common law at the federal level,[124] it has survived tenaciously in the common law of many states and has not been excluded by the federal copyright law.[125] This status quo has not been seriously challenged so far.

The time-sensitive element emphasised by the hot news doctrine has its unique historical background. It is not appropriate to introduce this element into the future datasets special property rights system. In *INS v. AP*, the INS followed on the heels of the Associated Press and kept copying factual news in the European battlefield reported by the latter. The amount of factual news that happens every day is actually relatively limited. According to the majority opinion, the issue in dispute is whether a single or a few pieces of factual news in daily coverage should receive some protection.[126] The dissenting judge did point out that the factual

---

[122]See Yang Aoyu, 'The Evolution of Information Misappropriation Doctrine in the US Law and Its Implications to the Protection of Data Property Rights in China' (2019) 11 *Political Science and Law* 161.
[123]Victoria Smith Ekstrand and Christopher Roush, 'From Hot News to Hot Data: The Rise of Fintech, the Ownership of Big Data, and the Future of the Hot News Doctrine' (2016) 35 *Cardozo Arts & Entertainment Law Journal* 303, 318.
[124]*Erie Railroad Co. v Tompkins*, 304 U.S. 64 (1938).
[125]*Barclays Capital Inc. v Theflyonthewall.com, Inc.* (2011) 650 F.3d 876, 894.
[126]*International News Service v Associated Press* (1918) 248 U.S. 215, 234–37.

news that the defendant plagiarised every day only accounted for a small part of the news sent to their clients.[127] The majority opinion supports the protection of factual news, but it did not set a quantitative requirement on the amount of factual news. It means the protection can be extended to a small-scale collection of factual news. In later factual news cases, the amount of disputed data entries rarely reached a massive or a substantial level as the large-scale datasets described today.[128]

Some people might think that in the NBA case where the elements of consideration in hot news doctrine are refined,[129] the fifth element – the defendant's use of information threatens the incentives of the plaintiff implies a large amount of data. Only after the factual news plagiarised reaches a certain amount will competitors save substantial collection costs, thereby gaining a competitive advantage and threatening the plaintiff's incentives for production. This analysis has some truth. However, the amount of data required here depends on the production cost of the data entries. If the production cost of a single factual news is high, then following the logic underlying the doctrine, the requirement for the amount of data may be very low. Therefore, from the practical application of the American hot news doctrine, we have reason to believe that the hot news it protects is not of the same scale as the large-scale datasets we are discussing here.

Without a specific requirement for the amount of data, the US courts naturally rely on other elements to reduce the negative impact of the legal protection of hot news. The key element the courts have chosen is to emphasise the time sensitivity of the factual news, which significantly narrows the scope of protectable information and shortens the term of protection, and thus effectively reduce the negative impacts of the protection. Otherwise, with the passage of time, more factual news may flow into the society and various ways of reuse may appear, continuous protection will significantly increase social costs.[130]

The US hot news doctrine might be a good solution to the challenge of highly time-sensitive factual news and their collections, but it does not fit for the protection of ordinary large-scale datasets. When the number of ordinary data entries in a dataset increases, the negative impact on freedom of expression in the public domain reduces or even ceases to exist.[131] Thus, the special property rights regime no longer needs to rely on the 'time-sensitivity' element to reduce the negative effects. Moreover, as the collection cost and commercial value of ordinary datasets increase,

---

[127] Ibid, 249.
[128] For a detailed review of the US judicial cases on the hot news doctrine, See Yang Aoyu (n 122) 151–56.
[129] *National Basketball Association v Motorola, Inc.* (1997) 105 F.3d 841.
[130] Richard A Epstein, 'The Protection of "Hot News": Putting Balganesh's "Enduring Myth" About *International News Service v Associated Press* in Perspective' (2011) 111 *Columbia Law Review Sidebar* 79, 84–86.
[131] See Cui Guobin (n 1) 11–13.

the legitimacy of a longer property rights protection is strengthened accordingly. China's judicial practices also suggest that the problem of inadequate protection for ordinary datasets has become increasingly prominent. All the datasets disputed in high profile cases, like *Dianping* and *Baidu Map*,[132] are not as time-sensitive as the hot news in the US cases.

For the above reasons, future datasets legislation should no longer use the element of time sensitivity to limit the scope of protectable subject matters. But it is not denied here that China might need a separate regime to protect single piece or a small-scale collection of factual news with time-sensitivity. A solution similar to the American hot news doctrine might be worth considering. Further discussion is beyond the scope of this article.

6.3. Technical measures

For the datasets concerned in this article, Japanese and Korean legislators adopt the anti-unfair competition model to provide protection. As a prerequisite for protection, the data collector must take 'electronical management' or technical measures to restrict the public's access to the data.[133] This is equivalent to an 'opt-out' mechanism with a default rule of no protection. If the collector does not take technical measures, the public will need not to worry about the risk of infringement. It looks good to the public. Thus, some Chinese scholars believe that electronic management measures, such as robots protocol or IP address restriction measures, should also be a prerequisite for protection in the future Chinese legislation.[134]

Under the Japanese or Korean law, technical measures have important functions. Both laws provide a broad protection for datasets by restricting subsequent unauthorised acquisition, use, and disclosure of the content of datasets.[135] The requirement of technical measures can reduce the negative impact of such a broad protection. In practices, not every collector needs such broad protection. Once a dataset is made available to the public, many collectors only need to prevent others from communicating the same content to the public. Thus, they may not take technical measures to prevent subsequent accesses or other uses. If the law requires a collector to take technical measures, the public can easily identify the collectors who have not taken technical measures and leave their datasets in the public domain. In other words, the requirement of technical measures reduces the subsequent users' information cost in avoiding infringements and expand the freedom in the public domain.

[132] See (n 2–4).
[133] See (n 43).
[134] Kong Xiangjun (n 15) 14–15.
[135] See (n 43).

However, under the property rights regime proposed by this article, the value of technical measures is much lower than that under the Japanese or Korean law. As mentioned earlier, the proposed regime requires a protectable dataset to contain a substantial number of data entries and entail a substantial investment, and it only grants the collectors the right of public communication. According to common sense, collectors of the datasets that pass the subject matter test, usually are unwilling to let a third party to compete by copying and then disseminating their datasets. If the proposed legislation imitates Japanese or Korean law by requiring collectors to take technical measures to show their intent to seek protection, it will increase the collectors' business cost without redemptive values. For the third party, the real challenge under the proposed regime is not to perceive most collectors' intent to protect, but to predict to what extent he can copy and disseminate the dataset. Apparently, technical measures are not helpful in resolving this problem. Even if technical measures are taken, the public still has to relying on the amount of data they used and the collection cost they saved to predict the legality of their behaviours of data uses.[136] As the cases of Baidu Map, Dianping, Sina Weibo have suggested, whether the defendants have substantially copied the plaintiffs' datasets is always a key issue in determining infringement.[137] Only a circumvention of technical measures should not be viewed as an infringement, otherwise, the protection would expand to every small piece of the dataset, which would be too broad and over restrict the freedom in public domain.

In addition, the law's requiring technical measures will cause inconvenience to the public who access or use the datasets. As we know, some data collectors provide services directly without taking complicated technical measures, which greatly facilitates their users. If the collectors are required to take technical measures, some users will be excluded from accessing the service, and other users will incur higher cost to get the services. Imagine complicated technical measures being applied to search engine services, map navigation services, or social media services (such as Weibo), and all users are required to go through a complicated authentication process before obtaining the services each time, it will cause inconvenience to almost every user. If the court cares about the inconvenience to users or the cost to collectors and only allow collectors to just take symbolic technical measures, it will actually make this requirement a formality losing its practical significance. For example, if the requirement is met by simply requiring

[136]Prof. Kong has a different opinion. He claims that the requirement of 'management measures' could reduce the uncertainty in determining infringements because the court would no longer need to decide if the defendant has excessively scraped the data and substantially substituted the plaintiff's service. In other words, it is much easier to determine if the defendant circumvents technical measures than determining if excessive scraping or substantial substitution exists. See Kong Xiangjun (n 15) 14–15.

[137]See (n 2–4).

all users to register online and accepting their request indiscriminately, it would be difficult for the public to perceive the collectors' intent through the collectors' adoption of technical measures because such technical measures are so commonly used. Another example is the robots exclusion protocol that bans web crawlers or other web robots. Some believe it is an acceptable technical measure under the future law.[138] To take such a measure, an ISP only needs to put an instruction (several words) into a machine-readable text file called 'robots.txt' in the root of the web site hierarchy.[139] The cost is close to zero. If the new property rights regime treats this as an acceptable technical measure, probably all the collectors whose datasets are able to pass the subject matter test will take such measures. Such a technical measures requirement can hardly achieve a meaningful legislative goal.

Based on the above reasons, this article takes the view that under the proposed limited-exclusive-right regime, data collectors should not be required to take technical measures to protect their data content. In the future, if the protection will be extended to reproduction or other uses of the datasets, it may be necessary to consider the requirement of 'technical measures' similar to that found in Japanese or Korean law.

7. Conclusion

Under the existing intellectual property law framework, it is extremely challenging to fill the gaps in the legal protection of datasets. In the past, the hot news doctrine of the United States and the EU database directive represented the attempts made by the international legal community in different scenarios – small and middle-scale data collections or databases. However, they have not solved the problem of protecting large-scale public datasets that we need to face now and in the future. At present, we have not yet established a high degree of consensus on basic issues such as the necessity of protecting public datasets and the choice of legal regimes. In this context, it is difficult to discuss the detailed eligibility requirements of subject matter under the future property right regime. But, studies on eligibility issues in turn, will affect decision-makers' views on the more fundamental issues such as the justifications of the protection for public datasets and the choice of protection regimes. Therefore, we cannot simply wait until the fundamental issues are resolved before discussing the issue of specific institutional design – eligibility rules.

[138]See Kong Xiangjun (n 15) 14–15.

[139]For a detailed introduction to the mechanism of robots protocol, see Wikipedia, 'Robots Exclusion Standard' www.en.wikipedia.org/wiki/Robots_exclusion_standard (accessed 15 February 2022).

Based on the current academic research and judicial practice, this article assumes that Chinese legislators will adopt special property right regime to protect publicly available datasets in the future, and only grant the data collectors limited exclusive rights (right of public communication). On this basis, this article discusses the eligibility requirements for the datasets protection and conclude there should be three principal requirements: the data entries of the dataset shall be made public, it shall contain a substantial number of data entries and the collector shall incur substantial collection costs. Through these requirements, the special property rights legislation can be distinguished from the US hot news doctrine and EU database directive and achieves different legislative purposes by protecting different size of data collections. Moreover, the new law will be connected consistently with the existing trade secret protection system and copyright, and effectively balance the interests of data collectors, competitors and the public. Except the above three principal requirements, future property rights legislation needs not to consider as eligibility requirements additional factors such as the legality of the collector's data-collecting behaviour, the time-sensitivity of data, and the adoption of technical measures. This author hopes that the analysis of the above-mentioned eligibility requirements would shed light on the direction of future research or institutional design on datasets protection.

Disclosure statement

No potential conflict of interest was reported by the author(s).

Index

Note: Figures are indicated by *italics*. Tables are indicated by **bold**.

FSC
www.fsc.org
MIX
Papier | Fördert gute Waldnutzung
FSC® C083411

Kolibri 360 GmbH
Ferdinand-Jühlke-Straße 7
99095 Erfurt, Deutschland
produktsicherheit@kolibri360.de